D1456787

United Spectrum

United Spectrum

The Unity of Nature and the Division of Man

LEVI MORRIS

Order this book online at www.trafford.com
or email orders@trafford.com

Most Trafford titles are also available at major online book retailers.

© Copyright 2011 Levi Morris.
All rights reserved. No part of this publication may be reproduced, stored in a retrieval
system, or transmitted, in any form or by any means, electronic, mechanical, photocopying,
recording, or otherwise, without the written prior permission of the author.

Editing by Arthur Lizza
Illustrations copyright © 2011 by Jesse Morris

The author gratefully acknowledges permission to reprint selections from:

Excerpt from THE HOLE IN THE UNIVERSE © copyright 2001
by K.C. Cole, reprinted by permission of Harcourt, Inc.

"The Elder Brother's Warning" by Alan Eriera.

Confessions in The Fathers of the Vol. 5, New York: Fathers of the Church Inc. © 1953. Used
with permission: The Catholic University of America Press. Washington, DC.

Printed in the United States of America.

ISBN: 978-1-4269-5544-0 (sc)
ISBN: 978-1-4269-5545-7 (hc)
ISBN: 978-1-4269-5546-4 (e)

Library of Congress Control Number: 2011902743

Trafford rev. 02/17/2011

www.trafford.com

North America & International
toll-free: 1 888 232 4444 (USA & Canada)
phone: 250 383 6864 ♦ fax: 812 355 4082

Contents

PART 6

List of Illustrations

INTRODUCTION

One may find the views presented in this book to be debatable, unrealistic or even radical. This is to be expected. Reasoned skepticism in the face of the revelation of new concepts is both commendable and intrinsically necessary for true understanding. It is a natural reaction to scrutinize new ideas and compare them against the beliefs that comprise your current schema of reality. I urge you to keep an open mind, to let these ideas sink in, and to allow yourself to enjoy them, because understanding only comes when we value it and commit to it. The comprehension of truth can be arrived at through many different avenues. No matter how credible or dubious it may be, living peacefully requires ones' awareness to be inspired, exploratory and introspective. Each of us has the ability and responsibility to recognize the veneer of illusion and to see past it to behold the truth beneath. Appearances can be deceiving, if they are all one looks at. I felt the need to write this book because so many of the things I have come to understand have helped me to see the world in a new and beautiful way, and I feel that I can impart some of this same vision and understanding to those with whom I share these words. My lack of distraction and intense curiosity about all of the remarkable and fascinating things I've come across and observed has enabled me to notice the profoundly deep relationship between all things. The more I observed people, and life in general, the more these feelings of deep awe and subsequent concern began to grow, and I began to write it all down. In 1901, Albert Einstein said "What a magnificent feeling to recognize the unity of a complex of phenomena which appear to be things quite apart from the direct visible truth." (Moring, 2004). This book is my attempt to express the unity of nature to a species that is destroying the world because of our division.

Writing a book about the many aspects of nature is like putting a ramshackle picture frame around a masterpiece in motion. In similar fashion, capturing the essence of natural and human behaviors within the meager scope of symbolic text has severe limitations. So it is also with the omnipresence of that beautiful and constantly unfolding work of art that is the natural reality of the world and the universe around us; capturing this essence requires the lively and concentrated awareness of the reader and the observer, who make it their own. Children are not alone in naturally tending to desire immediate answers, to quickly judge and jump to conclusions. As adults, we too are often seduced by the enticements of taste that masks substance, of superficial pleasure and flashy colors that are only a shimmer of the essence of reality, and we often pursue these instead of the depths of the vital nourishment of life, in much the way a child seeks candy over Brussels sprouts. I urge you to read these words with a childlike openness and enthusiasm that may lead to a deeper understanding of the reality beneath the flash. Feel free to read slowly and thoroughly or to skip around in this book, because although it can be read in the conventional linear fashion, reading what interests you first and then coming to the rest later also works. Read in the style that works best for you.

Over the next few years, there will be a large-scale transformation. In times of transition, there is turbulence. Life is a cycle, just as the seasons are. Earth needs periods of change to allow for further change. The changes on Earth that we are living through are as understandable as they are necessary. Think of it as a volcano, an agent of change that brings death and destruction before giving rise to life and renewal. It is an infinite cycle, with beginnings and endings used only for points of reference and ease of communication. When it comes down to just how we made such a mess of things on Earth, people rarely change unless they see the dire consequences staring them in the face. We act more readily toward problems than we do in preventing them. The dead, the criminals, the garbage, sewage and overall pollution we generate, the famine and war in our world—none of these are things we want to deal with, as they are unpleasant and harsh emotional burdens we wish to deny and escape. The denial of truth, however ugly it may appear or feel, sustains unhappiness, and only provides a quick feeling of stimulating, superficial and counterfeit bliss due to the denial of the reality of our intentions and their consequences. It is "out of sight and out of mind" as it's all whisked away, and that's generally just fine by us. We probably wouldn't literally sweep dust under the rug, but for matters of real importance we do this often. Even if we do see the consequences of our actions, humans have a real knack for getting used to things such as taking our way of living as acceptable and nature for granted. Life, just as the world as we know it, has been coming to the end of one cycle after another since it began. Many ancient civilizations and spiritual and scientific insights have converged at a consensus that points to great changes in the world at the end of the present cycle. It seems very presumptuous to pick a very specific date, such as the year 2012, but when we do the research and add contemplation, perhaps it is not so arrogant, and it is not really the "end" as many people think of it, but a beginning. The year could even be 2050. What earth-changing events may happen and when they may occur is not as important as why they will happen. Ask people what they think of death and they will most likely describe it as an "end" as well. It is true that some think of death as an end, but many others feel it is a beginning; it's all in how you perceive it. We all have our respective beliefs and views. If you have views you choose to change, then that is your choice as well, but it concerns me when people are so convinced of their beliefs they choose not to change them based on tradition, or self-righteousness, or even just stubbornness. Add the swift judgments we all seem to make, and natural change is ignored for as long as humanly possible. As you read this book, I suggest that you have an open mind and try not to hold on to your beliefs, as so many do, as an identity and security blanket. People kill for their beliefs, even if those very beliefs prohibit murder. Explain that one. It is up to the reader to take what he or she feels is important and true in this as in any book. To see how our planet has become so unbalanced, we must look at nature and humanity both individually and as a whole.

This book includes the following parts:

Observing as an Individual looks at the senses and our common interpretations of them. Consciousness, the ego, fear, doubt, belief and our biological needs and behaviors are some of the chief elements of experience philosophized here.

The Fall of Man and Critical Mass examines the effects of humanity such as: the continuation and escalation of war, a growth economy resting on fossil fuels and the abuse of our surroundings, overpopulation and the imminent collapse of our modern way of life. This section also looks at the possibility of drastic increases in solar activity and other cosmic forces likely to affect Earth in the near future.

Middle World—The Lost Splendor of Normal proposes that aspects of life considered to be humdrum are actually quite fascinating. This section also discusses trees, evolution and the relationship between science and religion.

Shape, Scale and Intensity—The Languages of Beauty combines fractal and Euclidean geometry with concepts such as nothingness, infinity and symmetry to illustrate the many ways in which nature is expressed.

The Elegance Behind the Beauty explains the astonishing physics of electromagnetism, gravity, spacetime and quantum mechanics as simply varying faces of the singular beauty of nature.

A Land Beyond Compare explores teaching, its limitations and further describes the relationship between life, death, duality and unity.

PART 1

OBSERVING AS AN INDIVIDUAL

*No man is an island, entire of itself; every man
is a piece of the continent, a part of the main.*

(John Donne, *Meditation XVII* in *Devotions
upon Emergent Occasions*, 1624)

Conflict and illusion exist only when one's perceptions of reality are
limited to their self. The metamorphosis of conflict into love is only
possible with a simple and total understanding of how and why we
create these illusions. We must also recognize *all* forms of conflict as
serious and illusory if understanding is to be realized. Why focus on
all these negative aspects of human behavior and all the depressing
issues facing nature? Because the understanding of what our illusions
are reveals the limited awareness that creates them. The solution is in
totally exposing and understanding the illusions, which effectively
reveals them as a problem and eliminates them. I wish to point out our
innocent and misled perceptions so that we can see clearly and without
any undue suffering, like a fly showing its fellow swarm a way around

an invisible and nevertheless painful window after we've been banging into it for far too long.

All facts and theories aside, people will believe what they desire to believe. People steadfastly hold onto their traditions and beliefs because they feel these are a part of them, and many people can't seem to change or let go of their long-held belief systems. With all due respect, we are a pig-headed bunch. We cling to our beliefs because we think they make us who we are. People die for their beliefs. Both sides of a "religious" war murder and die for their beliefs and the "glory" of their gods. Belief in science or religion is all a matter of faith, which is how new information is filtered by our credibility meter and personal experience. Over the centuries, religions have adjusted their parables and doctrines according to the changing authors, translations and values that change alongside our modern lifestyles, governments, cultures and societies. In science, the "laws" that are developed are in fact only high degrees of confidence or faith, until they are reevaluated and refined in the face of new evidence. Science has seen its laws and models change many times, and it is fair to say they will change again in the future. For example, Newton and Einstein gave us insight, centuries apart, into the nature of gravity and light, yet we still don't fully understand them. Still, both Newton and Einstein deserve praise for their impressive insights into the unified nature of reality.

Concerning the issues at hand, if people don't suspend their lopsided and burdensome beliefs, and experience a personal revolution of insight, then we will continue on our course of collective suicide and global destruction. We have been painting ourselves into a corner for some time now and it's time to look up. People who believe that an apocalypse is inevitable can affect the future and cause a self-fulfilling prophecy with far-reaching consequences. With the majority of the world believing in some sort of end-of-the-world scenario, this is more than just a point of discussion; it has and will continue to have real effects in the world of politics and warfare wherever religion and the contemporary ethos of the masses influences politics, which seems to be the case with the majority of politics. The perversion of nature's or god's will to suit our selfish desires has unintended consequences. We put ourselves at odds with nature by simultaneously submitting to it and believing that we are capable of dominating it. There might at one time have been a possibility of combining the two aspects of domination and submission by pulling back from both extremes, but it's too late now, and nature is poised for revolt.

We believe what we choose. Why hasn't anything been done to tackle climate change or to dramatically reduce our oil dependence? The economy is always number one, because it supports our jobs and our families, which are most important to us. We don't live in a democracy—we live in a capitalist paradigm where ambitious opportunists take advantage of people's misgivings and create this thing called "progress." Is this something we can all be proud of? Free trade and the pursuit of happiness are mere façades that companies and organizations use to make lots of money. Nobody takes on any job without a "what's in it for me?" attitude. No one is accountable; no one takes individual responsibility for human caused global issues because we are a part of a much wider and faulty species. It's always the government's fault, my boss's fault, the other guy's fault. I'm just doing my job, I have to pay my mortgage, I need to put food on the table. We are a guilty people who know what we are doing. On the other hand, we are innocent as children because if we knew of a more peaceful and balanced way of behaving we would certainly act accordingly. We live in a society ruled by all the people who have created it to rule themselves but then we only see the game or representatives as responsible and not also each player that supports it. Humanity is essentially a single person multiplied. We also live in an animalistic, instant gratification society and have domesticated ourselves because we are social animals and the luxuries and exploits of nature and others are plenty when we work together to make kings and slaves to our selves, our kingdoms and each other. From an inflated survival perspective, like any side-effect ridden pharmaceutical mitigating only the symptoms, the short term benefits outweigh their long term consequences and alternatives. Foresight is so near-sighted for some individuals and institutions that we cannot see past the problems of our own day-to-day lives and lifetimes. Long term is one hundred, five hundred, a thousand or even a million years from now, not a measly five or ten. This explains all the problems resting upon the speedy destruction of the Earth. We live for today. We need to live for the past and the future, because they are the same thing. Reality is not foresight or hindsight alone.

I propose that living in the present, with a conscious regard for both the past and the future, is what is needed to live with true wisdom and insight. It is the feeling of the *now*, the feeling of each moment arriving and departing. Insight is now sight. Insight is a holistic approach to things. It is an ongoing epiphany. This particular kind of "sight" creates a different kind of desire and a subsequent kind of action we all must self-actualize to reach our material and spiritual potential in this material and spiritual life. We are receivers and projectors of reality. Like a television, we get a signal, rearrange the information, interpret it into a useful image, and then project this onto our canvas of a world. It is a realization of reality, a sense of unity, respect, and love for each other, and Earth should be included in our collective intention. At present, we are mostly void of these virtues and this is why the changing of cycles is necessary. When I say "sight" in this context, I mean not only the ability to look, as most of us can do, but a wide, circumspective observing, both outside and inside of you, with full consideration for the prior, present, and future.

Belief and Faith

There are more things in heaven and earth, Horatio
Than are dreamt of in your philosophy.
(William Shakespeare, *Hamlet*, 1601)

Beliefs are based on choice and exclusion and are thus partial and conditional whereas faith is based on complete trust and acceptance which is unconditional. Happiness is not circumstantial. It is unconditional love. Love your enemies unconditionally. This is probably one of the hardest things to accept in this book because it so strains our normal thinking. The unconditional includes forgiveness. War, divorce, and all of the human conflicts that are increasing today, are ultimately caused by the inability to forgive and accept. Forgiveness is the acceptance of what is. This is known by many as faith. Forgiveness is the reconciling or union of good and evil and the relaxation of high and unrealistic expectations upon men and women, young and old. We're only human. What if we all truly loved our enemies as much as we did our most beloved family members? Unfortunately, the world does not live according to this paradigm. Misery loves company, just as love does. We are born from light, and in order to live as intended we need to see more than what our eyes show us. In the eyes of the person who forgives, a transgression truly forgiven is no offense at all. The intention/act of forgiveness is a form of acceptance and love that completely alters the resonant energy of all kinds of conflict or so-called evil. In the light of acceptance, how can one knowingly and intentionally "sin" if one feels connected to everything, a connection also known as love? If one has the awareness and intention to receive and radiate love, how can sin or conflict exist? How can one be sad or angry if they truly have the intention of forgiveness and acceptance? Love and accept the hate, injustices, and conflict in your life. We have a limited consciousness, limited free will, and limited awareness of the beauty of life as a whole. This is our individually perceived reality. We view God, free will, and everything in this existence based on our beliefs and our personal experiences. Surrendering to the infinite unknown is certainly a leap of acceptance beyond reason, and it is like no other leap you will ever make. Enlightenment is the awareness and understanding of the Universal or God, of self or spirit, through experience and openness. The ultimate truth and beauty is enlightenment, and it can be seen and felt in this world, in every touch, however sensual or painful, in every taste however delicious or disgusting, in every sight however beautiful or ugly, in every smell however delightful or repulsive, in every sound however melodious or discordant, and in every thought and emotion however pleasing or distressful. Truth goes beyond imagination, because imagination is too often limited by memory and experience within the context of our restricted and egocentric individual lives.

We must see the beauty of God as Nature, and Nature as ourselves if we are to have this awareness and enlightenment. Because if we do not, we will continue to be ignorant, deceived, lacking insight, and we will accept and become caught in the illusion and its consequences. Our restricted awareness of universal intent determines what size filter our consciousness uses to view the world. Our body and behavior grant us the ability to explore and observe reality whereas the desire for truth unites us to the beauty of it. In other words, life gives us eyes and the love of sight gives us life. These are two sides of the same coin. Our purpose in life is to live according to its truth. We let in or shut out beauty in different magnitudes and durations. Commonsense reality used in our everyday life is only a partial piece of the whole truth. In this way, the majority of people are divisive, unhealthy and conflictive, which keeps the body sustained and the mind busy, stressed and depressed with routine to-do lists, work, bills, traffic, children and relationships but at the cost of any explosive refreshment to their weary eyes and drained lives.

Belief is an exclusive view of reality, and faith is the trust one has in it. All choice is limited, because one is uninformed and/or misinformed. People often say that seeing is believing, and yet there are so many things people believe in that they have never seen for themselves. What makes someone believe something? If something coincides with your personal experience and there are few, if any, incongruities, then it is more likely to be believable. Furthermore, if someone who went to school and has credentials (a doctor, lawyer, judge, professor, or scientist) tells you something, what they say about their area of supposed expertise carries increased credibility. People tend not to believe certain things for a variety of reasons, such as what they were taught during their upbringing, whether or not the belief sufficiently agrees with their previous experiences; they will even reject a belief if, in their minds, it just plain old doesn't stand to reason. Some may not believe certain things simply because they are too negative to comprehend or appear to directly oppose their own belief system. We often want to know exact details and have concrete evidence, and if those details are too vague or are even moderately inconclusive, we may dismiss a concept entirely. It shakes our inner world. When confronted with imminent danger that can't be avoided, we are not satisfied with a simple warning. Because if that is all we get, we tend to not take it seriously, particularly when the people warning us aren't giving specifics or making a big enough deal out of it.

As we all know, dogma means an established and unquestioned belief. In other words, we believe what we want for whatever the reasons. The majority of people used to think the Earth was flat. In the past we used to think Earth was the center of the solar system and even of the universe. Humanity had no clue to the existence of microorganisms or black holes. How did we get from there to here? We were curious about nature and we investigated it. Each and every one of us has our own agnostic view of certain things, which is defined as an uncertainty or lack of faith. Our view of reality is based largely on the belief in our senses and how our brains interpret its information. People who say that belief is reality might choose to believe in a pantheon of gods and goddesses or a flat planet. They may choose to dismiss the existence of microorganisms, gravity, atoms, evolution, that they won't die or any other belief that seems crazy by the standards of earnest observation, and thus, for them, these beliefs are unequivocally real and true. Concerning beliefs based in ignorance, dogmatic acceptance, careless observation, fantasy, imagination and fabrication: if you had one hundred percent unwavering belief and certainty in the whole of your mind as to their reality, then yes, your beliefs would be 'real', but only to your mind. Belief is founded in both truth and illusion. But obviously our senses and perceptions tell us what is "real," don't they? We don't actually know what we think we know. We think we know what is real, but reality has a knack for hiding things from our senses. Now then, when we suspend the act of believing, we suspend judgment and selective observation, and we are left with the reality of what actually is. One can be so deeply immersed in what is being observed that the act of believing is erased and we see things as they really are. The act of judging or choosing stops us from seeing the whole reality. Belief is based on thoughts, memories, experiences, judgments, and their combinations resulting in a usually self-serving conclusion. This is very regimented and particular and leaves little to no room for the possibilities that exist. In a sense, belief or choice ignores much of what reality has to offer. Faith is another matter, not of kind but of scope. Faith is when we give up our control and let things be as they are. Ideas are based on thought, and our experiences and memories are used to navigate our world. Humanity categorizes, measures, observes, relates, and believes. We separate and categorize, then we compare what we have selected to form a relationship of similarities and differences in order to provide relative descriptions. If we recognize a pattern, which is just a repetition of events or findings, we grow more confident in our categorizations, and we then reach a higher degree of trust in these beliefs, further solidifying them in our minds. All scientific and spiritual beliefs are based on high degrees of certainty. Nothing can be proved or disproved with absolute certainty to anyone unless the person wants to choose and accept the evidence or viewpoint if it's sufficiently understandable and pleasingly agreeable to their own view. Most people are utterly convinced of their generally unexamined feelings and opinions' of what is real or not. This is because their experience of reality is taken for granted as quite real. Whether these views are founded in reality or only restricted to their own personal experience doesn't seem to matter because how could their experience of reality possibly be, for lack of a better word, unreal? Ones' unexamined perception of reality is not unreal but is rather naturally adapted to be limited and self-serving. The conviction of ones' limited ideas, thoughts and beliefs *as* a complete and pure representation of reality is an innocent and self-(pre)serving deception and is common to all life forms. Humanity is a force of nature that has taken ideas, thoughts and beliefs to levels far and away from nature's reality and intention.

People believe, or choose, only what they are aware of (knowledge), and this circumscribed, depreciated understanding of things splits the view of reality into a believable and an unbelievable dichotomy. As children we play make-believe, and as adults we continue to employ this method of entertainment, except that now we have become lost in this habit and in the illusion. How can one believe something if one isn't aware of it? As my wife puts it, "What I don't believe, I'm unaware of," which is to say everything we are aware of in our psychological construction of existence is perceived as either actual or fantasy by the mechanism of choice, which takes portions of the reality of what is and includes, excludes, or imagines it. We are convinced of the validity of our individual perception of reality by both the chosen acceptance and the denial of everything of which the truth of reality is comprised. We believe in what we pay attention to; we confidently believe in sensory "proof." Perception is belief, belief is imagination, and these are what we want to believe in. Faith is a receptivity and openness to a choice-free view of the world. Beliefs can't be overtly forced, but the art of persuasion can be a subtle and effective substitute. Persuasion can be from social influence as well as through one's own internal justification. Many stray from what "is" into a world of thought and illusion by self-justifying conflicting feelings and actions, which further reinforces that degraded level of awareness, and all for the sake of a shallow and fleeting sense of happiness.

Persuading or simply pointing out things in an influential manner can be undisguised and forthright. It can also be an almost imperceptible guidance toward accepting something through passive or active approaches, from both the side of truth and the side of deceit. Our view of the world is also altered by the perspectives of people we appreciate and respect. The weird part is that once we accept something as true we tend to be committed to that conviction, even if the original conditions under which we accepted it have changed. This is the slippery bait-and-switch that emerges from many, if not all, choices. All of this has to do with choice. Of course, plants, insects and animals make instinctual and reactive as well as thought out and deliberative choices, but they are necessary and complimentary to their surroundings. Whereas our decisions are needless and conflictive to our surroundings and ourselves, because of our divisive intention which spreads the imbalance of these unintended consequences in the wake of our obsessive-compulsive desires and actions. Decisions are made by weighing options and our scale generally sways toward oneself. Nature and all the organisms living as nature don't create any unintended consequences; we do because our desires and thinking is excessive, self-centered and antagonistic to the intention of nature and its organisms as a whole. We have separated ourselves from nature. In order to create an enemy and conflict, a choice to distance and separate is always the first step. Choice is accepting one view or position while denying other alternatives after weighing all the presented options. It is a judgment based on our thoughts and our experiences in the past. Choice and belief are mechanisms of separation. To choose is to exclude and as a result, ignorance, or conflict, is a deliberate choice. The awareness of absolute love, or life, is effortless and cannot be forced. Conflict is forced and chosen to happen whereas love just happens spontaneously.

Do We Love Our Children When We Go for Broke?

Although it may not seem obvious at first, we care more about ourselves than we do about our children or grandchildren. This is a difficult statement to accept and an easy statement to get upset about. Of course this simply cannot be true, can it? We love our children and would do anything for them. But stop and think about how our shortsighted demands and our ceaseless assault against nature, for the supposed benefit of our loved ones, will affect them and their families beyond one or two generations into the future. We are rushing nature as if every day is Black Friday, because nature is abundant and we are greedy. What we leave behind is all that our children have to look forward to. People still don't seem to get this. You love your children, but you are leaving them an Earth in ruins. When we die, this world will become our children's only real inheritance. What kind of legacy have we really left behind? Whenever any of us tries to decrease our "carbon footprint," we just can't seem to get ahead of ourselves. Each of us consumes fresh water, food, clothing, electricity, gasoline, forest products, and synthetic, manufactured goods every day. The bare minimum for the survival of nearly 7 billion people is becoming increasingly too much for the Earth to handle. No amount of well-intentioned Greenpeace programs, carbon credits or anything of that nature will solve the problems our planet faces. Only by eliminating our illusions and decreasing our numbers through the restraint of human propagation and the collapse of our life support systems will there be a balance and appreciation of the everyday beauty we presently forsake. These ideas at first sound horrible, but think about how effective and unavoidable they are in leading to a world of balance and awareness. Change must come from the inside of every individual first otherwise the obvious alternative is suffering for many more people than there are today due to war, famine, or disease—probably all three. We are too many consuming too much, and nature always has a way of balancing things. That is the essence of nature. If mountains rise, weather eventually brings them down. Similarly, if more and more people consume too much as we rise to our own modern "golden age," like so many previous civilizations, nature will inevitably bring us back down. The end of a cycle is the realization and fulfillment of itself.

There will always be people who are afraid of truth and death. These feelings of fear, of separation, death, pain, or whatever are like being in the sunlight yet feeling cold. Some people enjoy the comfort of being "blissfully" ignorant and unaware. It is a narrow view of life that masks the beautiful truth of our seeming predicament. "Out of sight, out of mind" is the same as "out of mind, out of sight." Realization puts people in a place where they have to acknowledge that which they want to ignore, and they then find themselves in a position where they have to change how they think and act. This rude awakening to reality conflicts with three of the most universal of human traits, the avoidance of peace and uncertainty, the attraction to self-indulgence, certainty and conflict, and the desire to possess life's beauty.

Picture Perfect

People choose to focus their time and attention on whatever pleases them most. We like something, so we take a picture of it to remember it. Taking pictures, among the many other forms of attachment, is an apt example of our almost insatiable compulsion to glean and possess that has gained my concern of late, not because what we desire to remember or keep isn't worth the effort, but because it has gained an unbalanced priority in people's lives. Pretty much everybody takes pictures, thanks in large part to cell phone and digital memory technology that make it easy to take unlimited snapshots. Pictures are just a common and easy example of the preoccupation with memory that many people have. It isn't only picture-taking; it could be anything with the same intention of making something special and the attempt to possess it. Making moments special makes others less special, raising something up brings the rest down. Striving to seize an image, feeling or moment implies the possibility of its loss which then implies its possession. There is no possession or attachment unless it is related to its opposite: loss or detachment. Taken separately or together, loss and possession are illusions. Death is a huge sense of loss and we see this loss in every passing moment we cherish and wish to save or capture. It's all innocent enough, but so are many other things that end up causing suffering later on. Living without attachment or detachment can be difficult, but it's not impossible.

Life is just one big motion picture with endless things to make a handle out of and hold on to. The moments we have, love, and remember are the ones we feel most connected to. This truth should be so simple. I don't blame artists or lovers of moments, because there are endless beautiful and unique moments, things, people and events we all want to remember over and over again. We view our past as if we are outsiders, disconnected, looking in on the scene, akin to Scrooge on his fateful night.

Now, the pictures that we take will never recapture the full experience of the moment and will inevitably be forgotten, given enough time. We take pictures of things we want to remember, but what about the moments that are forsaken? Are they not good enough to be remembered, or are they willfully forgotten because these experiences do not evoke pleasant thoughts and memories? When does one moment end and another begin? Have you ever taken a picture of something you didn't want to remember? What does this say about the moments not thought of as special and not remembered or captured? When the world is truly seen as it is, then what is seen in every moment becomes as rich and rare and as beautiful and precious and full of life as the moments on either side of it, because in reality they are all the same present and infinite moment. We feel a need to hold on to this eternal moment because of fear, greed and insecurity, and there are so many beautiful things we wish to have and keep. This endeavor is ultimately in vain. It is impossible, selfish, and against the flow of life to possess anything. Taking pictures or capturing moments is like shooting a bird from the sky to get a better look at it, only to see it lifeless when taken from its natural motion in flight. All moments are fleeting. Taking a picture just isn't the same.

It's all about the moment, not about capturing it. Have you ever taken a picture of a cloud or a sunset that did not turn out as you'd hoped or expected? Why is this? The moments, when seen as they are, as ever-present, need no thought of capturing or photographing them because they are as transient as the thoughts, memories, emotions, and feelings associated with them. When one experiences the total awareness of the observed as it really is, that person rightly lacks any desire or wish to freeze the flow of creation, change, and life. That is, when one is immersed in the now, there is no concept or notion of oneself in the future observing a moment from the past. Nevertheless, it is hard to blame people for taking pictures, because there is so much beauty in every single eternal and indivisible moment. How do we distinguish one moment from another? This is the illusion that divides and isolates reality into chunks of moments making one better or worse than the others.

Shunning pictures and all of the rest of the memory-possession business is just as silly as the preoccupation with it. An excessive preoccupation with picture-taking or the complete refusal to take pictures, both conflict with the flow of reality as it happens in any given moment. The resistance of ones' desire to possess and remember moments, by jumping to the polar opposite and totally avoiding still images of the past, creates a disharmony with "what is" because of the internal struggle to resist ones' actual desires. This creates, inside ones' mind, two opposing forces between "what is" and what one feels "should be." These polarized methods of excessive attachment and detachment are forces that push against reality and enable conflict to flourish, not only limited to the example of picture-taking but in all manners of fighting and pushing against anything considered less than ideal, less than just, less than righteous, less than desirable and less than satisfying to ones' values. Neither extreme possession nor escape will create happiness. It's the same as the contrast between an angry person who denies their feelings and holds them in and one who embraces the anger and suddenly releases it upon any suitable outlet. Holding in anger only builds it up while releasing it only allows the wellspring room to be built up again. Neither approach brings about peace because like any volcano there is stability for a period but it eventually loses its top. The inextinguishable fire and mounting weight hidden deep within continues the build-up/release cycle. The force of unnecessary conflict and desire, instead of being fostered or ignored (allowing the root of conflict to remain ever-present) must rather be balanced, neutralized and dissolved by understanding the whole nature of attachment, detachment and conflictive desires. The polarization between a fixation on possessing reality and avoiding reality are mindsets of our left and right hemispheres and are conflictive, whereas the simple acceptance of reality combines and annihilates both. The mind finds any middle ground of opposites to be a contradiction and doesn't readily comprehend it. It's like holding an egg so tightly to keep the chick inside warm and alive that it breaks, or doing the opposite by suddenly dropping it in its nest so that it breaks on impact. It is possible to have an in-between approach in which one must neither hold on nor let go, but rather allow the moment of now, like a fragile egg, to grow with natural grace and without misguided human assistance.

So take pictures if you want to, paint paintings and write words. Just understand them as plaque build-up in the free flowing arteries of reality that have the potential to grow into outright blockages. Don't get too preoccupied, and be okay with letting it all go. Whether it is a sculpture, or a tombstone, painting, photo, or book, we wish to capture that which is most ephemeral, which is life, love, and beauty.

The Wind and Stone Are in Our Breath and Bone

The stone with which we build our pyramids and churches and skyscrapers and cities was created by the same cyclic pattern as our own creation. Heat, pressure, and time created all stone, from limestone to granite to diamonds, all of which are simultaneously created and destroyed in cycles. Stone has been associated with permanence, certainty and timelessness ever since man began using it for spearheads, tombs, pyramids, the Dome of the Rock—the most spiritual place in all three Abrahamic religions—hieroglyphs, petroglyphs, Freemasonry, and quartz crystal technology. Stone supports life, from the dynamic rock of the Earth, with its natural creations from oceans to caves, to mountains and forests, which are pivotal to our existence, and stone can also destroy life, like the asteroid that killed the dinosaurs and the pebble with which David killed Goliath. Stones of all shapes, sizes, colors, and other different properties create our world as we know it. When we die, we most likely will have tombstones placed over our graves. Fossils are preserved over millions of years, the biological matter replaced with stone, and so ancient animals that were not turned into oil or other fossil fuels become the stone which is their epitaph. We want to be remembered and live on after death; that is, we want to live on in our paintings, our names, pictures, books, tombstones, our genetic legacy, and our memories, and we attempt to survive and conquer the finality of our bodies' death in a million other ways. We want to leave our mark on the world, and have we ever! We want to exist in people's memories and not be forgotten which, to many, is the same as never having existed at all. This is about as self-centered as we can get as a species, and it's only a futile attempt to hang on to the transient life we enjoy for a few short years. We generally feel uncomfortable about the unknown, and as a consequence we tend to hold on tightly to the known. Does the anxiety of the unknown, leading to the inflated motivation to possess more objects and knowledge than is necessary, explain why we are so curious? Is curiosity simply a behavioral mechanism that allows for the transformation of the unknown into the known, thus creating, in no small part, a false sense of security and certainty? Maybe it's also that we are just naturally curious because we think the universe is beautiful and love to connect to it by observing, interacting, and discovering more about it and ourselves. It takes energy to be curious and also to love. However, the good thing about curiosity and the similar creative intention of love is that it is like exercise; the more energy you put into it the more you receive in turn. Distractions of attention through ignorance and sensory indulgences, for example, slow the process of allowing love to enter and exit seamlessly, and this is due to disproportionately spreading thin and/or over-focusing awareness. I believe love and curiosity are the wonder and openness one has about things, and is as innocent and lovely as looking at a rainbow or the stars when we could just as easily not.

Memory—Reality Seen Through Smog in the Noggin

Memory is an imperfect perception that alters reality in everything from color to shape and size. It gives us our ability to live and to live well. It allows us to reminisce, imagine the good and bad times, and to think. Our mental representation of life is called a schema, and without it we wouldn't last long. It's a partial view of reality, but it works well enough for us to get by. It's one big fudge factor full of compromises, by which I mean it's not without advantages. If it works don't fix it, but what if it needs work and we don't think it does? Memory has the hidden disadvantage of not just being foggy and spotty, but sometimes also being a downright fabrication. What we remember might be not at all what actually happened. However, for all intents and purposes no one cares about this too much because the process of memory, however fuzzy, photographic, emotionally weighted, fabricated, and flawed it may be, does a good enough job in an evolutionary sense to persist as a proven method of survival. Memory is an evolutionary compromise that tips the scale toward the benefit of the organism, but what is lost in this natural selection is a complete and accurate reading of reality.

We like remembering only what we want to remember as is seen in most photo albums. Our memories are drastically skewed by our intentions and emotions, which are inextricably attached to them. They add a heavy and burdensome weight which drags them into illusion. We all create illusions, whether on purpose or otherwise. Our natural bias is a compromise away from reality and toward advantages for ourselves and the species. Our memories project into the future to make the present better, but this projection of illusion has gotten way out of hand. We want to manufacture the present into our own view of perfection but, in between remembering the past and projecting it into the future, we end up missing the true perfection in front of us entirely. The thing is, the present is always perfect. The process of thought, which only exists in the ideas of past and future, is missing the reason why humanity is utilizing it, which is to survive and flourish in the reality of balance and peace. Instead of living a life of reality and peace, we live in the conflicted model that thought has created in the mind. When tuned out of the inspiration of nature, the art of living becomes blatantly contrived. This incongruity with nature is where our manmade, idealistic, conflictive, and thus counterfeit lives are rooted. This is a perfect case of losing one's way along the way. This is not just one or two people, but the entire human population! It is our short-sighted, perilous disconnect from truth.

The Method of Our Madness

It is the tool of observation itself that deceitfully separates us, as observers, from that which is observed. How we use our observational tools and our trust in their completeness are also factors in the loss of peace and the rise of conflict. We have pulled at the thread of creation that has woven itself into harmony and we are now tangled in it. Done in balance with the natural tapestry, this thread-pulling can of course be a significant benefit to all organisms. It only serves to create a more beautiful and unfolding masterpiece; however, humanity has shown that it doesn't know how to weave with nature and instead gets caught in a self-inflicted conflict. Although the benefit of ingenuity does not reach a ceiling of excellence, and biologically is not needed to live within our means of survival, there is of course more to reality than what our sensory endowments allow us to cultivate and harvest. To aid in our survival, our senses and mental gymnastics have essentially domesticated reality into something of an abstraction—conceptually more predictable, mechanical, and manageable. Domestication, or fear of uncertainty, has made nature humanity's bane. The whole concept of navigating through life with habitually reactive and unexamined thought as well as sheer instinct leads to the perception of division and conflict and the unbalanced reality we see before us. The way of life can only be acknowledged when there is a clear insight into both the true nature and the limitations of thought and instinct as a single balanced survival system. We have concepts translated into words and sounds, then analyzed, evaluated, and interpreted into different words and sounds, and then each person translates them into their own personal meaning relating to their interpretation of that experience. This is all based on thought, memory, the isolated past, and the isolated future, all the while leaving the actual communication, the here and now, absent from their reality, when in reality that is all there is. This "enlightenment" is slippery, because it is not something one can grasp like an object, although we spend our lives chasing these things trying to hold on to all of them—grabbing at love, a shimmer of sunlight, a gust of wind. Try as we might, with loved ones, beautiful moments, or even the beautiful entirety of one's life, the intention to possess what is loved is ultimately fruitless. The entire concept of possession has its place in reality but not in the fullest sense. We want to hold on and not let go of all things precious, and who can blame us? As futile as these endeavors are, we all agree that this is useless, greedy, and silly. Yet at the same time it evokes a warming of the heart because it shows we all have moments we consider precious. The intention to hold on sprouts from the root of fear and ego and is the cause of all our problems. It is pointless. If you knew the pictures you took would never capture the fullness of the moment and they wouldn't last past your taking them (this is how we try to take and hold the uncatchable, which is life), would you still take them, fully knowing the unnecessary nature of the act? Or would you enjoy the moment and become consumed by and immersed in it, once you realize that you are the moment? Everything is all one in the same moment. All fear is the sense of losing that which is, not so obviously, an illusion.

The Art of Discovery

How many people don't question their beliefs? This should be common practice, and you should not be fearful of your reality changing, but rather excited that you can create and maintain the balance of reality alongside nature based on your desire to come to a fuller understanding of yourself and nature. Doubt, curiosity, and suspicion can arise from the desire to understand oneself and one's surroundings. With these feelings come confusion and uncertainty, however, because of these doubts and the presumed increase of clarity and understanding that follows; like pain or a problem searching for its solution, they consequently aid in their own subsiding. Discovering things about "outer" life and "inner" life is what connects us to the greater universe. Revealing and understanding what has been discovered, or reclaiming the recognition of beauty, requires interest and value as it relates to the inquiring person. Knowledge is awareness acquired from instinct or experience, and it is retained and grown upon because of its lasting value relating to the organism in which the knowledge resides. As a person is a part of life, inquiry about oneself is included in the exploration of nature. If one does not find reality and/or oneself interesting or of value, one will not see the full beauty of these things and will not care about or value life enough to learn, doubt, or discover the beautiful curiosities that abound. A blind eye toward the value of beauty, for whatever reason, is a blindness from the reality of nature and from ones' self. Interest and value are followed by doubt and curiosity, which are then followed by learning, understanding, and discovery. If any aspect of comprehending life is left out, the whole process is left incomplete and reality is then viewed as ugly, malicious and separate. The perception of flat out conflict and ugliness in nature and in oneself creates dichotomous world views about you and I, us and them, we and they, life and death, good and evil, past and future, heaven and hell etc. When we understand the process behind something or when we get an idea connecting things previously perceived to be unrelated, we become enlivened with inspiration, and this is the feeling of knowing God, creation, and your greater self. Discovery is a greater understanding and appreciation of things. Discovery is an act of creation, because in the awareness of reality, you are not only acting creatively, you are the force of creation itself. Discovery/creation is an awakening, a passion, an inspiration or breathing of nature's constant and simultaneous birth and decay. It is known to many as enlightenment, *moksha*, nirvana, or being reborn. Like every cell in one's body, we are all really being reborn constantly; we just don't see it. This is the revelation of genesis or the genesis of revelation. The eternally flowering tree of life is withering and blossoming simultaneously. The way to enlightenment or rebirth is to come to the understanding that the universe's purpose, along with everything else in it, is for us to completely experience love/god/nature/ourselves in all forms, as it is, right now. This is the "Theory of Everything" that physicists have searched for or the relationship with God that the devout have longed for, but because it is love, it makes sense that many haven't entirely found it yet in their equations, objective lenses and passed along traditions and experiences. One must be their own guide and ask and answer their own questions. Truth cannot be entirely found through others; any expressions of truth from anyone other than yourself are humble arrows that point to you and in all directions. A partial understanding of the whole of truth naturally leaves a certain level of ignorance about what is left, which thus remains unappreciated. When acquiring knowledge, we mainly see the limits of our own reality, and then we exult in claiming that we have conquered nature and understand it, when this is really only the thoughts we have about ourselves. We are deceived by separation. Almost all things related to the acts of man have been motivated by separation, and we see the projection of our own consciousness on ourselves and our environment. When we feel separated, we act accordingly. Understanding the whole truth of unity is the biggest endeavor we will have to face and it is why we exist; failing to understand the whole truth is why today we view everything—including birth, life, and death—as separate. It is why discovery is art, because how can uncovering truth be as beautiful as it is and not be called art? Being aware of beauty and truth and acting with the motivation it brings is the equivalent of being the creator. When you create or observe something beautiful you are an artist, and in this process there is a unity in which the artist and the art become one or the observer and the observed integrate into a single flow of movement. We create with our consciousness. When we dream and think and ponder the universe, we are creating what we observe by the way we choose to observe it. This explains the double slit experiment and hence quantum physics (see p. 260). If individual reality is partial and thus illusory, then this means that relativity theory (a theory explaining the interpretations of our world through a localized or relative consciousness) is also partial and illusory, which in turn would mean that quantum physics, with its individual observer effect and discrete particles, is therefore also partial and illusory, because it is based on the premise of isolated fragments and closed systems within the absolute singularity of the universe. These theories are incomplete in that they address only an individual's consciousness observed through our many filters. The art of discovery is feeling and understanding the blossoming truth and beauty of life from the preceding and subsequent seed or spark from which it flowers. Discovery comes simultaneously from within one's psyche and from the "outside world." There is no distinction of one or the other as separate. We can experience the beautiful truth in life and death because they are the same thing, just as space, time, energy, matter, God, and you and I are. We are already everything—we just have to discover this. We simply need to see past the illusions, which are fragmented views of the complete reality, caused by our self/localized consciousness to see this fractal reality. It is the art of discovery that creates infinite joy and awareness in every moment, and which brings a greater awareness of what life is about.

This might sound like an impossible undertaking, but it is nevertheless true: the universe and everything in it, including ourselves and others, can be understood if we want to accomplish this; all we have to do is open our eyes and discover what is already there. However, in order to seek we must already have an inkling of what we are seeking, and to find this is to simply recognize what has never truly been lost or misplaced at all. Our attention has been weakened and even lost in distraction and misdirection while the nakedness of reality patiently waits to be recognized and appreciated. When we find what we are looking for, we realize that we haven't really been separated from it, because it becomes more a process of reconnection or illumination. In a sense, it hasn't gone anywhere at all; we simply haven't been reunited, or have failed to recognize it. So when we seek, we find what we have always had, all along. We bridge the gap between the separation, not from what we have lost, but rather from what we have not recognized or have not seen. When there is no sense of time or self, there is nothing to fulfill, nothing to seek, and nothing to find. In mathematics, poetry, painting, or any other medium one chooses, you will find artists who say theirs is a creative art, while others will say theirs is a way of discovering what is already there. Creating is discovering what is already there, just as discovering is the art of creation. Any art is beautifully both.

Doubt

How can anyone be so sure about anything? How is it that we are able to screen and so casually dismiss so many things while just as casually embracing, with all our hearts, other things? Where do we get our convictions? How does anyone *know*? If someone says something that is true but that nevertheless sounds fantastical to the listener, they may doubt it because it conflicts with their individual schema of what the world is and of what is true and possible. They may respond by asking, "How do you know?" as if the storyteller might be lying or has no authority over what they are speaking about. Doubt has its place. So does an absolute conviction in truth, but how can one discern truth from untruth with any certainty? They are essentially polarized from what is real and what is not with nothing in between. This, I believe, is simply the delusion of a conflictive mentality. I personally don't believe in ghosts, but does it matter whether I do or not? A person may doubt the existence of quarks or quantum physics, but does it matter whether they do or not? There is ample evidence for the possibility of both ghosts and quarks. Ghosts, apparitions, or spirits may actually exist; however, for me, they just don't seem probable. That doesn't take away from my view of beauty nor, I expect, does another person's disbelief in quarks or black holes dim the lights on their perspective of reality and beauty. However, illusions always have unforeseen and unintended consequences. Moreover, if one believes in a monster under their bed, this can cause problems, because it interrupts the reality of getting a good night's sleep. Alternatively, this also means that if one believes in the Easter Bunny, lucky leprechauns, or Santa Claus who brings joy to children on Christmas Day, that person creates an illusory yet undeniable happiness.

Does this mean that Saint Nick or any other fairytale should be welcomed because it brings joy to a person? How can the idea of Santa be, for lack of a better word, wrong? Recall that ignorance is not bliss. Children and adults alike can believe in an illusion for a long time. Some will eventually find out the truth and may react with despair, or perhaps eventual acceptance; others may live an entire lifetime not knowing anything different. So what is the distinction? Due to this convenient tool of conditioning and control, in the case of Santa Claus, a child who is told that if they behave according to the rules of parents or authority figures, as a reward they will receive gifts. Whereas if they are naughty or disobedient, they might be punished by a withholding of gifts and a lump of coal in their stocking and might have a distorted, conflicted, and less beautiful perception of reality. This may seem like minor stuff, but I deeply wonder if people have a hint of doubt and awareness about the misguided and self-assured convictions they have built with their conflictive views of reality. If one becomes sad or angry, one only has to look to oneself for responsibility. Woe is you. Illusion spreads itself and creates conflict. However long one chooses to look toward conflict and away from the beauty of truth, the beauty remains, however unseen it is. If you fail to look at the beauty of the truth, you persist in missing it. The power of your firmly-held convictions must not mean that you cease questioning things, if only to keep from becoming self-righteous and misguided as things change and the moment of life flows by. Don't be too sure of anything, unless of course you *are* sure of it. Doubt is a sense of healthy skepticism about the known that makes some people uncomfortable, but I think it's good in a way, because it makes people curious and extends the boundaries of their awareness. Comfortable people who lack doubt are static, stagnating, and not moving with the flow of creation. There is no conclusion and no end to the known or unknown. This isn't to say that there is no peace; it is possible to have a union of opposites when there is an awareness of both together, for example, the known and unknown, doubt and certainty. As with all things, balance and proportion are crucial to forming a harmonious perspective.

Doubt is a concept of belief which, like all things, is open to interpretation. I doubt things I am unsure of, for instance, my proficiency, without instruction or practice, to be a pilot or to climb rocks without a rope. Another example is my own personal doubt in the existence of aliens with, let's say, skin with slug eyes instead of hair. I may be completely wrong and, in all probability, based on the Drake equation (which suggests the high probability of alien life, based on the multiplication of stars harboring habitable planets residing in every galaxy in the universe), there could be innumerable species far stranger than the one I just described. These examples are just an illustration of how belief works and how it can change the way we look at things. New things are scrutinized on the basis of our past beliefs and individual experiences. People tend to believe what they are first presented with. An example of this is the halo effect. If a first impression of something or someone is positive, we then tend to explain away subsequent negative aspects of this impression, even if negative traits accumulate. The reason is that, since our first impression was a positive one, everything that comes after must compete with that initial impression, because we compare a person's subsequent actions to our first impression of them. I am often surprised and always amazed by the fact that there are so many things that seem impossible based on our conventional wisdom, seeming common sense, and personal experience, and yet they exist. People are apt to say, "When I see it with my own two eyes, then I'll believe it." But in this age of special effects and computer graphics, even this doesn't work anymore. Anything can be made to look real. We have faith in our senses because only through them do we acquire our perceptions of material reality, upon which we must rely to navigate toward things we need and want, and to steer clear of danger, pain, and the things we don't want.

The Brain, the Senses, and Perception—
A Misused Multi-Tool

The brain is the organ responsible for the advantageous interpretation of sensory input, thereby creating the critical behaviors of the organism necessary to survive within its own self-created psychological realm and the world at large. Mind and matter are reflections of each other and can be imagined as a Möbius strip with one end turned 180 degrees and connected to the other end to create a one-sided strip with two apparent mind and matter aspects turned into itself. The mind is the perceptions we sense from the activity of the brain. The brain is our computer hardware and the mind is our software. This Möbius example can further include: quantity and quality, action and reaction, north and south, and any other face-valued opposites. The brain is like a spoiled brat, always wandering from memories of the past and projections (expectations) about the future, all the while never fully enjoying and being aware of the present (which is a superposition of all three aspects of time). We hop, skip, and jump from past to future, missing the now in between. The brain is always changing its shape. It changes with every thought and emotion and every piece of sensory information that it receives. This is called brain plasticity, and it lasts until we die. Physically, the brain is the consistency of congealed leftover spaghetti or Jell-O. It is very soft tissue, which is why it is contained in a fluid-filled sac inside a thick skull. The softness of brain tissue enables us to physically, and subsequently psychologically, reshape and grow our brains with relative speed. In other words, our brains are made to be able to move or reshape, just like Jell-O. The apparent non-physical changes the brain experiences, such as thoughts or feelings, actually create physical changes in the neural pathways, which interconnect areas of the brain like a tangled yet very effective superhighway. Most of our mental tracks are individual/narrow and one-way; they are scattered side roads leading to many dead ends. Generally automatic and hastily constructed, these gravel roads are filled into the brain's neural network without any real plan or layout with respect to the whole process of consciousness. They scramble to address the constant onslaught of thought traffic and, as a consequence, these roads get tangled up in themselves. Thoughts grown from a perspective of separation serve to isolate and categorize abstractions grown from reality, instead of allowing a clear connection and harmony among all roads to create a paved and integrated expressway, like an interstate highway system. Perspective and intention greatly affect the observer's consciousness; the acknowledgement of truth can be more of a self-reinforcing roadway—whether conflicting or harmonious—of awareness. Form equals function and the brain is a very appropriate example.

Self Consciousness, Hive Consciousness and Absolute Consciousness

I feel that an individual's consciousness—always a philosophical hot topic—is, like all things, far from adequately described or even understood through ones' mind in its entirety. Consciousness is, for an organism, a mental process that allows for perception. I believe it is largely an emergent process or behavior that derives from the number, relationship, and interaction of neurons and glial cells brought about by the experience of innumerable sensations, and their subsequent interpretations. Emergence is when new characteristics arise from amplification, and the feedback throughout this process. Does the concept of consciousness include all consciousness? Is consciousness the mind of all matter, the cosmic inspiration or breath of life residing in the totality of all natural phenomena? And, if this is true, does it mean we have the same consciousness as a grain of sand, or a tree, our neighbor, or even God as the entirety of existence? Are we just getting a slim, scaled-down taste of the whole? We have the same spirit or soul as everything else that exists. We separate and say "my" soul only due to our own experience. Ones' consciousness is the perception of the relationship between oneself and everything else. We act and react to various stimuli based on certain laws and we have come to accept these due to the recognition of patterns. Consciousness is the biological equivalent of water condensing and rising to create a cloud and rain. "Individual" water molecules or neurons each do what comes naturally without any idea or goal to create a rain cloud but, as they collect, a cloud, mind or awareness emerges. In a cloud, these forces create electrical charges, which result in a rainstorm with lightning and thunder. Consciousness, like life, is the storm which creates itself, and awareness of this storm (self-awareness) is our chance to see reality as it really is. This means that when atoms (or intentions) are orchestrated in a particular manner, then consciousness can arise. Consciousness is the orderly process of atoms emerging as the awareness known as the observer/subject, and the things we observe are deeply entangled in the process of awareness called matter, the observed or object. Self-awareness (an awareness of the universe as the greater self) requires both sides of this single equation of experience for reality to exist. Reality is a process made of a conceptual string consisting of two intertwined and indivisible strands called the observer and the observed, thus creating a singular reality. The full realization of consciousness is when the orchestra of the universe is tuned to all "radio stations" at once, and these interactions create the consciousness of creation with itself. All stations, when united in harmony, don't create white noise or interfering static but, in the context of reality, they create reality itself. Any storm is a choreographed conglomeration of many factors, and one gust of wind or lightning flash can affect the whole storm, just as a thought, observation or memory can affect the whole consciousness. Awareness exhibits the readiness for use, but also abuse, caused in no small part by the overuse in choosing to believe in segregation, categorization and thus division and conflict. Made by all organisms, these instinctual and reflexive decisions based on a narrow benefit to ones' self, and more direct groups relatable and identifiable to one, are beneficial to every system of nature because they are all interrelated and self-regulating. We have commandeered nature and are asleep at the wheel, caught deep in our dreams. We primates possess strong senses of individualism, self-importance, as well as moral and ethical agreements of right and wrong which vary from culture to culture. These ideas of right and wrong usually only pertain to the human species and favor the people in the religion/society/government in which these highly devoted and cult-like beliefs concerning what is desirable sprout from. You can't spell culture without cult. If selective and egotistic awareness is repeated and grown upon to the point of familiarity, habit and obscurity; one must only look at the global predicament induced by the feedback loop of our socially molded human psyche to understand the consequences of limited, divisive and thus conflictive awareness.

Consciousness is the awareness of awareness—or one person's reflection and narrative of what he or she experiences and thinks about reality. A person's consciousness is their lens to life's beauty. With consciousness as a reflection of awareness there can be a blurriness of focus due to asymmetric proportions between the perceptions of beauty in nature and in oneself. Consciousness is a lens to an unimaginably beautiful world, but the lens may be large, small, foggy, dirty, crystal clear, unused, properly used, or abused. The lens of consciousness is formed largely by using the coarse grit of survival struggles and, since we are a social species, the more refined sand of relationship skills with other people, being largely that of the dynamics within the units or cells of society: the family. The roles of both parents and siblings allow one within these cells to learn from one another and then use these skills when needed. The longer these basic survival skills are required and passed down the more they become etched into our DNA becoming instinctual over the generations. The majority of all family orientations in the animal kingdom behave in this teaching and supportive *all for one and one for all* family manner. For individuals limited by their specialties, this allows them to become a part of a system that is self-strengthening. As specialties or modern professions are quickly diversifying, allowing one to master certain aspects of life, learning from other's disciplines also has its survival advantages when starting a family of ones' own. In a way, an individual is a family unto themself by the way the roles of each family member overlap and support those of the other family members. A mother and father teach their children how to live as adults, mothers and fathers. Likewise, a child teaches their parents how to be children. A single person, family and society can be representative of humanity because they are what humanity is made of. Our ancestors are not dead but live within every cell of every one of our nearly seven billion bodies. An ancestor or present descendant is the whole of humanity just as much as a blade of grass and soil upon which it rests is a meadow. The biggest problem facing humanity now, and since antiquity, is to understand oneself and our home.

Undivided Attention

Each of us thinks we have our own separate, personal consciousness in our own brain in our own body. This view of oneself, and as a result, everything that we view as not our self, makes us feel clearly separate from everything and everyone else (think how people generally hear only their voices in their internal narratives). We perceive things through our senses and have them interpreted by our brain into something comprehensible and useful. The brain is a localized area that houses our over 100 billion cells. These cells, called neurons, switch on and off, creating pathways or patterns for memory, skill, knowledge, and everything useful and practical to keep the mammalian organism alive (from dreaming to personality to our sensory perceptions), all wrapped up into one personal reality. The brain can be compared to a computer. We each think we have our own brain inside the limits of our cranium. The brain interprets the information collected by the senses from outside as well as inside it. The brain sees no sharp line between what it thinks or imagines reality to be and what reality actually is. These interpretations and inferences made by the brain are what we call ideas, beliefs, opinions and feelings, which reside not in the reality "outside" the processes of the brain but in the transformations of reality made within it. This is where the mind or consciousness takes on a world of its own. These thoughts, ideas and perceptions arise from the activity of the brain which serves to bring only a slice of reality, albeit quite a valuable slice, to ones' understanding of reality. Every thought or idea is limited by the benefits and hazards we habitually weigh and render from the interpretations of reality made within the brain. This is why we all think of the universe and each other in terms of finite and separate objects. Ones' knowledge (as ones' mental reality) is reached by the filters of the senses. By the process of evolution which has tuned our senses to be of substantial benefit, the brain and mind, as a result, is a finite, categorizing, practical and useable tool that only has a limited access to truth excluding the perception of the entire, unified and infinite reality of nature. Look at the universe and consciousness as the World Wide Web. It is not a localized thing; it is everywhere, as a ubiquitous and amorphous process through thin air. It's not until we hook our computers, or brains, up to this information energy that we are said to be conscious, as we traditionally think it to be. Likewise, we are not separate and isolated beings as most think. These ideas of ones' own special soul with personality, likes, dislikes and so on are just the process of thought coping with the idea of losing itself. We have the same soul or eternal life force as everything else; we just choose to perceive and possess a certain portion of it and say it is our own. The soul of the universe is material as well as immaterial, just like one's body, thoughts, personality, morals, character, and so forth. Neither the brain nor heart is the house of the soul or consciousness; it just connects to it, like a radio connecting to the universe through radio waves, serving as both the radio and the individual stations with fractal frequencies. The computer or radio has intricate circuits and parts like the brain or heart. However, when one looks inside it one doesn't see any information, images, or music because it is a process. Our consciousness is the radio that receives awareness through vibration as our neurons live and die simultaneously, like a breath allowing life to enter and exit seamlessly without attachment. By swimming with the flow of life, we become all radio stations at once. Then there is no need to tune in, as we are the orchestra; we become the music, including the material that receives it, because we are both the receiver and the received. It's like a live performance where the performer and the audience become the performance. A profound, and seemingly incredible level of truth is that your consciousness (or the awareness of the awareness of yourself and surroundings) from your viewpoint is only one viewpoint among the infinite viewpoints in the singular creation. You have a sliver of consciousness that, as a whole, is shared with everything from Adolf Hitler to your parents to a worm or an alien from across the universe. On the other hand, there is the classical perception of the brain that says it is the house of the soul and of consciousness, which of course it is because there is no place that consciousness is not. However, like a Russian nested doll, conscious reality is a house inside a larger house, ad infinitum. The brain, knowledge, and thought have taken precedence in our civilization, because the value of human reason originated in the ideas and thoughts themselves. Whether the classical sense or a more unified sense of the brain/mind, both are true to the perceiver when looked at through one paradigm or the other, so the choice of what one perceives is up to the perceiver to a large extent. Everyone is correct in their view of anything—just to varying degrees. That is, the whole of truth is always partially understood by any individual, and however correct the individual view may be, led by limited thought and experience, it will always be more or less precise but never quite complete. As soon as whole truth is understood, grasped by the mind and articulated, the very act of this process dilutes reality and makes it partial.

We often think that if we swim with the flow of nature we will sink or end up somewhere we don't wish to be. Evolution has helped us to recognize many things and to ignore just as many others. It is a double-edged sword embedded in this carrot-and-stick motivation seen in all biology. The brain has a threshold for collecting information. We can absorb and interpret only so much information and so many images within a certain span of time. Our brains, like all organs, have their limits. When too much information is received, much of it is ignored and/or blurred beyond recognition and usefulness. This means we can only have a few thoughts and process a few images per second—anything slower and we can distinguish it as separate entities, but anything faster and it all blurs together. Think of a strobe light, or think of motion pictures. Back in the early 1900s, early motion pictures were seen to flicker as they created the perception of motion. When we are subjected to a life-or-death situation or any other threatening or enlightening experience, our flicker frequency effectively doubles (from its normal thirty-two frames per second) to allow more information to be absorbed in the same amount of time. This is why in such situations time appears to have slowed or even stopped. We experience a heightened awareness of being in the moment, the "now" of the flow of life, which is a timeless, escalated and peaceful form of awareness related in some respects to the fight or flight response. This fight or flight response sends the body into the control of the subconscious, which is where much truth hides as well as where addictions such as alcoholism or drug abuse originate as mechanisms to avoid or escape stress. The escape response not only causes addictions, but I also believe it is a main reason for the pandemic of ignorance and unawareness that has swept the globe, all in an attempt to get away from the perceived distress of painful realities. There is a desire to remain oblivious even if only temporarily and dishonestly. Anyone who believes in the statement "ignorance is bliss" is therefore speaking from an individual and misinterpreted experience, and thus *cannot* know what they are missing. Ignorance is the same as denial. This is a main reason for the depression, sadness, hatred, violence, apathy, and general unhappiness in the world. Escape compounds. We are blissfully unaware until we have no choice. Then it is the constrained psychological movement of ignorance itself which is the cause and the effect of conflict. If we pay no attention to our consciousness, if we allow our escape mechanisms and ignorance to take over, it is our subconscious mind that then rules many of our decisions, habits and some really rather important choices we should be aware of. When one becomes aware of a part of their subconscious it disappears into the transformation of consciousness. So shouldn't we actively choose to be more aware of our consciousness rather than perpetuating the real and adverse effects of our selective awareness and thus exclusory ignorance? Consciousness involves thoughts, feelings, ideas, perceptions, sensations, emotions, and dreams, and it is the awareness of being aware of these. Although there are well over 100 billion neurons in the human brain, simply being aware of being aware is not the definitive explanation of consciousness. We have all had the experience of "losing ourselves" in something we are passionate about without even being aware of it, whether it was an amazing song, painting or book. This does not mean one is unconscious, but rather one is for the moment unaware of the illusion of the self. Consciousness is one of the most misunderstood concepts in the world today. Some believe consciousness has evolved along with the physical adaptations of plants and animals and see humans as comparatively highly evolved and thus highly conscious. Hogwash! In order to have life there must be some kind of awareness at work, so everything which is alive has a consciousness or awareness, but not necessarily a self-awareness—a reflection of this consciousness or awareness. As human beings, we sense this as a kind of soul, internal dialogue or reflective voice in our heads that sounds much like our own voice. Rocks, air, DNA, trees, pitcher plants, dogs, cats, fish, bacteria, the inexperienced, the learned, and the brilliant all have a certain level of awareness. Each has its individual point of view. But, frankly, each of us has a drastically scaled-down perspective. Even with a full and vigorous imagination, we can only imagine what we can conceive of with our thoughts, and that is based on past thoughts, memories, and experiences. Our imaginations are surely not an all-encompassing immersion in the creative process that is the complete flow of reality. Real imagination or creativity is the release of active control along with the acceptance of the flow of creation. Genuine imagination as creativity is spontaneously unpredictable and beautiful as well as being rife with possibilities of all kinds; this happens when one is in tune with creation in such a way that they become the creative force of creation. Popular creativity is the process of a human mind manifesting an individual imagination based on manipulations of cultural and individual knowledge, personality, and experience. Full imagination is an infinite and timeless awareness of the actual and the potential being synthesized together in the same moment. Relativity makes things different for each observer, as does quantum physics. Both of these theories of physics point to the observer as integral and central to the observed reality so definitively that it would be completely negligent to deny it. However, they are both incomplete in that the observer, however central, has internal conflicts, and all the observations that he, she, or it makes are incomplete and flawed. True creativity is allowing the freedom of physics (or creation) in all of its variety to flower in sync with one's self. Oh, how the infinite simplicity of physical truth mixes and conspires to emerge and present to itself such a complete and awesome beauty that everything unwittingly obeys!

Perception

Is it the interpretation of our senses, along with the senses themselves, that gives us the perception of reality and existence, of ourselves and consciousness? Perception is the act of observation that bridges the separation between the perceiver and the perceived, or the observer and the observed. True and false are separated only by judgment, thought, and observation. There is no real separation between any two contrasting things, because there is really no individual observer to observe with judgment, distinction, relation, choice, and belief. Opposites are so utterly inseparable that they dissolve into each other and melt into one thing, as neither can exist without the other because there really is no "other." Pretty romantic, isn't it? This truth exists in all the opposites one can imagine. Observations of existence (as seen through classical eyes) bring a sense of separation. All fear, anger, sadness, and conflict, as well as everything our limited perception (and hence understanding) sees as good, such as love and pleasure, still has its opposite inescapably attached to it. If someone observes something involving hate, violence, etc. the observer naturally becomes entangled in the experience and may under some circumstances find their emotions absorbed into the same attitude, and react like a mirror, absorbing the hateful, violent demeanor into themselves. Once this happens, the conflictive energy reflects back to the event and individuals causing it, as well as redirecting it in almost unlimited ways. The hatred rarely stops at the beginning, but instead creates a long line of destruction past the point of its apparent origin. If you hate hatred, you are just further separating and continuing the cycle and become just like the object that you hate. If you hate hatred, what is the difference between what you see and feel as hateful and yourself? If you feel it, you are it. The beauty is that everything one can say about hate can just as easily be said about love. The difference is that the latter is an aware and peaceful process.

Intuition

Intuition is a tap on the shoulder from all past experiences which hide in ones' subconscious. Ones' basic attention placed upon any given situation is quite the scratch on the skin upon the body of reality. Intuition is synonymous with inner knowing without actually understanding why—and for good reason. Intuition does not have to be rationalized at the particular time that it arises. This is known as the art of discovery. If there is a feeling or a little voice that is strong enough for one to be aware of it without completely understanding it, that's intuition. It rarely makes sense compared to our conscious knowledge and left-brain reasoning. Some people refer to intuition as a gut feeling, or as what is sometimes known as flow. Good, rational decisions are usually based on factual information or knowledge. Great decisions are often simply a product of intuition. But what is intuition? If you make a pro and con list and, at the end, for some unknown reason, you still do not agree with the logical choice due to some unresolved itch, that's intuition! Intuition is a rush of subconscious information pushed into ones' awareness which usually occurs when ones awareness is captivated and dilated during an enlightening experience or the fight or flight response. Flow is when your mind is completely immersed, open, and dissolved in the present moment and nothing else. This is when the observer is aware of the observed as a single unit or action. The athlete making the big play, the artist in the grip of inspiration, the scientist making a discovery, the mother seeing her child smile, every person with a passionate inspiration or enlightening experience all have this feeling, however indescribable it may be. It occurs naturally by simply doing and not analyzing. These people are said to be in flow. You can call this instinct, or a connection to God-consciousness, or surrendering your intention to that of the universe. Feeling flow feels right; you feel you belong in that particular space at that particular time and beyond it, even transcending space and time. Being in flow can be called Nirvana, Moksha, or Enlightenment, and there are varying intensities to this experience. Being in flow, for most people, is likened to concentrating a thought or intention so much as to alter the very phenomenon that is being observed. When in flow or in a heightened state of consciousness, you can move past this observational focus and experience the absence and presence of consciousness simultaneously. This is a surrender of individual consciousness and an acceptance of the one true consciousness and intention. Keep in mind that when people talk about intuition and "gut feelings," these may well be their prejudices and instincts masquerading as a deep and unknown knowing of truth. Or they may be the biological and social imperatives that underlie our subconscious habits, and which may only feel like intuition.

Dreams

Sleep accounts for over a third of our lives, so it is important to understand what goes on during this time. Sleep is necessary for the body to recharge and give itself a tune-up after a long day. Sleep also allows the brain a chance to sort out all the information it has collected. Consciousness is said to be when someone is alive and aware of being aware of it. A view of consciousness when we are sleeping is called a dream, and its definition is also under much debate. What are dreams? The definition of a dream is, for the most part, inconclusive despite much speculation. Dreams are images or perceptions of any subconscious experience occurring during sleep, usually occurring during the stage of sleep called rapid eye movement, or REM sleep. Dreams can seem quite real, and of course they are, but only to the being experiencing them. The subconscious mind is the same as the conscious mind, except that it is relatively less apparent to the observer during their waking life. Aristotle once said, "Dreaming is thinking while asleep." Dreaming has also been theorized to be an explanation for the feeling of déjà vu, which translates as "previously seen." We can dream of events or circumstances and forget them when we wake; then when this déjà vu moment happens we get the ambiguous feeling that the event has happened before. Just because we forget a dream doesn't mean it didn't happen; we just can't recall it (this dream recollection is usually experienced as a déjà vu). There are recurring dreams in which we dream the same thing over and over again. There are frightening dreams called nightmares or night terrors. Some people seem to be able to dream only in black and white, while others dream only in color. Dreams can involve images, smells, sensations, emotions. Sleep and dreams strengthen memories and help us learn. If humans don't sleep, they die; whereas dolphins, for example, can sleep with one hemisphere of the brain at a time. Dreaming or imagining excites the same area of the brain with the same intensity as perceiving or sensing something that is classically considered to be real. This is why some dreams seem so real and vivid. Sleeping, besides allowing maintenance to the brains cells, gives us insight. The model we create while sleeping seems random and unreal, and of course some or all of it could be, but it could also be a way of understanding our world more than in our waking lives. I think dreams are, among other things, a way of tapping into the subconscious world of our minds and letting our egos take a break also. The philosopher Descartes and some Hindus and Buddhists have suggested that dreams are actually more real than our waking reality. There is a type of dreaming called lucid dreaming where the dreamer has the awareness that he or she is dreaming and can effectively alter the environments, circumstances, and characters in the dream. Is nature having a lucid reality of herself, whereby what is emerging and evolving in the universe and biosphere is the direct result of her infinite acumen and perfect intent?

When we dream our brains are actually more active than they are in our waking lives. In dreams, space and time skip, jump, speed up, slow down, and reverse but alas, we are unconscious of the amorphous nature of space-time in our waking lives. Dreams are only possible when our normal, rational, and limited consciousness is temporarily suspended. Or maybe our waking life is a temporary suspension of our dreams? In either case, dreaming may create clarity and provide a certain kind of guidance through the layers of consciousness, similar to the undercurrent in a river. Many say dreaming only helps retain important information and useful memories, but I think it also goes beyond this. How can we fully understand dreams or higher consciousness when our awake, fully conscious mind is set on fear, preconceptions, and self-inflicted rules so much of the time? Dreams reveal insights and visions people have about the present and the extended present, or future. Some add extreme importance to dreams and surround them with divine powers. Some postulate that dreams are less important than we think; however, our reality is a jumbled, confusing mess that during the day is always "on," receiving and cultivating sensations, experiences, and on-the-spot interpretations which carry over into our dream sleep. These improvised interpretations may not be entirely effective, so it is conceivable that when we fall asleep our brains keep working, but in a different way that sorts out these thoughts, sensations, and memories. Sometimes we need to dream and sometimes we don't. We dream because we are missing something in our waking life and our brain remains awake, sifting and making sense of the day's catch, while the body repairs itself as it sleeps. Dreams are a second look at reality manipulated by ones' mind in order to come to an understanding of the sometimes intricate and fast-paced world that we are riding along with. I think dreaming is a way of steeping and reinforcing sensory information and experiences while the collecting stage of the brain takes a break, in the same way an author writes a book in moments of inspiration or wakefulness, then revises and edits it later for the sake of clarity.

Our reality is interpreted by our consciousness, as are our dreams, so they are both really the same process, just different in terms of the degree or intensity of awareness. Dreams, as well as experiences in our waking lives, are unconscious and conscious aids to understanding ourselves and the world we live in. Dreams and waking experiences that bring confusion and conflict emerge from a cause; whether it is due to simple amusement or forsaking ones' total awareness to their self and/or surroundings, either way the effect of being aloof to peace and understanding is the same. Some dreams may be important and some may be more for entertainment's sake—the mind doing gymnastics, for instance. Have you ever had a dream that was completely bizarre being simply the unrestrained imagination feeding on itself, or a dream that was so fantastical and silly that you simply disregarded it as such, only to find some meaning in it weeks later? Isn't it wonderful how even the meanest and angriest person can sleep as peacefully as an angel? Hitler probably slept like a kitten, snoring away deep in his REM sleep. Dreaming allows for the partial suspension of the ego, while still allowing us to retain our wakefulness and observer quality.

The Vibratory Senses—
Made by Nature to Notice Herself

The scent of a flower garden, the taste of some fruit or fresh bread, a tickle or a pinch, a captivating melody, the sight of a beloved face smiling or the setting Sun fading into the starry sky—how and why do we sense the world around us in the way that we do? Isn't it utterly amazing that we, as well as all other life, can sense anything at all? An individual's personally experienced reality is narrowly and crudely sensed by the sensory organs, which are only as sensitive as they need to be in order to help us navigate this world as best we can. Our senses use vibration and contrast, from our eyes to our ears, in order to sense or detect anything. If there were no variety, metamorphosis or flux in nature all would be invisible, untouchable and uniform. The on-off, plus-minus duality is the vibration of the universe and is classically viewed as a discontinuity due to nature's fondness of vibration and periodicity. Nature is not discontinuous and it is a common mistake to view periodicity as a break of regularity or continuity. For example, an electromagnetic charge in the brain (from the eardrum, for instance) creates an on-off signal that we hear as sound. If we look at something, the absence or presence of photons reaches the retina and creates a charge. This same on-off signal also creates perceptions of smell, taste, and touch. Waves exhibit a back and forth motion but it is a singular motion. These waveforms exist throughout the universe and in ones' consciousness as varying brainwave frequencies. The individual consciousness is obviously not created and contained exclusively in one's mind. The brain (being made from the very intention of the energy and matter that it senses) receives vibrations from its surroundings via the senses like a radio tuner, television antenna, or Internet connection. The awareness of one's self and one's consciousness as that which it senses and is conscious of is genuine self-awareness. This is why we are both the observer and the observed. We are not separate from our senses and sensations. We are these feelings as we feel them. All awareness is self-awareness. How wonderful it is to sense anything at all! You are what you sense.

One Vision, Two Eyes

When we pivot our two extended brain marbles to something worth looking at, how is it that we can perceive the scramble of light waves as a thought-and emotion-evoking image with shade, texture, color and motion? We sense light when a light wave's source or reflection propagates photons aligning with our line of sight. We don't see objects, we see light. Light waves/particles enter through our lenses, which focus, reflect, and refract the light, and these degrees of intensity travel from the retina to the rods (which detect less intense light for better night vision) and cones (which detect color and higher intensity light), where this information is made into a message that is sent through our optic nerve to the back of the brain upside down. The brain then flips the image and senses these binary codes of positive and negative electromagnetic signals as a sight that is colored, shaded, textured, moving or still. It is amazing how electromagnetic waves (light) transform into electrochemical signals such as the cascade of thoughts, emotions, and feelings our senses gather and harvest, only to have a narrow fraction deemed valuable and utilized by our mental conditioning. The pupils of our eyes contract and expand like a camera shutter, breathing like the pores on a leaf or the skin, or a heartbeat controlling the flood of photons which tickle our rods and cones with varying intensities. Our eyes effectively breathe in the light we see, and just as the word *inspiration*, from the Latin, means "to breathe," we selectively see what we want and, like an asthmatic, often do not breathe a full, satisfying breath. Seeing is the unitary movement of the opposition of the pupil's contraction and expansion, opening and closing. Both eyes are floodgates that allow for a smaller or larger river of light, but it is a single flow.

Smell

How do we smell? When we smell a sweet flower or a foul skunk, what is really going on? Smell can't arise from vibration, can it? Well, sure, everything does. Each molecule has a unique vibration and thereby produces a specific "noise" that is detected by the olfactory system. This is another perfect example of form and function, because different elements create different molecules that make different vibrations. So when you smell cut grass, autumn air or vanilla you are, in fact, sensing the vibrations of the molecules that reach your olfactory organ, which then interprets these movements into electrochemical signals which are further interpreted by the brain as something with that specific, distinct smell. We smell things as good or bad for a reason. Things that smell pleasant probably taste pleasant also because taste and smell are closely connected with each other. We consider excrement to be absolutely repulsive, yet a dung beetle would be perfectly content making a meal of it and home in it, perhaps while considering us as the crazy ones. Things that don't benefit us right away benefit scavengers such as rodents or birds and decomposers such as insects, fungi and bacteria, which can in turn create a benefit for plants which then will be able to benefit larger herbivores and carnivores once again. Plants and animals have specific likes and dislikes which allow organisms to have a fair share at all the forms of food (or organisms) that are constantly reproducing, growing, transforming and decaying.

Hearing

Our ears exist, and are formed in the way they are, so we can detect pressure waves in the air. When we listen to music, the wind, or a voice, how does the vibration and movement of the instrument, the air or the vocal cords create something that sounds pleasant or not so pleasant? The process of hearing begins with pressure waves that travel at Mach one or about 330 meters per second. These waves are channeled via the curves of the ear which then hit the ear drum in the ear canal. The inner-ear includes the cochlea, the seashell-like organ in the inner ear which allows us to hear. It is a basic golden mean or spiral form (see p. 215). The cochlea is filled with a watery liquid that moves in response to vibrations coming from the eardrum, which moves from the pressure of waves hitting it in a range from twenty to twenty thousand hertz. As the fluid moves, thousands of "hairy cells" are set in motion by pressure waves which convert that motion into an electrical signal. This fluid also gives us our sense of balance and makes us dizzy if we slosh it around too much.

Touch

Pain, as I'm sure we all know, is not simply an automatic/instinctual and physical feeling. Everybody knows what pain feels like, but how can something interact with one's body and cause the sensation of pain? Pain is a distinct feeling directly entwined with all of the other senses (as all senses are already connected to each other in varying degrees). Although all of the senses are more or less connected, many think of pain as a sense distinctly related to touch. Physical pain can be general and achy, or localized and sharp. Thirst, hunger, headaches, cramps, sprains, strains, breaks, pulls, cuts, scrapes, gashes, punctures, bruises, burns and all the rest are the body's way of letting us know that we need to do something to stop what is causing this message. It makes sense that our tools for sensing would be subject to pain, because too much of a stimulus past a certain threshold would damage the equipment, much like a stereo blowing its speaker. Pain, however, is not only objective and sensory, as some may think. It is also, like the other senses, highly subjective and emotionally weighted.

For some people, pain can even be perceived as pleasure; this makes sense because the nerves that perceive pain and pleasure are the same. Paradoxically, pain is a defense mechanism that gives the brain a signal to stop whatever is causing the pain. The body has a high receptivity for pain, but this receptivity can be low in certain areas. Usually the greater the concentration of nerve endings the more potential there is for pain (or pleasure) and the greater the need for protection from injury, thus illustrating the beneficial role of evolution in sensing pain/pleasure in selective intensities in higher and lower prioritized areas of the body. High and low nerve concentrations allowing for more or less pain or pleasure also exhibit the dual—and seemingly opposite in their interpretation—sensations one may feel with the same nerves. Pain and pleasure are quite the conditioned carrot and stick. In addition to pain being an automatic and instinctual response, it appears pain is also a learned awareness, meaning it is conditioned over time and experience. Pain can be called a state of mind. People can feel pain before, during, and after the stimulus. Pain appears to be not a thing, but a concept of a process, and therefore if you observe or are conscious of pain then you will perceive pain. Amazingly, hundreds of people around the world are born without a sense of pain and because of this, they must be extra mindful of their movements and surroundings. Just like pain, fear is a conditioned response designed to protect the organism. Animals feel fear and pain; so do plants and, in fact, all biological life. Emotional pain is just as real as physical pain and can be quite excruciating, such as the empathetic feeling of someone else's emotional and/or physical pain, heartache, anguish, stress or mourning for a deceased loved one. If plants can feel physical pain, is it not possible for them to also experience emotional pain? I think so. Emotional pain is an awareness of a dis-ease affecting any relationship, whether perceived socially or individually. It is a feeling of disconnection from love, joy, esteem, belonging, or recognition. Maybe plants don't have all these complicated social needs, but they do have an instinct for self-preservation, and they can experience empathy when one of their own is hurt and consequently experience fear. Pain and its partner and opposite, pleasure, are not divided from one another by a sharp line, but connected by a blurred and sliding scale of intensity that is created by adaptation and learning. A hot bath feels nice, whereas boiling water would be excruciating. Having your back scratched feels great, but administered with glass or nails jabbed into your skin, it would have you howling in agony. Too dark and one is blind. A middle ground of light and dark allows one to see but, again, too much light hurts the eyes and one is blind yet again. Below the vibratory threshold of pressure waves, we are deaf, whereas a range of moderate amplitude sound becomes audible, and extreme pressure can damage and rupture ear drums. When it comes to our senses and, in the wider context of nature, life thrives best in a balanced middle world without extremes at either end. Sensory intensity and proportion are sensed as pain and pleasure. Our collective human experiences have created in our instincts or DNA many carrots and correlated sticks to aid in our survival. Losing a limb in an accident certainly would hurt, but in some patients it hurts more afterwards. This is called phantom limb pain, and there is a simple and amazing therapy to reduce this excruciating, unbelievable pain; a mirror. How beautifully simple it is to be able to ease one's conscious and emotionally weighted pain by placing a mirror next to the remaining limb and have this symmetrical image of the lost limb destroy any sense of pain for the time being. A similar treatment for shock upon a sudden amputation is to simply conceal the injury and ease their anxiety by talking calmly. Focusing on pain or any other sense only intensifies it. This is apparent when one focuses on pain and in the raised sensitivity of the rest of the senses in the blind. The body's purpose is to stay whole and healthy, which is its natural state of harmony. Pain is a lesson meant to be learned quickly.

In addition to the usually considered senses, we also have six more senses called interoceptive senses. Through these we have many angles through which to sense the experience of life. One is called equilibrioception, or our sense of balance. This is based in our vestibular system and, as mentioned previously is also responsible for hearing. It is a system of fluid passages within the cochlea that sense balance. The organ is called the inner ear or vestibular labyrinthine because it resembles a labyrinth.

There is also the sense of kinesthesia, which is the awareness of one's body in space and whether it is accelerating or moving relative to other objects and things, including the sensation of the presence or absence of gravity. We have a sense of psychological time (i.e. memories and imagination). We sense time as processes and objects in space flowing constantly forward and have a generally incorrect understanding of reality due to this inadequate interpretation. Our ability to sense time is caused by the flow of our thoughts relating to the space in which our experiences occur, from memory to the projection of thought to create confident expectations and stories concerning processes and movements in the physical world. The sense of chronological time, such as changing and moving objects, is just the movement of objects and oneself in space. Time is measured by physical variables related to other physical variables, so our sense of time is simply a sense of moving, thoughts, objects and space. We see this flow of creation as a progressive, forward direction set in stone, but it is actually fluid, symmetrical, and everywhere. Thermoception is another sense—the awareness of temperature differences, or the presence or absence of heat. Stereopsis is our depth perception. We need two eyes to form a binocular relationship to perceive this particular dimension in space. Finally, we have relatively weak magnetoception, or a limited sense of direction based on electromagnetic fields. All of our senses are based on the polarities of oscillatory movements in waveforms. Taste receptors are connected to smell receptors as well as to sight and all the rest. All of the senses are interconnected, some less and some more. The perception of touch, for example, can be affected mechanically, chemically, or thermally.

Taste

As soon as one smells, looks at, and puts food in their mouth, the process of digestion has already begun. The empty stomach tells the brain to use the body to look for fuel. The eyes assess things that may be nutritious and tasty and then the nose smells them to ascertain whether they are edible and whether they would be pleasing to the tongue. If food can get past the tongue, it has generally passed the point of no return. Taste buds cover the top of the tongue, and can distinguish which molecules are tasty and beneficial and which are disgusting and hazardous. The discernment of sweet, sour, salty, bitter, and umami allows the organism to find appropriate fuel to maintain proper functioning of the body, brain included. In developed countries, with readily available food and drink of both healthy and unhealthy varieties, this sense of taste, coupled with the brain's behavior of craving what it thinks the body is missing, and the not-so-ancient instinct to gorge whenever possible, causes one to perhaps overindulge from time to time. Our agricultural success and modern economy/society have created a lifestyle conducive to sedentary living as well as a prodigious supply of junk food tailored solely to the senses. Our brains have not caught up to our unnatural foodstuffs and ways of living, so many eat and drink based on taste and, day by day, become overweight which, not so long ago, actually was a sign that the nutrition of food was healthy and filling. The proliferation of material consumerism and obesity is connected. Our unnatural way of living has created a life of excess as well as a general misdirection away from what satisfies the stomach and the person as a whole. The perceived lack of, and thus manmade excess of, things that stimulate the senses are certainly not limited to taste, but really include their interpretations and the senses as a whole.

All senses are, at a fundamental level, the same in respect to their polar contrast stimulation. There is a stimulus, or flipping switch, where a nervous cascade effect leads to the brain, to be picked up and acted upon like a fly hitting a spider's web. Every taste and touch, sight, sound, and smell is a connection between the aspects of oneself and the observable world. From the combination of every sense emerges a single sense of reality and, if it is understood, one can see that what is observed, one's sense of it, and oneself as observer are all one reality. This perception brings satisfaction and balance rather than dissatisfaction and excess.

Thought, Ego, and Fear—Three Layers of a Veil

If the doors of perception were cleansed every thing
would appear to man as it is: infinite.

(William Blake, *The Marriage of Heaven and Hell*,
quoted in Erdman, 1793/1988)

Thought, ego, and fear together comprise each person's sense of self, self-preservation and feelings of separation. They are a trinity that creates humanities' bipolar disorder of stimulation and sorrow, mania and depression. Thought, or the process of mental activity, divides reality into the actual and the abstract, splits the present into the past and future, alters what is into (our narrow view of) what should and shouldn't be, and so on. Each aspect of thought, whether it be the ego, fear, emotions of all kinds, making choices and decisions by means of comparison and categorization, viewing events as a duo of cause and effect, clever ideas or moral concepts of good and bad, all serve in their own way to harbor and exacerbate division and conflict. Thought divides reality into a perception of difference and separation that creates conflict. Thinking transcribes reality into a partial yet usable form the mind can play around with, like adding the live action movements of an actor into a computer and transforming these into a movie scene or video game. Thought is certainly not without its benefits, such as the list detailed earlier; however, it is only the higher understanding beyond thought of what reality is, how and why thought acts, and what distortions thinking makes of truth that can alleviate the divisive symptoms that thought can cause. One can truly think rationally only when there is an awareness of unity which thought, ego and fear fall short in seeing. Awe puts a direct end to conflictive thought. Ego creates a dual and false sense of me and you, we and they, superiority and inferiority, etc. Fear creates a false sense of loss and separation. Ego and fear are children of thought and are always active. In light of this, full attention can never be given to reality while thinking. This incessantly active tool needs to unlearn what it has conditioned itself to believe as important and true and be able to turn itself off to be able to see clearly, even for an instant to begin with. Without this peaceful insight, due to a purely spontaneous lull in the mental process, I believe humanity is pushing itself into a deeper cycle of fruitless unhappiness, conflict, and strife leading to probable self-destruction.

There is of course beauty in thinking and having a sense of self. My writing this book would not have been possible without it. The beauty of these self-reflective processes presents itself in a wide variety of ways through all the nuances of art, science, and emotional expression, but it all transpires at the expense of the pure sight of reality in the attempt to communicate it to others. Despite our progress, in a sense, in expressing ourselves in art and technology, our specialty in self awareness and thought are not without their difficulties.

Burdensome Birth and Chewing Our Cud

In proportion to our bodies, humans have the largest, as well as one of the hungriest, brains in the animal kingdom. As infants, our brains consume roughly sixty percent of the energy that the body needs. This energy requirement is reduced to about twenty percent in adults, which is still remarkably high since the adult brain accounts for only two percent of the body's weight. Our brain is also a fiend for oxygen which is why a fifth of our blood is routed to it. As we all know, the brain is a crucial and highly active organ of the body and as such, requires much of the resources that the body attains in order to perform the feats of inner and outer cognizance that it does. Babies are born with a very limited sense of self which makes them cry, cling and suck. This primal and innate awareness of self supports their attraction to sustenance, safety and love and later matures into a full sense of self by about age five. This creates a strong and possessive "mine" complex and the possibilities for spoiling and catering to the sense of self which creates greed, envy, egocentrism and thus violence, aggression, undue emotional hardship and overall conflict. Moreover, human babies are all born before they are finished developing in the womb. This is because their heads are, at the time of labor, already quite large and heavy compared to their tiny bodies and the mother's bipedal orientation makes the birth canal rather small compared to our four legged relatives. Humans have quite painful and complicated births with many family, friends and medical professionals supporting the mother and child during this dangerous time as well as throughout the child's life. Caesarian sections are on the rise and complications from wisdom teeth are common if not extracted. Human babies, as well as adults, have disproportionately large heads compared with other animals. It might seem that our brains and surrounding skulls are getting bigger to cope in an increasingly complicated social dynamic and decision-rich culture. In lockstep with our changing brains, our jaws, the foundations for our teeth, appear to be getting smaller because we rely more and more on our food to be tenderized and predigested by our fires, mixers, blenders and cutlery instead of the naturally endowed knives and grinders in our mouth. Our teeth are made to break down food into smaller pieces so it can become covered in saliva and allow easy travel into the stomach for further processing. Our jaws are shrinking because our teeth are being phased out of the process of digestion. The usual number of teeth is becoming excessive which crowds our shrinking jaws. Our wisdom teeth, the third molars on each side of our jaws, are nearest to the joint where the mandible attaches to the cranium and are the last teeth to emerge between eighteen and twenty-five years of age giving them their name. It makes sense that these are the teeth which face the first struggle against the increasing size of the braincase. Molars are specifically made to grind. This is why the teeth of herbivores, as opposed to carnivores, have large molars because of the raw and fibrous plant matter they ingest. Ruminants, such as cows, have strong jaws, prominent molars and four stomachs to aid in breaking down cellulose-rich plants such as grasses, hay and other cereals. Modern man, on the other hand, with his omnivorous dental set is eliminating the hassle of eating raw, chewy and tough meat and plant matter, which can be difficult to digest. In addition to wisdom teeth extractions, our weaning from difficult-to-digest foods may also partially explain the rise of appendicitis and subsequent appendectomies which appear to be more of a modern affliction to our digestive systems. The mammalian jaw is unique in the sense that it hinges directly to the jaw instead of having a few bones in between the jaw and skull as non-mammals do. Thus any change in shape to the cranium due to the expansion of the brain will directly affect the jaw bone as well as the teeth nearest the area where the skull meets the jaw. I feel the evolutionary compromises of brain size and diet changes induce complicated and even life-threatening premature births and dental/digestive issues down the road of adaptation. Our artificial and social surroundings value our visual appearances, competitive egos, social and decision-making skills and fear-bred domestication more than the inner structures of our bodies because these socially selected characteristics have become more important, from a survival perspective, than easy births, extraction-free wisdom teeth and appendixes, lots of insulating fur, weaker senses of self and limited social skills. Paradoxically, self-domestication of the human species may be balancing this brain inflation by making our brains less active, specialized and thus smaller as is seen in other domesticated animals. Still, for now at least, the benefits outweigh the disadvantages because regardless of our strong senses of self and our constant thought process clouding reality along with our let's say, problematic bodily transformations, we have doctors, midwives, dentists and many more specialized occupations that support these human adaptations to the cities, societies, economies or unnatural surroundings in which we live our everyday lives. Increased thought and senses of self, our big heads, our shrinking jaws, appendicitis, difficult births and our fearful reluctance to live with the ways of nature are all part of a single social package humanity is adapting itself to. This creates a deep and total dependency with our unsustainable societies and as a consequence, both become tied to the same self-inflicted and precarious fate.

Thought, ego, and fear are ways of understanding our world, and what a light in the dark they are! There is beauty in thinking and having a sense of individuality; however, these methods of experiencing the fullness of reality will always be a one eye open/one eye closed situation, serving to reveal truth, but because they represent a split of perception, they will always omit the true depths of life. A sense of clarity requires a real revolution, as there's only so much cleaning one can do with dirty water.

Our hearts and minds march to the beat of a single and omnipresent tune; however, like everyone with an iPod these days, we are all listening to the same song, but we are shutting out each other's version of it. Our egos are our earphones; this is the individually perceived relativity of the absolute. Treated in isolation, as our minds tend to treat things, a number, person, or thing becomes static and unchanging, but when seen as related, open, and connected to the whole context, numbers and people become free and ever-changing processes. Thought, ego, and fear isolate things and impart to them a strict dimension of inanimate and inert material structure, which stands at odds with the natural interconnectedness and radical metamorphosis of numbers, people, and things. Isolation, as in a system or state, is a human creation of the mind as a means for dissecting reality into manageable, bite-sized pieces, when the truth is that any system or state exists only as a single, open, and fleeting movement in the whole observer/observed creation.

Excess, ignored and misconceived ego, thought and fear are like skips on a disk, where the music keeps on playing but we jump off the track and into our own world where we miss so much. We are a cunning and yet unwise species. The ego, together with its thoughts and fears, is a combined method of viewing our world and it has worked quite well up until the present moment, where these views are coming into a clearer resolution as to their compounding "unintended side effects." Our misconceived world is a direct result of our misconceiving it. It is both our gift and our Achilles heel. Ego is what mostly all our thoughts and actions are based on. When we describe ourselves, we start with what we've done, followed by what we think, decisions we've made, the things we have or own, etc. etc. Intentionally let go of this view, and try not to become distracted or lose sight of who you really are. The reason I say don't lose sight is because people have very short attention spans, especially when we have these entertaining illusions constantly distracting and blinding us, not unlike the thin surface of the water with the Sun reflecting into our eyes and blocking out the depths of beauty.

Naturally, all organisms work this way. People separate themselves from their physical bodies, actions, intentions, thoughts, and feelings. It seems so natural, but is it really, when one thinks of how many things we are a part of or connected to? Where does the inside end and the outside begin? Most would say the surface of the skin. We breathe in the world and exhale ourselves; we eat, drink, and release waste back to the Earth to be elegantly recycled. We share ideas, thoughts, and feelings. Ego, thought, and fear have grown out of place and proportion and have gone from medicine to poison. Medicine balances and makes a person whole through healing, while in contrast a poison is an excess that creates an imbalance. Poison is a medicine that tips the scales too far. Thought, ego, and fear have become toxic to their host, and there are a lot of hosts with this disease. It is a flower that has blossomed and is now rotting past its prime.

The sense of "I" or "me" is our sense of self and is responsible for thought and fear just as they are in turn responsible for the perception of the ego. They feed each other well. The illusion of a separate self gives us real feelings of pain, confusion, self-importance, bigotry, fear, and suffering. Together we must reconcile with this illusion of duality to embrace the inevitability of the "death" of the self and thus live ones' life as a compliment to the process of all life. When it is relative and exclusively observed, we lose sight of its unity. We lose sight of the infinite, which is complete love. Our mechanical mindset has created a narrow and focused perception that loses sight of the full beauty of reality. Thought, fear, and ego all serve to help us see the surface images in front of us; however, they blind us from seeing the deeper process and connection of things below the distracting skin of the ocean of existence.

The Bane and Beck of Fear

Be not afraid.
(Jesus Christ, Matthew 17:7, *The King James Bible*)

What is fear? What are you afraid of? It's really all a matter of a sense of loss, isn't it? I have something I value, I fear being separated from it and the possibility of never getting it back. Humanity shares many common fears: losing one's life, family, friends, memories, knowledge, physical abilities, security, food, job, money, home, possessions, comfort, sense of belonging, pride, and any and all other cherished things. All fear is a sense of the "me" "losing" something. Like a sense of self or security, fear is a motivation aimed at surviving, not in seeing truth. Fear is a thought grown from the thought of a desired future. The sense of loss is an idea grown from the belief in possession. Like our coveted knowledge, fear gives us our individual reality (imagine a person frozen in terror at the sight of a large spider compared to someone who is unfazed by arachnids). When one experiences a loss of the known, one sees into the unknown. The loss of the known, or past experience, can be profoundly saddening and terrifying and is precisely why we fear the death of ourselves and our loved ones. It is simply impossible to comprehend the process of beauty beyond the known, commonly viewed as loss and death, through the confined avenues of understanding such as thought, ego, and fear. Additionally, many things we think as so obviously known are still unknown when it comes to their essence. Fear of death or any other fear arises from the unknown, which is really all there is. Pristine reality is only found in the vast and unknown wilderness of nature and in the unhampered, unprocessed wilderness of one's mind. The increase of false senses of security that knowledge has given to our collective human mentality has created rapidly expanding pockets of certainty and society the world over. Our age could appropriately be defined as a war against the wilderness in ourselves and, as an extension of ourselves, against the uncertain realities of nature. We love creating certainty in our minds (i.e. patterns, knowledge, and memory that create a future) in an uncertain world because it makes us feel safe, in control, and comfortable. This is only too natural, of course. We must have a clear understanding of our own thought process as well as a sense of humility, uncertainty, and doubt toward what we think we know. This leaves openness and acceptance of the now, which is, like the unknown, always new and all there is. Everything else is past and future, which is thought. Do you see how our extreme love of something such as thought (a limited tool just as an eye, ear, leg or any other mechanism is) has caused so much conflict?

We love our country, so we protect, defend, and fight. We love ourselves or one another and again we protect, defend, and fight. We love material things, and so on it goes. We turn love into fear, conflict, and hate so easily because we can't comprehend losing it when we have invested so much time, thought, memory, and money into it. We have elevated and practically deified a process that simply makes choices based on limits. It is the repeated cycle of thought: recollection, translation, interpretation, application, analysis, synthesis, and evaluation. When we focus our awareness on the self or progress or whatever it may be, we effectively shut everything else out. I liken this to the state of our modern world, populated largely with specialists, wherein we find precious few "Renaissance men" who are capable of contemplating and creating a variety of things as a whole, while most of us look at our world through eyes half shut, with only a narrow flashlight to guide us through a shimmering midnight darkness. This leads to the feeling of fear, loss, and separation.

It's Not the Dark We're Afraid of

Are all of the things we fear losing based on our drive for survival? Our ego, being tightly linked to fear, is the mental aspect of our individual selves that drives us to live, to preserve our lives, just as our physical instincts impel us. Fear is natural, as can be readily observed in both animals and in people. Every organism wants to live, and fear is a powerfully effective survival tool. You are alive now because of this compulsion that has navigated your motivations and actions toward keeping the body alive throughout your years. Whether fear is an instinctual habit and/or a mental creation doesn't matter, because the effects are equivalent. Now the question is, can we survive both with and without these characteristics of fear? Fear does help in our survival; however, at the same time it is a victim of its own efficiency. Our preoccupation with, and our over-attentive reinforcement of fear can lead to chronic anxiety, phobias, and other psychological disorders. In this way the natural and beneficial sense of instinctual (and also rationalized) fear can be caught, manipulated, and magnified by our thought process to become a dysfunctional focal point, and thus a detriment to our well-being and survival. Unacknowledged fear (and, to a wider extent, ego and thought) permits the unbridled transformation of the beneficial intention of fear into an undisciplined and maladaptive mode which then becomes overactive, hindering one's well-being as a consequence. Animals other than humans don't really need self-reflection to rein in their behaviors, but with our enlarged minds as powerful amplifiers of instinct, self-reflection becomes crucial because we, more than any other species, need to understand how to operate this tool of consciousness by reflecting on our own thoughts and the process by which we think. This is called self-consciousness, and it is the awareness of being aware. The ability to reflect upon ones' self is meant to be exercised until an understanding of the illusion of the self has come about. Of course, other animals have this awareness, but we have largely forsaken this awareness in dangerous proportions concerning all life on Earth. If we do not understand our habits and fears as problems we have ignored, allowing them to breed and proliferate, they will act like a bacterial infection, parasite, or virus, killing the host and spreading without restraint. A habit or automatic behavior grows when unchecked. Like an oven, behavior does well what it's supposed to do; however, when left to the anxious mind of ever unsatisfied desires, it only serves to burn the food and, if left long enough without the recognition of its dangerous instability, the oven, or human habits, will engulf our home, or Earth, in flames. Instead of fear remaining in a supporting role in the act of survival, this ambitious and egocentric character so often takes over, and takes control of our thoughts and lives. Ignorance creates habit, and habit simultaneously augmented by thought and pushed into the subconscious and ignored, only serves to create imbalance and conflict. Instabilities arise, but they do not endure, because any perturbation is naturally self-stabilizing.

Hereditary knowledge or instinct, as well as circumstantial knowledge founded on an individual's memory, are based on survival. The involuntary brain stem and the voluntary brain are essentially the same survival tool. One aspect of the brain tends more toward automatic responses, such as the fight or flight response, as well as routine things we don't need to actively be aware of to control, such as our heart or breathing rhythms, and the other tends toward direct circumstance and things requiring decision-based action such as problem solving or communication. The more patterns we remember and understand (to a limited and necessary extent), the better we can navigate through life's benefits and hazards to our and our species' advantage. Our senses and our interpretations of them have led us to this point. All biological life forms are creatures of opportunity that must be in tune with the whole of nature. Our senses are limited to providing a balanced benefit of the intimate relationship between ourselves and nature. But our interpretations, egos, and fears have created thoughts and actions that range far from that balanced benefit to ourselves and nature. Some of us are trying so hard to change and domesticate nature—both nature at large, such as with agriculture, manmade waterways and mining, and even our own biological nature, such as through ideological conditioning, and both essential and nonessential medications and surgical procedures—and this push against what comes naturally is creating a world in conflict with itself because of the conflict of humanity against itself. We as a species don't like things the way they are and, as a consequence, we become intensely enveloped in the habit of attempting to control things or change them to the way we think they should be or the way we want them to be. This conquering, dominating, and overcoming mentality is the real thorn in the side of humanity. This mental thorn causes many of the situations that humanity tends to react to through separation, conflict, and restlessness. Controlling nature itself, or even our own biological nature, is not a question of whether it is possible, but rather a question of whether it is a balanced approach. Surely, it is not. We impose our small intelligence upon the unlimited wisdom of nature, which, as the Kogi people of Colombia believe, is the Mind of God (see p. 157). We have changed the flow of life into our individual (and very limited idea of) free will, and it is in conflict with itself.

Our conquering spirits will catch up with ourselves. Conquering is stupid and so is division, hence the popular war strategy "divide and conquer." Imagine how silly it would be to try to push a flower back into itself as it blooms! This is what we are doing to ourselves through irrational and imbalanced fear, and consequently we are trying to conquer everything in a feedback loop.

Fear is the natural defensive instinct of any organism, and can arise with or without thought. When it is unbalanced due to thought we get the kind of world that we have now. Some of the greatest fears are that of the unknown, in particular, death. The similarity between fear, cancer and humanity is as cold as it is fitting. Cancer is a mutation and is not a balancing aspect of natural selection except maybe in how it brings an organism's proliferation back into proportion with its surrounding organisms. Cancer thrives until it kills its home or host. Normal cells maintain a balance between life and death, whereas cancer is excessive and unbalanced. Cancer is when a normal process of cell replication necessary for the equal replacement of dying cells mimics a wildfire. Cancer is unrestrained growth. I believe that the understandable preoccupations with survival and fear of the unknown are the driving force behind the human suppression of enlightenment and acceptance of death which leads to a cancer-like overpopulation and a life of conflict with our host. This reservation against jumping into the unknown has led to society's fear of increasing certainty or knowledge. This leads to our current world, which is an emergent characteristic of so many individual fears and other imbalances. A person can be peaceful, however, in the context of nearly seven billion people; the masses magnify the discontented essence of each and every emotionally-caught-up human being as in a mob or herd. Our misdirected and unsatisfied essence is not diluted by quantity but rather, like the vastness and beauty of our surroundings, makes it ever more apparent. People are so afraid of the uncertainty of the unknown that they swing to the opposite and think that what is known is the key to satisfying this unquenchable thirst for certainty. Microscopes and telescopes—and science itself—can't bring us omniscience, and without introspective and contemplative wisdom we will always be afraid of the unknown. The greatest unknown is death, which is why we try to hang onto life as long as possible and leave our mark on Earth in some way, either by creating a lineage of genes and stories to be passed throughout the ages or by carving our faces into monuments so we will exist as a memory that "lives on" when in reality only the symbol or image does, and even that usually lasts for but a few generations. If we have to come to terms with the fact that we cannot live eternally in the material world in our present form, why not choose the next best thing, that is, to live on as a memory or concept which also, with enough time, will fade away just as our bodies will have done. You are a process in form and the process doesn't die. However, the form changes, and no matter how clear this is, our egos will fight it until the very "end."

The illusion of separation explains how our world clashes with nature and how our Earth has become so mismanaged. This separated view of reality is what brings conflict and fear to the table. These are illusions that have spread from the root cause of fear. Fear of the unknown is the fear of uncertainty. It is a fear of not knowing, of not being sure, of not having a solid grounding in what is next. We lie to ourselves concerning how much we know, because in the context of all things we actually know or understand so little that it is really quite funny—or tragic, if you prefer. Our most common fear of the unknown is the fear of death. It rules our lives in the sense that, needless to say, almost everybody on Earth believes death is a bad and fearful thing. The view of a separated universe causes us fear and makes us fear death and the unknown. If we know death to be a unity and a continuation, then there is peace. The unknown is to be embraced with awe and wonder, not fear, anxiety, worry, or terror.

When I speak of ending thought, ego, and fear, I don't mean doing so by getting drunk, escaping or ignoring reality, but rather through attaining an awareness and acceptance of what the present moment offers. Once the branches of fear and ego, growing on the larger branch of thought, are vividly seen as the imposing prominence on the tree of balanced consciousness, they disintegrate like salt crystals in water. Fear is an illusion with many benefits. It protects us from many things. However, as with all decisions, there is a compromise. We have elected and allowed mechanisms such as fear, leaders, governments, and all manner of control to exercise their beneficial duties unabated. These previously helpful assistants have taken on a downright preposterous domination over our lives. They have taken a mile when all we originally gave them was an inch. We allow our survival mechanisms to dominate our lives. Protecting yourself from harm, through the basic emotional response of fear, is a primary drive for any organism. However, when fear is used continuously due to exaggerated psychological perceptions of fear instead of physically threatening circumstances, survival becomes an unbalanced priority, because then the other needs such as love and self-actualization take a back seat. As with any process, any part left out leaves the process incomplete. We rely on our inner survival mechanisms to keep us from harm, but we are a social species and thus there are also societal survival mechanisms such as parents, and political and economic leaders of every echelon whom we rely on just as much. We allow these controls to dominate us inwardly as well as outwardly. Despite the clear benefits, there is a dangerous and disproportionate compromise in favor of that which dominates. Any movement of a domination/ submission or superior/inferior duality breeds a conflictive existence. Of course, dominance is seen in nature and is a necessary force for life to survive, adapt, and thrive. However, just as we have taken the fact and beauty of evolution and turned it into an idea of progression or artificial social selection, we have, because of our fears, mistakenly perceived nature as a largely dangerous force to be fought against and dominated. By continuously using fear as a lens through which to view the sublime beauty of nature in all its events, we have twisted the vast forms and amounts of life and death on this Earth into something quite one-sided, unbalanced, and temporary. Fear has its advantages, but as soon as it upsets the balance it becomes a burden. We have taken thought from our instincts and amplified it by our thoughts, which are also beneficial only when they are balanced by insight. We have allowed governments, as an outward extension of the inward domination of an individual's fear and need for certainty, to dominate our lives, because the alternative of uncertainty and danger is obviously less desirable. Since we can't deal with or properly understand fear, we outsource the responsibility for understanding this force to leaders or governments. This only makes things worse, as it only allows fear to grow unimpeded. Any government is created from the collective human idea of a governing head or mind, which includes fear to a large extent, dominating and controlling the body or population. A government is an outward societal manifestation of how we view ourselves. We view ourselves in the same bipartite, dominant/submissive manner, as a mind with a strong sense of ego, or nationalism, with fear as a strong sense of authority which we, the governed body or population, submit to in order to prevent undesired danger, pain, or death. We are all infants in the sense that we need a government to control us because we can't control ourselves. Governments enable a population to want and need governmental control, rather than being a good parent who allows children to grow and eventually govern themselves.

The more governments take control, the more our fears multiply and increase. They reflect each other. Look at the trail paved since 9/11. Fear exists only in the illusion of separation. This illusion has its benefits, which explains why humans are such fearful and consequently such effective survivors—and yet courageous survivors at the same time. The sense of fear allows for a person to confront danger, which we see as courage, or to flee it, which we sometimes view as cowardice. We pick our battles, then we seek out more. Both the fight and flight responses to dangerous situations have survival advantages; this is exemplified in the human species. We have a heightened sense of fear, but also a sense of promise and possibility in the future. Furthermore, if one wants to understand fear for what it is, one must not see it as bad and deny it on such grounds, because this is avoidance and ignorance, which only amplifies the separation and fear. The greater the illusion of fear, the greater the separation. However, like the caterpillar that turns into a butterfly, the fear when fully observed doesn't disappear, but dissolves and is transformed into something much more beautiful. It is not a feeling of fear by itself with you the observer watching it; you *are* the fear you feel and examine. It is not happening *to* you, but through you. You are your senses, thoughts, emotions, and fears. You are the sights, sounds, smells, tastes, textures, and the rest of all that you observe. Detaching from it and looking at it as an outsider creates fear and all other forms of conflict.

Maslow's Pyramid

In Abraham Maslow's well-known hierarchy of human needs, the top of the symbolic pyramid is self-actualization. Below this, from bottom to top, are basic needs such as food, water, shelter, security, and belonging, with self-actualization resting on their shoulders. Only when the basic needs below the apex or pinnacle of the pyramid are met can actualization of the self occur. How hard is it to self-actualize if we are too busy living our distracted daily lives? When I say "self," I mean the universal self or whole, not simply the individual. Only self-actualized people who can be conscious of more than their own needs can be true altruists and think of the world with every action, thus serving to compliment the world. The levels of Maslow's pyramid are meant to be acknowledged and flowed through as a continual process. One doesn't just eat and drink once, but every single day, and the other stages should be viewed the same way, as a fused and constant action of living. Every level is meant to be a stepping stone to the next and transcended repeatedly. The ego, like all other needs, is useful and at the same time achingly incomplete if made into a final destination. These stepping stones can be related to the emergent properties of "complex" biology, where so many factors have to be present and infinitely precise in order to allow for observation of the process of self-actualization. If any process is disturbed or removed, the entire system feels the reverberations of the seemingly inconsequential impact of the omission. The pyramid is quite the hierarchal image, and imagining it alternatively as an ever-flowing circle can help in portraying the interconnectedness of all the steps to self-actualization. Every step or act of self-actualization has within it every other, as it is a single process; this is how eating, drinking, breathing or anything at all can be a self-actualizing, spiritual experience.

Our biological nature obliges us to breathe and hunger and thirst for food and water. If we didn't have this automatic response to our bodily imbalances we would not survive long. Imagine a time when you were gasping for breath or extremely hungry or thirsty. These basic needs allow for the intake of oxygen, fuel and water for the sustenance of the body. We need to maintain our body heat (just below 100 degrees Fahrenheit), to be able to provide energy for our muscles and brain, and to move ourselves toward things we need and want and away from things we don't. We also need the building blocks of essential vitamins, proteins, nutrients, and minerals to rejuvenate our cells and maintain the body, or to heal it when necessary. These building blocks for our bodies are found in our food, which are, of course, the bodies of other organisms. In a way this is a basic step toward enlightenment. Bodily imbalances or nutritional deficits can distract from peace and well-being, and can make one manic, depressive, cranky, tired or irritable. But food has become so easily accessible and varied—and tending toward the less nutritious and more flavorful—in the developed world that the natural urge to nourish oneself is relatively easy and readily exaggerated, becoming a fixation that has resulted in the explosion of obesity and overindulgence. Our habitual senses do not perceive an unmoving, sharp line of division between necessity and desire, because of course there isn't one. This is why it has been so easy to move from one to the other without serious concern about these excessive desires. Not so long ago, when the vagaries of drought and other geographic and seasonal conditions created a scarcity of food, it was instinctually wise to stock up on food and drink in times of plenty. We are still running on this ancient wisdom, and our modern way of living is not a good fit for it. Imagine not eating or drinking; this is why we swing toward the extreme opposite.

The need for safety and security is ever-present in our world today. From the family with its strong, sturdy house with locks and codes on everything, to Homeland Security and police departments at all governmental levels, from local to national, safety needs are of utmost importance to everyone. But we go further than that: We want security in relationships, in our jobs, in our insurance policies, for our children at school and everywhere else they go, particularly around strangers. We want security in our finances, bets, and debts. Our craving for safety is obvious in territorial manifestations such as castles, forts, cities, states, nations, and pretty much anywhere human activity occurs, where structures and what we deem to be valuable exist. Safety is a crucial necessity, as evidenced by how anxious, stressed out, and afraid we become when we are without it. Safety gives us peace of mind so we can try to get a good night's sleep. Imagine not having security in the things you own, or not knowing that the people and pets you love are safe! This is why we take the extreme from this undesired mental image of total insecurity to a manmade world of near-total security, safety, and predictability. We see our world as uncertain; the freedom of nature scares us, so we condition ourselves to avoid uncertainty through ignorance or by confronting it and trying to learn finite concepts and ideas about the infinite nature of the world we wish to predict and be certain about. Humanity escapes the insecure and uncertain feelings of the world by leaning toward and fixating on its opposite conception—through the self-created sense of security in overdrive seen everywhere in human societies—from the simple, physical locks and walls we create to the more psychological routines, laws, loans, plans, contracts, guarantees, social and homeland securities, and insurance and pension plans.

The next stage in Maslow's hierarchy is the meeting of our social needs. These include the sense of belonging to a group and the sense of being loved by another individual or within that group. We are social animals and these specialized group needs are important for humans. This area of development for humans includes admiration for actions and ideas. We all know what happens when a baby does not receive love. Having a sense of love and belonging is essential in a group such as a family or other social arrangement, because without it the person may become withdrawn from society and, instead of having a sense of belonging somewhere, will have a sense of isolation and alienation, without a solid foundation of balance from oneself, peers and/or siblings. This is an imbalance of emotions that stalls the full development and flowering of consciousness. If one doesn't feel loved or doesn't feel that they belong, they will not reach the maturity and awareness that self-actualization requires. People can get stuck in this stage, constantly seeking a sense of belonging and the love of others. The sense of belonging is where many religions, clubs, societies, and businesses come into being and have would-be members scratching at their doors of aristocracy and exclusivity. People get caught up in this and miss the joy of real love and belonging. This stage of belonging conflates well with the next stage of esteem needs.

Esteem includes both self-esteem and the esteem a person receives from others whom he respects. The recognition of deeds, actions, viewpoints and social status ties in very closely to the preceding stage of belonging and love. The alterations or intensifications within the dynamics of esteem make the ego the major player in this level of self-actualization. The sense of self creates the need for social status and drives some to become kings, presidents, or tycoons striving for riches and reputation. Such people crave both self-esteem and the high esteem of others—subjects, constituents, friends, business associates—and they are known to have a high regard for or value placed on the self. However, excessive regard for the self makes it less possible to be humble, and empowers a person to think of themself as a sort of king of the world. This is egocentric and self-inflating beyond the point of necessity or prudence—or respect for others. Having an ego, no matter how necessary it may be, seems to cause as many problems as it solves, because even as it certainly aids in the survival of the species, a large ego does not permit a truly peaceful existence within our surroundings. The sense of self has grown into a sort of cancer in the mind of humanity. When the ego of a given species becomes too ambitious in its desire to preserve itself above all others, then the species, as well as the other forms of life it intimately shares this spinning ball with, will invariably suffer as a result of the imbalance of a single population's explosion and view of its own preeminence. The high regard for self creates the idea of entitlement and being special, with all others below one's self-perceived status. This is tragically evident in the oppressive monarchies and dictatorships of the past, but still exists in many varieties of governing hierarchies and governments today. And yet, self-esteem is essential to self-actualization, because a love for oneself is essential to gain a high regard for all other people and things. How good does your ego feel when you are recognized for your beauty, coming up with a good idea, or for doing a good job with your sport or hobby? Often the simple respect for ones' existence as a human being is all that is needed. People should feel satisfied with the humble simplicities of life and be accepted and recognized by others as sharing the same humanity that we all share. It is also true that people take this need and escalate it into a want or desire that goes beyond necessity, to the point where it becomes perverse and excessive. They crave to an unhealthy and unbalanced degree the pinnacle of status and high regard of the kind that we often see in movie stars and athletes, as well as other professionals who are at the top of their field and desire the kudos.

This is their addiction, and there are people who crave fame and power and money so insanely that their entire world is unbalanced. Hubris is pride that is overbearing to the point where it becomes a debilitating fault. Humanity is stuck in this stage, whether it is in the competitive, capitalist, economic growth model or the contained and selfish way we live our lives. There is currently such a motivation to be more, to be better, to be different, and to be ahead of the rest that it seems as if excess is the driving force of the growth economy. We live in an age not of balance but of dominance. It is everywhere and it is astounding to see how utterly ubiquitous it is in society. Note that each level of Maslow's needs is hardwired into the next as a continuum without any definite dividing lines. Self-actualization can be called enlightenment or any other equivalent word. It is seeing the truth of the process that we are individually and as members of a society. The majority of people in the world are caught in the hunger, insecurity, loveless, un-centered and egotistic selfishness of their unmet needs precisely because they assign far too much importance to those selfish needs. Hunger is just as important as safety, and likewise safety is just as important as a sense of love, which is just as important as recognition and self-esteem, which is just as important as enlightenment. One rests on the others because they all rest on each other. No one stage is better just because it happens to be at the visual top of the pyramid (Maslow's Pyramid, after all, is just a visual depiction of basic needs leading to apparently more complex), because each need is completely interdependent on the others. We often don't see or realize this interconnectedness, and as a result we have a world of opposite states—worldwide hunger versus obesity, locked doors and excessive security measures versus utter psychological insecurity, the superabundance of daily social, communal needs that are the focus of people's existence versus excessive egotism that inflates its versions of masculinity and femininity into irreconcilable comedic tragedies between men and women. The insight of illumination is the missing piece of the puzzle that makes everything fit in balance with respect to the whole. Hunger, safety, and the rest are all unstable addictions to natural processes and are in need of the remaining puzzle piece of self-awareness. Natural and healthy inclinations quickly turn into an unexamined habit of excessiveness and unrestrained indulgence. People are crazy—not only because they are seeing things that aren't there—but also because they are not seeing things that are there. This is the common thread that runs through humanity, which is reflected—or perhaps inflicted—upon our environment.

The beauty of life on Earth as it is—and as we know so little about—will profoundly change in our lifetime. Given its delicate nature, taking chances with such a rare blue-green jewel as this planet is unthinkable, yet it is happening as you read these words. It is too late for us. We are in need of a new beginning; however, history has shown that it isn't until we are at the edge of losing what is most important to us that we change. The sustainability of the Earth's resources is the most important issue facing us today. There are many who would argue that the economy is the most important issue but this, of course, is a part of the problem. The economy, with our burgeoning population, increasing pollution, and unchecked greed, all under the guise of "economic development" (which is the human condition projected onto its environment), are responsible for man's constant assault against nature and our fellow inhabitants.

Purpose, Free Will, and Questions

Do you guess I have some intricate purpose? Well I have...
for April rain has, and the mica on the side of a rock has.

(Walt Whitman, *Leaves of Grass: Song of Myself*, 1855/2007)

As our population grows and we continue to strain the resources of Earth, something drastic has to happen, and some things already have, such as the mounting environmental crisis, the rapid and continuing destruction of entire ecosystems, and the rampant and accelerating extinction of species as we grow. Whenever I try to talk to anyone about the concept of death, or more specifically the nature of the change that may come in the coming years, people always respond by asking, "If we are all doomed, then why don't we rob banks, or go on holiday until we die? If it's inevitable, then who cares? If you can't control it, then let's speed up the process?" or "What does it matter, then, if we stay on our course?" It's been suggested to me more than once that I stop worrying, and I've been asked, "What's the point in telling us this when there's nothing we can do?" I'm sure I've been misunderstood. Worse, I imagine I'm viewed as a fear-monger and lumped in with people who want to make a buck from the fear of death. For those who question my motives, and particularly for readers who experience fear or hopelessness in this time of radical change—or at any time in their lives—I hope this book suffices in bringing clarity to my motivations.

On the subject of purpose, why do we get up in the morning? Why do our hearts beat? One may ask, "What is my purpose?" Humanity has questioned its origin and the reason for its existence since the dawn of time. Questions multiply, such as: "Is the future decided by manifesting my own destiny, or is it simply fate—or even both? Is there no Creator, and are we simply evolved from chaos and random entropy?" Did fate bring you to read these pages or was it just randomness or curiosity? Whatever way you look at it, every experience and decision you have made in your entire life has led you to this single moment. The confusion and misunderstanding of truth leads to the asking of an important question: Isn't it the case that one only needs to truly understand why and how the question is posed to realize the answer? Understanding the reason and manner of the question posed, that is, the naturally incomplete but nevertheless pregnant question brings the question closer to a fruition, birth or answer. Understanding is not the meeting of two halves called a question and an answer, but a single curiosity of reality transformed and made clear. Perhaps a question asked is not even a question that is at all relevant to reaching its clarity, which is why asking a more appropriate question often leads to a less obstructed and timelier understanding. People say there are no stupid questions. I agree and, with all due respect to the people who ask them, there sometimes are just immature, innocent, or misdirected ones. All questions expecting a direct answer laid out in front of the questioner are essentially faulty because they are seeking the unknown through what they know. Any question is based in no small part on one's naturally misconceived expectation of its answer, which is based on prior knowledge. How can one understand a fresh answer that aligns previous knowledge into some wider insight if one has specific and unwavering expectations? The questioner probably won't accept or recognize the truth of any drastically alternative answer. Understanding a question requires openness to the answer, even if it is thought to be wrong when first received. An effective question is all the more simple and general, such as "Why do you ask?" A rhetorical question does not require an answer, but is rather a message or statement of fact or opinion, set in the form of a question in order to establish a desired effect, rather than asking a question to which an answer is compulsory. There are confirmation questions, which are questions posed with a solid hunch as to the correct answer, where the questioner just needs to hear a response from another for the answer to seem that much more believable. There are hypothetical "what if" questions which can lead to a greater understanding of things. A *koan* is a paradoxical question with no definite answer used by Buddhist teachers, among others, which, if pondered upon, reveals an answer and/or more insightful questions. A *mondo* is a question that requires an immediate answer, and the sheer spontaneity of the answer brings insight into the question. An effective question requires the questioner to deeply examine not only the question but also their selves. An answer should not be delivered on a silver platter without any serious effort on the questioner's behalf. Any worthwhile question is an expedition, and most people want to get right to their destination. Asking a question of any real meaning is a process, and in this process of searching the answers can be found. There is a danger in our instant-gratification society, because if one skips directly to the answers without any effort or care, one misses the essential truth and meaning behind those answers.

Commonly held beliefs about purpose are a human invention designed to find a reason for things we don't understand or repeatedly misinterpret. We create a loving yet vengeful image of a Divine Judge who resembles an anthropomorphic parent and stands in authority to guide our morals and actions. Chance or accident confuse purpose, and we are stymied by it. Purpose is an action of truth and beauty that is instant and constant. Purpose is the intention of the moment. It isn't a goal to be reached in the future like fate or destiny, but is the action that is taken by nature or simply going on right now. We think that if one decides, then acts, a purpose or achieved goal will come out of this as a reaction to certain methods, processes, steps, or what have you. This is a projection of the past and expectation of the future that is invented to make one's life artificially special and somehow separate from the true purposes of nature itself. We all think we have an individual purpose, and it is this sense of individual purpose that gets to me. This is why we are so misled by our own narrow ideas of purpose. Some people even think their purpose is to do any job that they really enjoy. To be special is to be better than someone or something else. This creates separation and conflict.

Anyone who asks a question is searching or on a quest for an answer—that's an obvious truism. However, humorously and tragically enough, many questions are self-misleading and misdirected, and rarely open to marriage with its answer. For example, either/or questions are posed with a narrow and exclusionary mentality, as are "many or one" questions, or any other question that requires picking one choice over another; these are dichotomous curiosities that expect a rational, specific and non-paradoxical answer. In any problem, naturally hidden, lies the answer. All questions are flawed, misunderstood, or ambiguous, due to the nature of the unfulfilled premises of the partially blind wishing to see clearly while expecting the fluid reality of the answer to conform to the illusion and limit of the boxed and bordered question. Changing the questioner's mentality is just as important as being curious; being interested enough to ask the question in the first place is equally important to fully understanding the answer. The answer is the same as a clear question, so in this sense there are no stupid questions, just a haze in our perception of reality. However, a confused question will only lead to a confused answer. Let's look at an example of a lost question that cannot possibly lead to an answer, and contrast it with a clear question that leads to its natural answer. First, the lost question: *What is the goal of life?* People have asked this question since antiquity, in an attempt to fill a hole in their unhappiness and find a reason for their life beyond the perceived ordinary, common, and flat daily living. One asks this question as if life and its goal are somehow separate, because that is how the person views life, as a process with fulfillment in the future rather than in the present moment. The questioner is expecting an answer containing a method progressing to an eventual conclusion or fulfillment and will not understand any other answer, because if they have to ask such a question in the first place, they will not be able to grasp any answer that is contrary to the entire basis of their query. The questioner must be entirely willing and accepting enough for their question to be restated clearly. There are many examples where a questioner will be more inclined to understand the answer when he or she has a flexible hunch and simply needs confirmation, and an experiment can be performed for verification. However, a question posed with a stubbornly steadfast presupposition as to the correct answer makes for a difficult time in comprehending any other answer than the preconceived one. The intent one has to question—or to have doubt in a healthy dose—and to experience a feeling of awe and wonderment is, in a sense, the question and answer as a single movement. A question might not even be intended to find an understandable answer, or to make sense, or make things "right," but simply to wonder, and as such is enough to engage in the discussion of interesting and important things. To wonder without expectation or doubt or a yearning to understand, but simply to be in wonder and awe is definitely enough. People tend to think that an answer is a conclusion to their questions. It is not. However overused the adage is, we must unlearn what we have learned, and this process must be continuous.

Questions are intrinsically colored by what we think we know and what we don't know. They are also colored—contaminated in a way—by emotion and desire. The answer is in the misconceived, almost pre-decided, question. How can a questioner solve his or her question? By looking at it from all angles; that's all. New angles give clarity to the immediate, which is a level of complete appreciation (also known as awe and wonder). If you look at a jigsaw puzzle, you will instinctively move the pieces around to get a varying perspective on it, whereas with other, more important things, we dogmatically stick to our unchanging and decidedly restricting view. Whenever anything horrible and dramatic happens, we always ask questions. However, this curiosity about the greater meaning of things is almost always missing from the pleasurable events in one's life. I think we are just too caught up in the moment to be able to reflect upon the event at the time. We always ask why terrible things happen, but ask yourself this question: When things are great, do we wonder why they are great?

Einstein's curiosity, creative isolation (or lack of distraction), and faith in truth are what gave mankind most of its revolutionary insights into the world of physics and science (although his very conclusions, knowledge of the times, and convictions as to their ultimate truth barred him from finding a Unified Field Theory). At what point does one recognize the truth when it's right in their face?

Where Did I Come from?
Why Am I Here? Where Am I Going?

Most parents shiver at the thought of having to attempt to explain the origins of human life to their children, not only because they have trouble explaining life and its meaning so that there is a clear understanding (and to escape from the situation unscathed by embarrassment on either side), but because we as adults have trouble figuring this out for ourselves. Indeed, many ask themselves this question well into their senior years. Where did I come from? What is the I? I is a sense of self that is ego and separation, a useful illusion. The ego is found in both the mind and body because the brain is an organ within the body. For example, our thoughts are a unique combination of our own perspective and experience while we have an immune system (including many types of bacteria and other microorganisms) that detects and attacks foreign agents. The brain regulates body functions such as: blood pressure, heart rate, digestion (including feelings of hunger and thirst), circadian rhythms, breathing, the fight or flight response and body temperature (including sweating and shivering). The brain doesn't function without the body, the body doesn't function without the brain and both rely on a sense of self together. In this way, the ego *is* an individual's process of thought *within* the physical processes of the self-involved body. This is why thought cannot comprehend the negation of the self, or the thought process, such as when the body dies.

The question "To be or not to be?" posed by Shakespeare's Hamlet is not the true question, because it is limited by the ideas of choice and dichotomy that only serve to split the reality of all things that exist (being in a state of being) into a choice between the solely human and egocentric being (or process of living) or its opposite of nonbeing or death. Why does one choose to live rather than die is what Shakespeare was getting at. Or, in other words, why do humans, or any life for that matter, exist and constantly choose to maintain this existence? The motivation to live is made by all things that are alive. The motivation to risk ones' life is usually made only when natural events threaten life yet humans are set apart from this because we risk our lives, commit suicide and kill others by actively maintaining, creating or searching out the kill or die, fight or flight conditions that threaten our lives rather than naturally occurring circumstances. People like the thrill of conflict and in this way, like enjoying extremely spicy food, a terrifying rollercoaster ride or constantly putting ourselves in conflictive situations, we are masochists. Despite the huge compromise of the total loss of peace, we like the physical and emotional gratification that often leads ourselves and others to pain and conflict. Our senses allow our ego to crave excess stimulation and thus conflict because it gives us something to fight against and propel ourselves forward into conquering new goals and feats of achievement which further strengthens our egocentrism. Conflict is the fuel in our egocentric vessels that allows us to push against something which effectively pushes us forward to new heights of meaningless achievement, over-stimulation and conflict.

Of course, human consciousness cannot be conflated entirely to the conflicts imposed upon it by misinterpretations of reality due to egocentrism. Being, as conscious awareness, and non-being, as the negation of traditional explanations of consciousness, is essentially the same process of connecting existence with itself through the act of creation/observation, but with varying degrees of appreciation of one's integration with it. When one is in a state of total awareness or bliss, one acknowledges the connection between the universe and him or herself. This is also true when one is totally unaware or in a state of non-being (we would call this death), where an individual's consciousness is believed to be cut off from the ability to be aware of the connection of things, but rather becomes the connection. In between complete awareness and complete lack of awareness is what we would call the regular life of the known, with all its cleverness and ignorance.

God, Soul, Spirit (or the Universe) is aware of itself such that existence can be observed through the creation of an observer from the very energy and material of what is observed. The universe lives as a single indivisible unit. I would therefore suggest that Rene Descartes' "*Cogito, ergo sum,*" or "I think therefore I am" (which is the ego talking and in this limited sense quite true) can perhaps be more appropriately tailored to "I am everything that exists whether I think it or not." In a composition that speaks of unity, one can't help but have paradoxes and concepts that are used interchangeably and repeatedly. This may produce unintended confusion for the reader.

We constantly ask questions about our origins and our destiny in order to make sense of the present moment, but the answers are most often viewed as lost, hidden, or unclear, exactly reflecting the person-observer in the moment as separate from them. These questions have been flippantly asked by toddlers and the aged alike without, for the most part, any settling answers. These questions lead us to structured life-models and religions, all systems of belief and purpose, fundamentalism, organization, government, as well as all the counter-structural movements against them. Some will offer their mechanistic and decidedly impoverished approach by saying we evolved from pond scum created by the Big Bang, and natural selection just runs its course. At the opposite end, some present a divine entity from afar bringing a "Big Bang" of its own, manifested by a divine spark of conscious intention. There are lumps of truth and beauty in both avenues. However partial our views may be, as long as a non-conflictive beauty is seen and shared, one should not get too upset or overwrought over these competing views. The point of this is that there have been hundreds of creation myths, whether from the Mayan *Popol Vuh* (the Quiché Mayan bible), which states that we have been made many times from mud to reptiles to monkeys to finally being made of corn, to the Christian Bible where creation took six days to come into being, Adam was made from dust and Eve was made from one of Adam's ribs. Their cultural styles and nuances aside, these countless creation views, or myths of creation, fate, or destiny rule most of our lives, but nevertheless many of us think we create our own destiny based on our free will. We came from the unknown, are in it right now, and will return to it because the past, present, and future are inescapably united. Not everything we think we know presents itself to our limited minds as a complete unity and reality. The reason life is so difficult to understand is that, with our survival and thus ego-based mentality dividing the observer from the observed, we simply have too much trouble seeing the totality of truth. In that case, how can the unknown possibly be known? This is more than a nuance of words. The unknown mirrors the need to seek and to fulfill. The seeking is really finding what we already have; otherwise we would not recognize what we have lost, but would, repeatedly miss what is right in front of our faces as we are doing. Fulfillment is a concept of something that is separate from being and becoming. An ego that is filled with pleasure, experience, or thought isn't really fulfilled and, I believe, misses the point of the real meaning of life. Real freedom is when we are aware of the unity of existence such that there is nothing further to be fulfilled, nothing further to become, and no being but universal being. We humans have lost touch with ourselves and consequently with our very nature. We are trying to regain clarity within ourselves through solely external influences rather than finding the light in ourselves and then allowing it to shine along with our surroundings. Our surroundings are always shining, but it is only within the realm of the individual's consciousness to reclaim the permeability and clarity he or she once had. One cannot completely rely on the very specific and personal lenses of others to view their inner self anymore than expecting clear vision by wearing someone else's glasses. Nor can one expect to find peace anywhere but inside one's own awareness first. Can one give the responsibility of their awareness to another? Can one be totally open to beauty when one's awareness is a barrier to it? In order to change the world, we need to stop this silly and utterly redundant game of hide-and-seek we play with ourselves. It's a waste of time to look everywhere for our inner self when we have a good recognition as to how inner insight can be uncovered, yet we still entertain the game by first looking everywhere other than within ourselves. Some people choose to ignore their inner selves and indulge in all manner of pleasure; others actively seek gurus, guides, and teachers and other models of external direction. When the narrow road that denies personal truth and attempts understanding entirely through the views of others is taken, one becomes fettered by a fruitless roundabout, dismissing the importance of one's own awareness at every turn.

Newtonian mechanics is true as far as it goes, just as relativistic and quantum mechanics are true as far as they go, but relativity theory and quantum mechanics are only improvements (albeit much more defined than earlier physical models) in the accuracy of measuring/observing physical experiments and events. They do not currently complement each other, and are thus incomplete descriptions of reality (and of course any description will always be incomplete relative to what it describes). Relativity only works with a dual approach involving an observer and what is being observed. Our personal method of relating our human experience to space and time is the orientation, but not the boundary, of consciousness. What you focus your attention on is what you are conscious of. If one only observes their individual slice of reality pie, one naturally risks being ignorant of the entire pie and where his or her slice fits in it. "Free will" is a matter of what one chooses to pay attention to out of all the things that are presented, and how one decides to respond in accordance with nature and nurture, as well as the constant laws of nature that are solid, determined, and yet dynamically fluid and open for change. Our attention span is short and there are so many distractions.

Free Will

The concept of free will is one of the greatest debates among philosophers and theologians and, like everything else, is a matter of interpretation with each interpreter, including you and me, having a somewhat valid interpretation. Free will is a process that is influenced by many things inside and outside of our "selves." Society, biology, gender, expectations, morality, law, and so on; we are pushed and pulled by them all. Insofar as I know, conventional free will is a contrast between acceptance and denial of the truth or, in other words, what is. Is there a way that a free man, fancying himself a prisoner, can free himself from his imaginary prison? Conventional free will is based on choice. With intentional and yet effortless care one can radiate and reflect the beauty of life and allow life to flow through one; conversely, one can resist, diminish, and distort this beauty. All choice is a compromise, and exclusion of one thing in the preference for another is only half of reality. Awareness of the whole is a choice-free observation. Free will is considered to be "one's own" possession, as with the personality and soul, but this individual intention is still living in the illusion of separation. One's free will is to accept and deny reality. Acceptance is peace and love, Whereas the denial of what is brings with it illusion and conflict. Denial is the choice our egos make, and thereby its energy is used to displace and disperse the flow of reality. Indifference is the same as ignorance or denial. Separation from separation is still separation. The embrace of acceptance is a non-conflictive and open awareness of what is and a clear view of what is not. Acceptance might be easily viewed as identical to indifference, except for the glaring omission of love in the indifferent, empty, and dull-eyed observer, whereas the accepting observer is far more alive, calm, aware, and peaceful. Acceptance includes love where indifference excludes it. The apathetic, disassociated observer has dullness in the eyes, where the accepting observer has a joyful glint. Both types of observer are impartial and indifferent but with a significantly distinct yet immeasurable inclusion and exclusion of love and awareness. True free will, as choice-less acceptance, is more of an ability in us all to be free and awake instead of the traditional concept of free will that forces one's awareness into the process of weighing options, deciding, choosing, and excluding. This is hard to explain and may not make complete sense at first. The power to create our own personal destiny is not something we individually possess and wield over circumstances. Our view of free will as leading to our own ultimate, individual little destiny is all so human and dramatic. But it is the awareness of freedom and beauty that is the guiding force (called love) that "chooses" for us. If you feel love, you can do what you wish; it is an intention that is self-aware and involves no choice, because things are clear. A complete view of free will must connect both the views of the superficial, finite, material, and the individual self, together with the infinite, profound, and miraculous, as with the union of the random and chaotic freedom that nature displays within its laws or natural tendencies. Indeed, a complete view of anything must include its inseparable and polar, or opposite, companion, reflected in symmetry. An individual, through thoughtful observation, is capable of seeing through the mentality of contrast and separation which, after all, only partially portrays reality.

Have you actually made every choice "you" have ever made? Even with free will, we must make decisions in reaction to actions or events outside of us. With this in mind, we have control of only half (or even much less than half) of any decision, and this is true only if we choose to exercise this power of choice to its fullest extent. We choose based on what is presented to us versus others' choices. All freedom of choice is based on thought, the past, fear, and ego, all of which are limited in an unlimited world. With the current worldwide recession and overall decline in the environment and human history that appears to lie ahead, this can make one feel pretty helpless (that is, either totally helpless or totally free). There are always different ways of looking at it.

When we understand that the process of weighing options and choosing an appropriate course of action is something that is isolated from the subsequent action, any other force involved in the process, exclusive to humanity as well as within one's complete control, free will becomes a misnomer. If free will is seen as the freedom of natural choice seamlessly fused with all of the actions of nature, then free will becomes something that belongs not just to humanity, much less to an individual person, but rather a singular movement of nature's intention. In this light, free will, like consciousness, is nature itself. Nature embraces all things in all forms and excludes nothing. A fly, a gust of wind, the Sun, happiness, sadness and everything else is an active process, and in that action all things express the freedom and will of nature together. Humans make active decisions, as do most living things, and call it free will. Imagine all the things we have little to no control over, from our bodily processes to the actions of practically everything else in our environment. Free will is not entirely what we think it is. Our arrogance and lack of insight has ascribed to free will a powerful and mystical value. We eat, sleep, and breathe in many different ways. We use our hands, chopsticks, or forks to eat; beds, mats, or futons to sleep on; we breathe gently or heavily depending on our level of exertion. We all eat, sleep, and breathe in ways that are environmentally, culturally, or circumstantially appropriate. We can't change the fact that we need to do these things; however, we can change the details of how we do them. Hold your breath and you will end up gasping for air. Stop eating for long enough and you will eat almost anything. Hold off sleep for a day or two and you will naturally fall into it because you have no real control over it. Your body, as nature has determined, knows what it needs. Preventing the inevitable might help you in the short term, but the inevitable or what comes naturally and in harmony with the whole always prevails.

If your will, thoughts, or intentions are those of balance, love, and change, you will be connected to the same overall characteristics as the universe. The universe is made of energy and all it does is transform, and in this transformation is untold harmony and beauty (as long as one doesn't get too attached to certain forms). Anything else is a dissipation of energy due to separation. Intention from a source of selflessness and love comes from the intention of the universe. All other ill-founded intention is separation and only breeds more of its source, which is fear, sadness, unhappiness, conflict, restriction, limit, and separation.

We can welcome self-organization. Our choices must be naturally selected with a view in respect to the whole. The variety of things we do is the same as the variety of life forms, no better or worse than others. We all choose to fulfill our motives of pleasure, peace, and love in whatever way they suit us and however many roundabouts or wrong turns we may take—just as we all strive to live, depending on our environmental neighborhood or circumstances. A camel, for example, is adapted to live in a relatively vast, open, and arid climate and therefore has more of a need for long, powerful legs and a hump or two on its back to store fat and fluid. Likewise, I can read a book in English and a woman in China plays the violin. We all live and do different things based on our environment and circumstances. Books are no better than violins and vice versa; they are just varying ways of expressing and experiencing beauty. We might not have continuously, consciously, and individually chosen to be alive, yet here we are, more or less choosing what to do with the lives we have. Life and the happenings in it are all governed by the laws and freedom of creation, including all of the parts that make up the whole. Free will is more than you think precisely because it is more than your thoughts. Destiny or fate is timeless and instant. It flowers instantly and eternally in the infinite process of cyclic creation.

Our natural tendencies are the stepping stones for our circumstances and at the moment of our stepping are just as important as any others. They are meant to be respected, acknowledged, and transcended wholly just as (forgive the cliché) each step of the journey is the constant destination in itself. The baby is just as important as the adult, and the bottom of Maslow's hierarchy is just as important as the top. Each relies on each aspect or form of itself; that's why they exist, because they have to exist in order for everything else to exist.

The awareness of what is dissolves and paradoxically incorporates what was and what could be—and what will be. Then one becomes in tune with the infinite vibration of creation, which brings forth the sensation of love to the highest degree, including and beyond the senses, into every action. So in keeping with unity, free will is the will not just of oneself, because that is strictly ego-based and is an illusion of separation. As for the word "free," it denotes freedom of choice, which comes down to making decisions based on many limited illusions of separation. So free will, as we have commonly come to view it, is the illusion that our individual selves or egos control our fate or destiny based on our sensory- and illusion-based circumstances and decisions. So conventional free will could be considered an aspect of illusion and separation. Free will is an illusion and, like all illusions, it is partial and misperceived. Free will is commonly misperceived as a divinely endowed human mechanism possessing the power, primarily, to choose thoughts and acts of either morality or immorality, righteousness or evil. Free will is a conscious technique involving adaptation, sociology, expectations, the predominant laws and religious views of a given time and place, and ideas of cause/effect or right/wrong, to name just a few factors. Will is a wish, desire, or force to control what is. It has clear benefits, but easily leads to excessive domination over things with increased frequency of use. Free will is seen in the behavior of all sentient beings, from a bug to a human. We see an insect or animal feed, fly, or sleep and say they are living on instinct, but do we know how much free will is involved in their lives? Because of their presumably lesser reasoning facilities, do they have less free will to exercise than us? Is free will a part of instinct and, if so, what if anything is in control of it? Our choices, whether we see them as free acts of personal volition incorporating factors of circumstance, benefits to ourselves or some groups, or as mood, subliminal persuasion, lack or excess of available options, the length of time it takes to decide, or the belief that freedom of choice is dictated by our evolutionary and social biology, are governed by the unspeakable beauty and precision of the laws of nature. This is a description of a controversial subject that, with some answers, only leads beautifully to more questions.

The Human Partition

Many believe that humans have a duality of wills, that there is a Divine Will that sometimes intervenes with our own will and creates our individual "destiny." The truth is, our will and the Creator's are one in the same. However, there is a great gap that we perceive as existing between, and so separating, our individually manifested free will from that of the Creator. Due to this misguided belief, we now see our free will as unsynchronized and limiting. Our free will isn't really ours, although it may seem to be. Our free will is the illusion that it is separate from everyone else's and all the rest of creation. How disconnected and upside down our thinking is! It is clouded by deception, doubt, and separation from unity. This leads to unrestrained or misunderstood desire, which only pushes one away from any kind of satisfaction. The universal intent is quite passive in an active sort of way, analogous to an individual who is active in conscious creativity yet passive in expression, or amusing and extroverted in expression but passive in a consciously receptive and nonjudgmental way. We have let our "free will" get out of hand, because we are a "fallen" species. There was a time when individual awareness was necessary, and at the present time, this remains even more necessary. We live and choose without the true awareness of nature's intent or the will of creation's oneness. As an aspect of the whole we (as a form of the whole) need to connect and realign to it. Then there would be no need for us to intervene with our unconscious and habitual selves, because there would be no unconscious or unseen area of the psyche and thus not two consciousnesses fighting for the spotlight. When we are aware of the connection to the whole, the subconscious or ignored and devalued consciousness combines with our awareness and moves from backstage to center stage. Our conscious awareness is the focal point of the mind's eye, whereas the subconscious is the blurred periphery. With the harmony of our awareness, there is a singular clarity of consciousness, rather than one focused and another out of focus, as in the case of partial awareness. In addition to those who believe we have a dualistic consciousness, some also think the left and right hemispheres of the brain might actually be two cooperating brains rather than simply the left and right sides of a single brain. The problems we have are due to an illusion of ego and the idea that we manifest our own purpose separate from the unified purpose. We have the spark of the divine, but misuse this spark as free will or personal consciousness to dictate, at least in part, where we want to go in life. Creation is telling us it loves us in every way it can, but we ignore this and remain deceived and deluded. In place of reality we recite to ourselves and families the skewed story of reality that places us as the lead characters who heroically conquer the dragons of nature and strive to reach a destiny in which hero and mate can finally live happily ever after.

We believe in hate and conflict because they're true; we've seen them in others and in ourselves. When we hate others it is essentially the manifestation of disharmony and antagonism for our selves projected upon anybody *but* ourselves. We've seen them in others and felt them in ourselves, but the problem is that we believe that we are separate from others and think this is the extent of reality. It's perfectly analogous to believing that the colors of the spectrum we can actually see are the full extent of that spectrum, when in fact the spectrum is infinite and our eyes only see a fraction of a slice of it. Destiny and fate combined with possibility are what we call chance or luck. All chance, accident, or chaos is defined by very precise and fundamental laws. The determinism or unvarying precision of the physical laws of nature allows for the very freedom of its movements and processes. Through our belief in free will, we believe we can change the perceived random unpredictability of nature into order, but it is already orderly. With our narrow mentality, humanity can't predict nature's actions by human laws. Even nature can't predict the outcomes of its processes, because that denotes a sense of future, and nature only acts in the now. All of life's movements (governed by such aspects as gravity, electromagnetism, and nuclear forces) are so infinitely precise and perfect that we simply cannot conceive of that perfection, and this unknown is what we call chance, chaos, or accident. In a universe so open, free, beautiful, and precise, there is a characteristically unfathomable order. The finite exists within the infinite. This is called God, creation, love, or flow.

Chance or accident are simply the acts of unknown reason and unknowable explanation. They are indeterminable, just like all the things we think we know or believe we have reasons for, due to the limitations of our understanding, insofar as our crude sensory and reasoning faculties will allow. Chance or accident are simply the fate or reason we don't know. Every act, however big or small we think it to be, is indistinguishable from every other, and all are miracles. In other words, chance is the openness of possibility which is built into creation. The creator or creation is this force, including the possibility to see it. What is the most beautiful moment you've ever experienced? Imagine this moment being continual and generalized throughout your observations, not spread out thinly, but spread thickly and uniformly and concentrated everywhere from the point to the periphery of your experience and existence.

PART 2

THE FALL OF MAN AND CRITICAL MASS

Up to now we have ignored the Younger Brother. We have not deigned even to give him a slap. But now we can no longer look after the world alone. The Younger Brother is doing too much damage. He must see, and understand, and assume responsibility. Now we will have to work together. Otherwise, the world will die.

(Kogi Mama, *The Elder Brothers*, 1992)

As we all know, humans are killing Earth along with ourselves and fellow life forms. As long as we prioritize human life at the cost of the diversity of all life, we will quickly and steadily destroy both. We are our own worst enemy and it is not an accident just because our narrow intentions have inherently unintended consequences. It is imperative to learn how to observe, but we generally have so far ignored and excluded every beautiful moment or opportunity. The cause of the fall of man was (and, of course, still is) the awareness and belief in our misguided perceptions of reality planted in separation. Searching for happiness with an eye for separation is like putting your high beams on in the fog; you will only see more fog. I believe that our fall from grace (or reality) originated when humanity became aware of being aware, and we humans began to fancy ourselves gods of our own destiny. This happened long ago in our evolution, but it is repeated each time an individual child reaches this mental awareness. Do we own our destiny? Are we so self-isolated as to think and believe that we create our own world as we see fit, the way most people believe they have the wisdom to create their own happiness based on their "extensive" knowledge? This separation and sense of self ego is about as far away from God as one can be. I will talk more about ego and free will later on. You see, in the Bible, Satan created doubt and a strong sense of ego within Eve and Adam. This gave them the false sense that "if I eat this fruit I will gain knowledge of good and evil and with this tool I will be able to alter 'my' destiny or fate." In the Bible, all Satan did was deceive us in the same way he deceived himself, and in so doing turned our consciousness away from God and towards ourselves. This made us think we were capable of being separate, special, in control, and gods unto our self. This illusion separated humanity from creation and is both our self-inflicted illusion and the hurdle we must overcome.

Shortsighted Tunnel Vision of the Mind's Eye

Reality is what we perceive through our senses. Our senses are governed by the singular relationship of duality. It is the seeming opposition of this on-and-off discontinuity that creates the distinction of relativity theory, the observer and the observed, and quantum physics with its probability wave collapse all being due to our observation. Discontinuity is why things appear to have opposites, like waves, north and south, positive and negative, and relativity; however, the discontinuity is relative to separate observers and describes an absence of something. Continuity is truth beyond the separation of discontinuity. As a flame is put out, the same flame will reignite. All flames, however separate we see them to be, are all the same flame, and the same is true for water and everything else. Life which encompasses birth and death is not a discontinuity, but continuous beyond space and time and the experience of one's self. Birth and death are seamless; they are one and the same flowering of life. With this awareness, we can see ourselves in all things and can then taste the perfume of all things without even opening our mouths. Duality and separation are the most widely held dogmas or illusions in all of human existence and experience. Trust me, I know how crazy this all must seem. If someone were to tell me this a few years ago, I would have instinctively thought that it simply was not true. "Of course things are separate," I would have said as I shook my smirking head in incredulity. Perceptions have a tendency to germinate and grow when cared for.

An epiphany or revelation cannot be explained with finite words, or believed in any completely effective manner by exclusion/choice. Belief is an exclusionary interpretation of reality. It is a quite personal experience and can't be explained, only felt. A certain enlightenment, revelation, Eureka! Moment, or epiphany can come from anywhere at any time. If you recognize the illusion of duality and the widespread scope of its effects, you will see this deception everywhere. Granted, in the Bible God created light and separated it from darkness as He did with land and sea, man and woman, the tree of knowledge of good and evil, but it all came from one source and different views of the single creation. If you realize the truth of unity in one obvious instance where opposites combine, you will see it everywhere. The nature of humanity is a juggernaut that has little resistance to itself, although we are a profoundly conflictive species. We sprint forward with reckless abandon toward endless ambitions and endeavors and refuse to stop and think why. We rise to the occasion in time of crisis instead of preventing the crisis in the first place. Consider disease, crime, and every other preventable imbalance. We feel the storm, but not the breeze which subtly creates it. It is to nature's short-term detriment that the tool of thought has been such a successful creation and has developed within the limits and imbalance of separation at its core. Too much of a good thing is no longer a good thing. This is the bait and switch illusion of excess that uses the tool of thought to propagate itself. Our brains and thoughts are our inherited and compounding disease in this respect. Balanced or imbalanced, they both spread. The difference is that balance knows when to stop. Mayan civilization, Rome, and the civilizations of Angkor Wat and Easter Island collapsed through combinations of aggressive agricultural expansion, deforestation, overpopulation, and fixations on expansion and war. They weren't built in a day and they didn't collapse in one either. We are making the same mistakes as our ancestors but on a global scale. Soon the United States and the entire human empire itself will collapse under their own weight, just like societies in the past. There's no going back, so the only way out of this mess is through it.

It is our natural bias to separate, which is why death, among other major events in life, is seen as a loss and something we fight against for our entire lives. Thinking about it makes us slaves to it. Thought is a navigational system that, for many of us, is on autopilot. Fear, pain, pleasure, ambition, memory, expectation, the future, conditioning, nature, nurture, and ego are what drive us, rarely the full beauty of truth and openness.

Farming brought more certainty than hunting. Farming was a step in the right direction (as we all know the benefits of farming), but it has very plainly gotten out of hand. It has marched to the beat of the imbalanced human drum, not in harmony with nature. A disease of the mind is to always desire and want more. Desire serves us too well, to the point where, like eating too many sweets, it hurts us in the long run. Nature enables our actions by taking the passive approach. How long this will last, only time will tell. Mother Earth, like all good mothers (even with a brat of a child) will see only the good in him or her. She lives in her loving forgiveness as much as she can, giving benefit to every doubt. Viewing misguided humans through the lens of progression and the only divine animals on Earth only allows our actions to compound to the point of collapse. This is the way of exponential things. Things have gotten out of hand because they were never in our hands to begin with, and we blindly thought they were. We are finally starting to realize this. Self-destruction is nature's and our way of dealing with us. It's a bit like a bad scene in a movie that we have to watch to get to the next, perhaps more pleasant scene.

Oil and Population

The midnight oil is a candle we are burning at both ends. Oil is believed to have first been utilized by man about 3000 years ago somewhere in the Middle East. This was when the transformation of potential energy into kinetic energy ignited the wildfire of combustion we see today. It was probably discovered easily or even by accident, because oil is lighter than water and tends to migrate upward from underground. We have tapped all the easy-to-find oil fields and nowadays we are digging deeper and deeper into the Earth and finding less and less at greater cost. Petroleum, fortunately, replaced whale oil (mostly sperm whale) in the 1800s, as whales were being slaughtered to the brink of extinction and more of a supply was needed to meet rising demand. The global oil market began with the invention of kerosene and kerosene lamps. With the invention in 1879 of the long-lasting and commercially viable incandescent light bulb by Thomas Edison, kerosene lamps (again, fortunately) quickly became obsolete. Oil was plentiful, and there was a profit to be made, but where? Electric trolleys and even electric automobiles existed before gasoline and diesel automobiles, so how could the oil companies put this high energy sludge to work? Things really got rolling with the creation of the internal combustion engine and with it the modern automobile in 1910. This was the symbol of prosperity and the American dream. Ten years later, the mass production of vehicles was unstoppable. By this time there was no desire or need for electric trolley cars, or the bicycle lanes which had been the norm only years before. Highways began to crisscross the United States and the world followed suit. If you study a map of the United States or any other industrialized nation, it is amazing how many railways, highways, and streets there really are. These access trails are critical for any modern economy resting on the availability and necessity of transporting goods. All industrialized countries and their economies are designed around the use of oil (even many of the roadways are paved with petroleum byproducts). It is convenient, abundant, practically free, powerful, and liquid, all of which makes it easily mobile and indispensable in our modern world. It can be processed to create lubricants, all kinds of chemicals, pharmaceuticals, plastics, diesel and jet fuels, gasoline, kerosene, solvents, paints, tar, asphalt, and endless varieties of synthetics—the list going on and on. Yet a single century has seen the creation of a global oil market and probably the decline of availability. It is truly mind-boggling that, within roughly the span of 100 years, we could very well see the rise and fall of oil. We did not reach peak oil in the mid-1960s; however, we reached the peak at which we were finding it easily. Peak oil is generally defined as the point at which the extraction and supply of oil has reached its zenith and enters a stage of decline. Imagine a mountain climber who spends all day leisurely reaching a mountain's peak and suddenly realizes when he gets there that he is only at the half way point of his journey and must now descend the unknown terrain and gusty winds of the other side of the mountain in the dark. The continuation of the global fossil fuel industry depends, unequivocally, on supplying mainly oil, coal, and natural gas to the growing number of people and organizations demanding it. The peak extraction rate of the worldwide supply of oil will be, or is already, reached as a direct consequence of each and every individual using it, for a few basic reasons in multiplied and myriad ways. Oil spills such as that of the *Exxon Valdez* and the more recent oil-well explosion in the Gulf of Mexico will perhaps occur more often as we drill deeper and deeper to get what we need, but these oil spills detract from the constant oil spill that goes on every day. What is constantly pouring out of all the other oil wells around the world? This oil may be shipped in containers, refined and transformed into things we use; however, in the grand scheme of things the only containment nature has for this extracted muck is the entire biosphere.

Humans have artificially heated the planet with fuels made of fossils and, in the process, we have become so utterly dependent on them that they are now as vital to us as water. Since the world's growing population is profoundly sustained and supported by fossil fuels, they are truly as essential to humanity as water. Food production and transportation to the heating and cooling of homes to a nation's military and the various ways of earning a livelihood, all rest on fossil fuels. Accessibility to fresh, potable water is also on the decline, so I suppose a few more short years will tell whether fossil fuels or water become the greater concern for humanity's survival. We are the only species whose exploding population is the result of our massive exploitation of nature and her ancient fuels, and we and a host of other organisms in our wake are at risk of dramatic decline because of this.

Every business in our globalized economy relies on the demands of its customers, and collectively creates our planetary economy. An economy gives people what they desire, at a price, in that the same people desire the same things. Our civilization will fall, as all the others have. Our widely unacknowledged precarious way of modern living will quickly change just as it comes into focus. Ever since the mid-1960s, we have been finding less and less oil in smaller and smaller deposits. We are now over a decade into the 21st century and there is no stopping the exploitation of the bonds between hydrogen and carbon. Irresponsibly and without much thought, we are all making our bed in such a way that sleeping in it will be restless.

Oil is humanity's energy credit card and the debts are being paid heavily, instantly, and irrevocably by nature. Oil is an energy-rich substance that is vital to transportation and agriculture. There is a truck/supermarket symbiosis that creates human biomass, pollution, and everything in between. Our lives are subsidized worldwide by oil to the tune of 100 million barrels a day. Almost everything we have, want, or need can be tracked to the energy and versatility of oil. This energy came from the Sun in the form of photons, the carriers of light and heat which were transformed, used and stored by ancient plants. Oil supply is what economies and exploding societal growth are made of or built upon. Without a constant flow of this liquid gold our routine would be in for a dramatic change that would put the global economy in a state of shock. The United States and the Westernized world are not by any means ready for a disruptive shift away from oil, despite increasing prices, environmental stigma, and shrinking supply; ever-increasing demand only leads to increasing dependence. It isn't only the amount we use but how speedily we are using it. Whether by human consumption or by natural processes, the end of our global management, the cessation of human domination over nature will have the same effect of collapse. These are different styles or methods with identical effects. If a life-sustaining ecosystem is ruined by man or climate change, another may eventually take its place. If all, or almost all, of the Earth's ecosystems are destroyed by either the heavy hand of man or the extremes of global weather (perhaps ultimately caused by man), most or all of humanity will fall along with it. If the life-giving properties of nature here on Earth suddenly gives out, we die.

Peak oil is when the maximum extraction rate of oil has been reached and subsequently enters a period of terminal decline. Energy underground in the form of oil does not come from an unlimited spring. Once it's gone, it's gone. Many experts in the field posit that peak oil has already been reached worldwide. Peak oil is also known as Hubbert's peak, so named for Marion King Hubbert, an oil researcher who worked for the Shell Oil Company in the 1950s. In 1956, Hubbert predicted the United States would reach peak oil in the year 1970 and, lo and behold, in 1970 it happened. He also predicted global peak oil in the year 2000, but at present we have no definitive way of determining that. However, gas prices in the near future might be the proof that most people need; they will certainly be the proof that people will feel the most. Definite proof leading to action in this case would come perilously too late. Of course, there are alternative and renewable fuels such as wind and solar power; however, as long as there is a profit margin large enough to keep the greedy and in control interested, oil will always reign as king. The largest oil field in the world is the Ghawar Oil Field in Saudi Arabia. Since its discovery less than 100 years ago, Saudi Arabia has extracted well over a trillion barrels of oil from it. This oil field represents half of all Saudi Arabian oil production, and the production from this particular oil field has now fallen below half of what it once produced at its early golden age of extraction. Peak oil is inevitable, if not already here. Many countries, including the United States, Japan, Mexico, Venezuela, Iran, France, the UK, and others, have reported reaching the peak of their oil supply in regard to the demand that currently exists (and is growing). What will happen when the oil we are so stupidly and so mindlessly dependent on stops flowing?

Overpopulation—Trouble in Paradise

Unlike the plagues of the dark ages or contemporary diseases we do not yet understand, the modern plague of overpopulation is soluble by means we have discovered and with resources we possess.

(Martin Luther King, Jr., *The Dominant Animal: Human Evolution and the Environment*, 1966/2008)

It is a small world, and the number of humans it contains is growing fast. Shall we blindly follow our instincts into the future at the peril of the entire biosphere, not to mention humanity and all other life forms dependent on it? We grew from nomadic tribes to settled farms and villages, towns, and cities to national and global unions and institutions. Things aren't what they used to be. We have taken instinct and, with our learned behavior and ideologies passed down through the generations, have tailor-made it into something absolutely incompatible with nature. When we compete with other animals for anything, we inevitably win. Urban sprawl and slash-and-burn agriculture allows for the expansion of humanity but at the cost of displacing the habitat of all other wild organisms. It's not the survival of the fittest anymore, but survival of the most fearful, the most ignorant and most bluntly powerful. Of course this competition with nature is a self-imposed conflict based on fear. We consume land, sea, plants and trees, animals and fish, coal, oil, minerals, water, and everything in between only as material commodities with no real view of beauty attached to them. This is a very narrow and impoverished view of things, a travesty against nature and a forceful slap in the face against the Creator (which is creation itself). In a world of cycles, what goes around comes around, and this slap in the face of creation is no exception for those who have desecrated it. We take and use the Earth and throw back what we see no use for in the form of garbage and pollution, and even the things that we treasure ultimately turn to garbage and are added to the pile. The beginning of this large-scale production and mass taking of resources occurred only about two generations ago. Ambition, convenience, and greed were not inventions of the Industrial Revolution by any means; nonetheless, since then good *and* bad intentions, along with scant foresight, have impacted the Earth more than anyone could have imagined possible.

Population and oil have an intimate relationship. In basic terms, the more oil that is found and utilized, the more people there will be. When Jesus was born about two thousand years ago, worldwide population was estimated at nearly 200 thousand people. A thousand years ago, the human population was estimated to be around 310 thousand. By 1800, it was 978 million. In the year 1850, we surpassed one billion. By many estimates, it took over 100 thousand years to reach the first billion at the height of the Industrial Revolution. Spanning the late 18th and early 19th centuries, it was a time when oil and mechanical innovation were quickly exploited. This was a pivotal time for humanity. We went from farmers to city-dwelling consumers relatively quickly. The urban distance from coaxing our own food from the Earth was the beginning of a saddening trend away from the direct touch of the pure generosity of nature. Eighty years after the first billion was reached, we arrived at our second billion in 1930, and only thirty years later the population reached its third billion. Forty years later, in the year 2000, human population had doubled to six billion people living on Earth. As of 2011, we are just shy of seven billion drinking, thinking, eating, frightened and beautiful people. The majority of population increases take place in developing countries. One reason is developing countries have higher percentages of farmers and, in contrast to industrialized nations in which the retired have varying degrees of financial security, farmers generally have to rely on their many children to take care of them in old age and to take over their farms when they pass on. This is why they are compelled to have large families. A large family is their retirement plan.

We live in a time on Earth like no other. We are living in uncharted territory (as always). If it is true that history repeats itself, this means that history's lessons, combined with global proportions of population never before seen, gives us a scenario for dire global change, whether it is due to any mixture of human ignorance and the inevitable forces of nature. Either way, history is full of specific examples of both. For thousands of years, the balance between births and deaths was in relative harmony compared to now. Think of over-population as a company with an imbalance of employee turnover. We are employing more people than can be maintained, yet adding more all the time, while few are getting fired. The company is full, and one must not imagine that this can go on for long in any closed system. Eventually, everyone will suffer the consequences. And worse, when there is a higher concentration of humans who live too close to each other, who in essence invade each other's space, war and all other conflicts are absolutely inevitable. Either the company is made sustainable enough to survive, or the company folds. There is a theory put forward by English economist Thomas R. Malthus in the early 19th century that roughly stated that a population will tend to increase dramatically while the ways of sustaining the population will increase relatively slower, resulting in a lack of food, water, and so forth which, as a consequence, will eventually and drastically deflate the population by means of war, extreme poverty, environmental degradation, disease, dehydration, and famine. Malthus may have been off in his prediction of how and when this would happen, but the main concept remains increasingly probable as the population increases and uses up the Earth's resources at a steadily increasing rate.

Population growth may seem innocent and natural enough. Who in their right mind would argue that there's a problem with so many new beautiful mouths to feed? However, the very real pressures on nature are echoed in the quote at the beginning of this section. Our basic instinct is self-preservation, which includes procreation. How can nearly seven billion mammals control their basic instincts for the good of the future of the world? Can this actually be done and, if so, have we waited too long and ignored our responsibility? We exclude that which we are not conscious of. Is this instinct or extinct? This is our ultimatum. There is an old trick passed down through the generations, similar to our eyes having a blind spot in order to have the keen vision we possess. We miss our self-actualization because we are too focused on the prize (our goals). We make the path or goals to happiness more important than the happiness itself. We get stuck in the method. It's oddly understandable that this is so common. Can old dogs learn new tricks? It is a biological imperative to fear, to hope, and sometimes to see less than there is (or all that's needed to get by). Can this survival mechanism that has served us so well be transcended and can we be fully aware, as it is happening, of this behavioral string tugging at our lives, in order to accept what we are and maintain a balance with ourselves, others, and nature? If we ignore our natural tendencies and instincts we become or remain their slaves, but if we are aware and we accept and overcome them, then we are free. These are the two faces of the coin of indifference. This is our ultimatum. If we can't find in ourselves a way to live differently and shed the core of all this conflict, then the fruit we share will be a world rotten and spoiled. Nature has her checks and balances, so there is no doubt that we will self-destruct and she will continue on. Any disturbance in an essentially balanced system will come along easily and go just as easily. Humanity is a blip on nature's timeline. The dramatic decrease (or even complete eradication) of the human population may be the most realistic and probable avenue nature has of uniting the problem with the solution and thereby canceling each out. However dire these scenarios may seem, they are no more stark and rude than the present state of the world: a festering problem leading to its own solution. There is a war on a multiplicity of fronts that is applying overbearing pressure on that which gives all life. Nature is fragile and can only take so much.

Economy Run Amok

I can get no remedy against this consumption of the purse:
borrowing only lingers and lingers it out, but the disease is incurable.

(William Shakespeare, *Henry IV*, Part 2, 1599)

Our current economic model is based on separation and does not follow the harmony of nature. What are the prospects for our continued existence if we cannot live without persistently pursuing an unsustainable growth economy, as well as seemingly not being able to live *with* it either, because it never seems to be enough? The mentality that fuels and drives the economy is founded deep in a conceptual misunderstanding that has serious consequences and detrimental effects, just as fear is essentially a purely individual and psychological reality with real and actual effects.

Glut breeds deprivation and deprivation breeds glut. Excessive prosperity is only possible at a great cost to nature and to others in the developing world. We are working ourselves out of a job. On one side of the world a heavy person eats their steak alone while on the other side a starving crowd eats clay. This imbalance is the same old unbalanced dichotomy of the very rich and the very poor, both looting nature in a free-for-all. This free-for-all will transform into a free fall. We hold on to the capitalist economic dictatorship because the alternative would be communism, socialism, or possibly hunger and joblessness for millions, and that is out of the question, right? Capitalism amounts to wanting to join the rich, not despising them. This model began to collapse right from its creation, much as all societies and civilizations built on the foundation of greed and separation have done. The *Declaration of Independence* states that all citizens have the right to life, liberty, and the pursuit of happiness. Why did Jefferson add "pursuit" in front of happiness as if happiness is an endless chase without any achievement? The answer is that happiness is not a destination, as most people think it is. If I have a house and a car and kids and I win the lottery, we think, *then* we'll be happy. I've got news. Real happiness is the complete awareness of love; it is not a goal to pursue solely by material or circumstantial means.

The economy, like pollution and all other human symptoms and conceptions, is a projection of the fragmented psychology of each individual who is a part of it. This is understandable, because whatever we create in the world we first create as a model in our minds. In a democracy, as in all governments, the government itself is simply a leader of collective consciousness, and the only difference between it and the individuals governed is a matter of increased scale, and hence power and influence. Government leaders spend money like we do, have trouble balancing budgets, try to grease the squeaky wheels so they can keep their power a little longer, and definitely make mistakes and learn as they go along. Or do they really learn?

The Thirst for Seawater

Our world today is all about faster, bigger, and better. Nothing gets in the way of progress. Progress is also separation from what is. Progress is the competition that drives excellence. This sounds good, but we have further perverted this striving for excellence into a competition to see who can make the most money. Why is money or the desire for excess money so important to so many? The United States was once considered the land of opportunity, but after so many have taken advantage of this once new land, is it still the land of opportunity? What did Bernard Madoff plan to do with his stolen fifty billion dollars? He was simply a hoarder as so many of us are, which is just an excessive enactment of a normal instinct. Why are billionaires seemingly so discontent and always in need of more? They hunger for greater wealth with an insatiable appetite. The reason is because inside themselves lies a bottomless pit. How does a trivial number representing a secular monetary value fill this profound absence of contentment and peace? It doesn't. It is a fleeting excitement or high, much like shopping. It fades rapidly, leaving one only wanting more. This thirst, however, cannot be quenched. It is like drinking sea water. We know, or don't know, that it's bad for us but we keep pounding back the saline solution. The American dream is slowly being realized for what it is. The pursuit of superficial happiness has its consequences and now it is time to face them. The land of opportunity and the American dream are now the land of empty promises and this American reality of greed has spread the world over. The current wage-slave economic model is fundamentally the same as any enslavement of the past. Look around: in our economic society, we are slaves to invisible masters and cogs in a machine that is running out of steam. The only difference between historic slavery and modern slavery is our collective conviction that we are intrinsically free, and anything but slaves. We work for the profit of others, we feed and shelter ourselves, we fight wars of independence and freedom, protect our dreams of a better tomorrow with overused fear and ego as the root causes. Whom do we work and die for? Why?

The economy is the cause, not the cure. The near complete absence of the power and influence of the overall economy, however it may inevitably come about, is the cure for its clashing ramifications upon the biosphere. To help illustrate my point, imagine how one might attempt to create a better vehicle by fixing an old, flawed one and using the same faulty methods and broken, albeit polished, pieces. It doesn't work that way, and there is no other alternative than what is being undone now. The illusion behind the economy is unraveling itself. We will always cling to an economy because we are completely dependent on it. The growth economy paradigm will only aid in its own demise. The complete absence of the cause—inflated ego and its effects—is the only cure, like solving a problem or removing a painful stimulus once we become aware of it. If the collapse of our current economic paradigm is only a partial collapse, leaving tainted remnants behind, human societies will simply rise and fall again and again as they have always done in the past. A human economy is growth maintained, much like cancer, so every economy is essentially growth unimpeded for as long as possible. Growth in nature is not maintained to an inevitable point of collapse, but rather sustained in a way that balances and stabilizes all life on Earth and not just a single species. Any society/economy is an outward manifestation of the inward intentions and desires of the people involved. Putting the greed and general lack of awareness and prioritization that created our current economy aside, we can have a trade system that doesn't only take from nature. This economic model would involve sharing, with an empathetic understanding of the interwoven priorities in one another's lives, the understanding of necessity and unbridled vainglory and knowing when too much is too much, all the while having the interests of nature involved in the whole, truly global, economy. However, as soon as people begin to think of nature as separate from themselves and as a treasure to be greedily exploited, things become conflictive again and we end up right where we left off, with a conflictive growth economy sapping nature of her gifts unabated and eventually collapsing under its own weight.

We have gone too far. As President Obama remarked, "The party is now over." The lesser of two evils to save the economy is to spend more. This is counterintuitive, in that we, our children, and future generations are given the bill, and they will inherit horrific global conditions. Let me ask you this, if you are in debt, do you spend more to offset your bills? We are living off the present and the future of nature and our dream is being realized, but at what cost?

We are consumers. This label is as accurate as it is uncomfortable. We spend and consume products the same way we eat, and it shows in our bank accounts as well as on our bodies. Both of these issues are emotional crutches centered on unhappiness and dissatisfaction with life that, if treated symptomatically, only serves to create more debt, bigger bellies, and the continuity of over-compensating with quantity rather than quality. The economic news that has dominated news channels lately is based on a concept—growth—and the narrow-minded confidence in it. The rate at which the Industrial Revolution took off, together with oil and population growth, was world-changing. Each country's gross domestic product, which is the measure of an economy, depends on high productivity and trading in the form of markets. There must be jobs, cars, food, and housing for the exploding population and oil for the energy needed to produce and expand. We have lived the last 200 years in a growth economy. There have been many hyperinflations during this time span, many occurring during and after wars, with the majority occurring in just the last 100 years. What the world needs—what humanity itself needs—is a steady state economy or SSE. The term "steady state" doesn't really define humanity as a whole. In fact, "exploding state" is a more apt description of the world's population. Achieving a steady state for the human population will happen only if global population is regulated in some way. In China, for example, there are laws governing how many children a couple is legally allowed to have.

Now, the mention of China and the regulation of population may seem like an ominous connection, and I am in no way suggesting that mankind itself should be responsible for, or is even capable of, regulating its own world population, despite what China has done. What I am suggesting is actually something even more ominous: As reluctant as I am to say it, there must be—some way, somehow—a dramatic decrease in consumption and consumers in order to bring back the Earth's natural equilibrium, which creates and sustains life. Nature always finds a way of balancing things out when they get out of hand. As rational, moral, and ethical beings we recognize the rights of all people to reproduce, to live prosperously, and pursue their happiness, but our success is our undoing, because our population growth, when unrestrained due to the benefits of oil and agriculture and technology, mercilessly interferes with the populations of other life forms and with nature as a whole, Earth's fragile ecosystem. Should that ecosystem collapse, the consequences for mankind would be unspeakably horrific. But it would be nothing more or less than nature restoring the Earth's natural and timeless diversity and equilibrium.

Spending money is what we do, even if it is borrowed and doesn't really exist. We borrow money using "credit" to buy things we really don't need. This is what got us into this mess in the first place. Buying huge houses beyond our means while borrowing money from greedy bankers expecting a huge return from leverage and interest, all of this is a vicious cycle with a definite plateau or ceiling for exponential growth. We have lent recklessly and spent likewise. Now, to solve this frozen market, we must thaw it by using the same method that created this vicious cycle, more spending. Am I the only one who doesn't think this will work? Flooding the economy with money or debt to get it moving on its merry way is the wrong idea because it is the very same idea that caused all this trouble in the first place. This "fix" for the economy is a quick and temporary job, like a shot of heroin into the arm of a dying drug addict. We create these problems and we can be the solution, but probably not in the way we hope or think. If each person that makes up humanity cannot see the need to completely understand their self and thus live peacefully, then the world will continue living in the suicidal effects of our combined psyche.

Granted, we have seen boom and bust before and we have recovered. This is what most people believe will happen, based on history. But people believe in these happy endings because, after all, how could we go on if we didn't? Hope is a survival mechanism that we all have, and look at how great it works! There are some who don't believe anything bad will happen to them in the future, as if they have some kind of protective bubble around them. This is based on fear and arrogance. Most people, from Baby Boomers to today's children, haven't really experienced difficult and troubled times. We have had it relatively easy. The economy is a strange yet understandable thing when seen clearly.

Hope and Greed

Excessive hope and optimism for the future unfulfilled can often leave people surprised and saddened. Hope is the belief in the fulfillment of a positive expectation in the future and is *always* linked to fear. Hope gives us a motivation, a rush to action, and so does fear. This is created by the ego and is the deliberate thought pattern that leads to a positive attitude instead of a negative one. We avoid the negative perceptions or aspects of life when we should embrace and accept them completely, instead of using the comfort and motivation of hope as a projected design of escape from things that we perceive to be negative. We need to accept all experiences as they are, and not just the moments we personally believe to be pleasant. Psychological suffering through unrealistic perceptions of hope can be illustrated by people who buy lottery tickets honestly hoping to win, only to have the odds beat them and leave them disappointed and angry or sad. Hope possesses a vast proclivity to skew the neutrality of reality into outlooks of aggression, mania, and depression, which are forms of opposition and conflict against that which is present, real, and perfect. Lotteries and casinos are multi-billion dollar industries that feed on hope and greed. Economic markets are strikingly similar; it's a fool's gold rush, but with a clever mask. We live in a growth economy that has butted heads with nature and won for too long. Now, patient and powerful, nature will gradually reclaim the world and restore balance. As this process occurs it is widely apparent that this societal collapse was not a matter of if but when, not maybe but how soon.

The current economic model does not complement nature and, because of this, it is inching closer every day toward its expiry date. Many may find reason to debate this; however, all counterpoints are ill-founded. The effects of our increasing numbers, along with the egocentric and conflictive awareness we all appear to harbor, are currently magnifying and compounding the consequences more than ever before. Capitalism is an economic system created and kept alive by this human conflictive awareness in which we don't despise the rich, but want to be them. This is the best current economic model we could come up with, and it is based on rotten, self-indulgent hearts. Technology is not the answer, nor is stimulus or anything else that helps the current economic framework survive longer than it should. It has gotten too big and has taken on a life of its own, much like a disease that kills its host and then ultimately will kill itself. We are throwing caution to the wind because it is a long-term process.

On a Foundation of Clouds

What is money? It is the collective agreement with a symbol that represents a value. Money doesn't grow on trees; it grows in thin air, like a cloud of credit and debt, but now the cloud is dark, heavy, and ready for its final thunderstorm. Money is a symbol of value. That's it! Like any monetary quantity, it's a number that is related to something of actual worth, such as a service or product. Throughout the years money has taken many forms and standards. It used to be beans, shiny rocks, and gold. Now it is the U.S. dollar. When we take out a loan from a bank, we make a promise to pay it back with interest. This promise creates the money to be borrowed and also creates the debt which is the loan to be paid in the future, only it's actualized instantly, while the money grown by this promise to create debt is only realized in the future as a distant consequence, and this is a major problem. This form of value creation is at the heart of our modern economy and it is really weird that we have built a society on something so imaginary and conceptually backward but, alas, greed never was the wisest of emotions. Simply put, in our society, dragged out and broken promises equal our modern economy. All credit is a gamble, and in a growth economy it is multiplied by every person that is a part of it. Why are all these reckless companies being given bailouts? Do we think banks and the government are separate institutions? Banks and governments are simply entwined ideas fed with trust. Since we have unlimited debt we have unlimited money, and this is why there are billionaires and so many people that have become so easily possessed by all their stuff. If you know how to work the economic system, it is relatively easy to be wealthy if desired.

The Herd Is a Dead Horse and It's Kicking Itself

Economic trends resemble a herd mentality, and markets are tools that reflect the creators and users. Markets are based on decisions made by cautious and alert humans. If they get wind of something negative concerning the safety of their assets, they become a herd, and if one twitches in this highly combustible atmosphere, there will be a stampede. This is called herd psychology and is the reason for booms, busts, and frozen markets. When I hear the word "bailout," I think of a sinking ship with someone being handed a bucket and scrambling to get the water out. One can only do this for so long. What should be done is to try to stop the cause, not the effects. You can bail and bail, but the leak will still sink the ship. When I think of stimulus, the image of a patient in a hospital being jolted with a defibrillator comes to mind. A stimulus may shock the system for the time being, enough to revive the patient, but for how long? Fear controls all rational thinking. We have now passed the "slippery slope," as many love to call this; we have fallen and shouldn't get up, but of course we are a tenacious bunch. We need an entirely different and practically impossible new approach. We have a severely myopic view of the economy and of the future in general. Since it appears obvious that mankind can't change the fundamentals of society, such as war, government, and the economy of our own volition, nature will now give these ego manifestations a helping hand in disguise.

I am currently living my twenty-fifth year of life, and the older I get the more I realize that age has nothing to do with wisdom (knowledge and experience perhaps, but not wisdom). Age gives more opportunities to learn, but if we are creatures of habit, then these moments, these eternal moments of now, are mostly forfeited and wasted. People say "Do whatever makes you happy." For the most part, we do what we think will make us happy. For the sake of argument, let's say that every day we progress toward our goals, step by step, bit by bit, and day by day. Do our goals represent our happiness? Like a mirage, a goal once reached disappears when you reach it. We seem to make our goals or paths to happiness more important than the happiness itself. Like the pursuit of happiness, once this abstract concept of potential is thought to be reached it often is not what we expected and we are left to pursue another goal. We travel down the road to get to a destination that can never be reached by the vehicle called ego. It feels good for awhile but, after a relatively short time, from days to weeks, your love for whatever it is dims and you look for something else to fill that illusory and self-inflicted void. Unhappiness does not prefer rich or poor, nor is one more prone to happiness than the other. In some respects the more rich one is the more entertained and easy their life may be, but an unnaturally easy life full of excessive comforts and luxuries is a shallow and superficial life of temporary pleasure. This meaningless and deeply unsatisfying attempt at true happiness is not a tree that bears lasting and satisfying fruit. A counterargument would be that money is a means to an end, happiness. So, if I have lots of money, it is a tool for growing happiness with less labor and more time to enjoy life instead of always cultivating a livelihood by the sweat of one's brow. I call this baloney. Of course it's better to work less and enjoy doing what you really want to do, but that is ego-based and not the path to real happiness, no matter how good it feels to the hands, back, and senses. We may have migrated from the forests to the fields and recently into the cities, but none of these steps vaulted our society into peace or bliss.

Molding our growth economy to fit nature's sustainable design was perhaps possible in its infancy. My view is that any action to save the current economic model is too little too late. People have a hard time changing, especially if what we have been doing for so long has eluded our control. These unwise intentions and acts have culminated, created too much too fast, and now it has become a runaway train. We, as a society, are all passengers on the Economy/Ego Express, powered by the confused desires that make us human, and all the conductor can do now is try to tell us what is ahead and when it will hit us. Scientists and spiritual leaders alike have told us what is coming, but we continue to ignore them due to our horror of its potential reality. Most of us either ignore our ability to change or accept that we can't. Either way, it leads to the same result. Collapse and renewal is the path to a new paradigm. How long will this global economy really last after it destroys the life-giving balances of this single, fragile Earth? We have created a successful global society to a fault by means of excessive abundance and excessive scarcity. It is our inflated/deflated disproportion against nature.

The Beaten Path of War

All warfare is based on deception.

(Sun Tzu, *The Art of War*, 6th Century BC/2009)

War is a struggle between two opposing forces. If an opposing force is absent then there is no remaining opposition because any bipolar force cannot stand alone. The mentality of conflict is an illusion at a fundamental level, and how effortlessly is this frame of mind translated into real wars! All wars begin from a gross misinterpretation of reality. This misinterpretation only breeds more conflict as it is willingly unleashed from one's psyche and transforms from a concept into actuality. The prevention and treatment of any war, however politically or personally complicated it may seem, is only possible from the simplest awareness there is: love. The clarity that comes with love brings a deep understanding to conflict and thus ends it instantly, without stages, vengeance, "peace talks," strategy or effort. Love is awareness that is self-aware, self-actualized. Love is the awareness of oneself and the "enemy" *as* love itself and if this awareness of connection is partial or broken, conflict will remain and continue because there is now an absence of love for conflict to fill.

There has always been conflict, going farther back than one cares to remember. The history of humanity is based largely on war. War is in fact a timeless continuum with small breathers in between, seen as times of relative peace with only smaller battles waging in between the larger ones. Moreover, when a physical and bloody war is dormant, the conflict merely transforms from a war on the outside to a war on the inside. Humanity has not gone a single second, let alone a generation, without some sort of war. After any stupid and bloody war is over and both losing sides attempt to return to their normal lives, they find they can't. They carry and spread the continuing conflict, anger, hatred, sadness, and depression into all aspects of their life in ways that one may not obviously notice. This unresolved conflict is multi-generational, essentially lasting the entire span of human history. War is a stupid and shameful waste and it bothers me when people glorify its battles and honor its participants.

There are healthy, balanced and necessary struggles seen in nature between plants and animals that permit the complementary survival and limited proliferation of a species where, simply by their surviving and multiplying, the interests of all the other species in relation to them are taken into consideration by nature's process of homeostasis or maintaining stability in a constantly changing system. When it comes to the human species, unhealthy and diseased conflicts are seen in the creation and maintenance of all battling nations, regions, religions, beliefs, ideas, politics, neighbors, co-workers, strangers, friends, family, husbands, wives, children, and across age cohorts. There has always been conflict. National borders are drawn with the blood of war. Conflict in nature is not really conflict because it has a purpose that, aside from arbitrarily narrow and isolated acts, beneficially affects the world at large. Humans, however, have taken what we ignorantly see as conflict in nature and turned it not only into something unnecessary and wholly different from what the process is and what its effects are into a violent misinterpretation of nature against ourselves and every part of nature. It is increasingly apparent that mankind seems to be the planet's—and our own—worst enemy. In the 20th century alone, it's estimated that over 200 million people worldwide have been killed in war. The majority of these deaths occurred, of course, in the two world wars, accounting for more than 100 million. They died not only because of bombings and artillery, but also through starvation and disease. People killed one another or died because of the fear, anger, and conflict present in each person behind the office desks, machine guns, grenades, planes, ships, tanks, atomic bombs, and all other manner of warfare and its support mechanisms. The illusions of fear and separation are the cause for all war. Our strong sense of fear, our hoarding mentality and our aggression used to serve us properly in the past. These behaviors have since become antiquated, because while they had survival benefits in the past, now they are less necessary and thus have become vestigial behavioral appendages stuck to our human psyche. Society, with its many social classes and processes of sexual selection, has even transformed hair and pheromones into almost obsolete vestiges of what they once where. We generally praise the animal behaviors of competition and aggression, but go to great lengths to suppress our observable animal commonalities by cleaning and clothing ourselves daily, trimming and shaving our hair, and masking our bodily odors. If we could see our behaviors, without the passive-aggressive effects of civility, as clearly as we see ourselves in a mirror, we would perhaps see our animal aggression disproportionately enlarged to something like a grotesque tumor.

World War II was the largest-scale war with the most casualties in human history, reaching about eighty million by many estimates. This war was the one that changed the world more than any other (although, when taken as a whole, all wars have greatly changed our global "civilization"), where nations combined forces to create two opposing sides on a massive scale unlike any other. The atomic bomb was invented and ended the Second World War; although it was used at the tail end of the war in the Pacific, it definitely sealed the deal. Our technological understanding has surpassed our understanding of ourselves. This is an extremely unsettling truth. Tensions in international relations have remained basically the same. Meanwhile, the tools that now can be brought to bear in inevitable future conflicts among nations present the potential and probable scenario of complete annihilation on both sides.

Playing with Fire

If we don't end war, war will end us.

(H.G. Wells, *Things to Come*, 1936)

We are six minutes to midnight, where midnight is global destruction. The discovery of atomic power and its weaponization was the moment in which humanity went from the ability to kill many to the ability to kill everyone. This created the doomsday clock, a symbolic representation that compares humanity's proximity to potential self-destruction to the ticking of a typical clock. It originated in the late 1940s, reflecting the threat of nuclear weapons and their proliferation, but now includes modern problems such as climate change and biological weapons, both of which can also be included in the arsenal of threats of major destruction to humanity and the biosphere. It would be more accurate to change the time on this doomsday clock to noon, but that's not how leaders/the majority do things.

Do you or your parents remember the nuclear preparedness drills at school? What is even scarier is to consider that, should we ever be informed that a nuclear weapon has been launched and is heading towards the United States, the response protocol (even if the nuclear weapon was somehow launched by accident) is immediate retaliation. In theory, the U.S. would "defensively" launch its own nuclear weapons in an attempt to destroy as many of the (presumed) aggressor nation's nuclear weapon locations as possible, in an effort known as M.A.D. or Mutually Assured Destruction. Has anything ever been more aptly named?

Ultimately, all wars are religious wars, because both sides face death and the afterlife and generally believe that God or something to that effect is on their side. Religion and war mix more often than not. Jerusalem's Temple Mount is the most important site of all three Abrahamic religions and is said, in the *Book of Revelation*, to be where the end times will begin before spreading throughout the world.

Countless scientists, humanitarians, religious leaders, and even politicians have warned of the potential for worldwide nuclear holocaust. The two superpowers that emerged following the aftermath of the Second World War were the United States and Russia, whose mistrust of each other spawned the Cold War. One of the crystallizing moments of the Cold War was the Cuban Missile Crisis, over which the two superpowers came alarmingly close to nuclear war. The Cuban Missile Crisis gives us good reason to believe those scientists and others, if we didn't already, who warned that nuclear war is a very real threat that is here to stay. The abolition of nuclear weapons by all countries is the only way to prevent nuclear war on Earth, but that surely will not happen in the near future. In the last fifty years, atomic weapons have become much more powerful as well as proliferating into the tens of thousands. Humanity's first problem of feeling separate from God and the second of murdering another have iterated or magnified through time and have directly created our war-dominated and tragically conflictive world.

The world currently has enough nuclear weapons to destroy all biological life on the surface of the Earth. By some estimates, over 100 thousand people died in Hiroshima, Japan on August 6, 1945, followed by another eighty thousand in Nagasaki on August 9th. Before and during the Cold War, the U.S. conducted over a thousand nuclear tests above and below the oceans as well as in outer space and developed many long-range weapons delivery systems. It boggles the mind to see the people of the world acting in such irresponsible ways.

Global Government

After World War I, the League of Nations was created to prevent another war of this scale. This did not succeed and, after the Second World War, with nuclear weapons now proliferating, the United Nations was created with the intention of preventing yet another world war. Of course, their intentions may seem to be in the right place, but the prevention of World War III is unrealistic given our human nature, which has not changed. Conflict in all aspects of human existence still goes on, despite our cunning and growing knowledge, to this day. There has always been war. All wars however they are separated by time, country, periods of peace or otherwise, are essentially the continuation of a single human war. In the Old Testament, the first battle between two humans is the story of Cain and Abel, but even before that it is said to have been between God and Satan, and also between God and the original humans, Adam and Eve. Cain, the first son of Adam and Eve, became the first murderer by killing his brother Abel. The weaponry of man has changed from stones and spears to remote-controlled drones and robotics. Remote-controlled simulations of battle situations have transformed into remote-controlled weaponry and, as a result, have made war into a virtual world, a computer game with the soldier far removed from the real consequences of their actions. I wonder if, in the not-so-distant future, soldiers will earn the Medal of Honor for their high scores reached from the comfort of their homes. What about the possibility of computer viruses and hackers taking control of the programs that govern the software and hardware of drones, robots, tanks, and nuclear submarines?

War is an economy booster. It took World War II to pull the world out of the Great Depression. War creates jobs, and the population needs to keep busy in order to get a paycheck and put food on the table. War stimulates economic growth, and both have become almost social deities these days, so keep a close eye on global economic decline and the escalation of current wars and the introduction of new ones.

The Greek word "apocalypse" translates to "lifting of the veil," which means a total presentation of truth long hidden by a curtain of illusion. Of all the end-time predictions and prophecies, Armageddon (literally a war to be waged between God and Satan on a hill overlooking the Megiddo Plain in Israel), which will precede the second coming of Jesus and his rule for a thousand years, is the only one that many religious people are consciously trying to bring to fruition. They want deliverance from the trials of this world, and work toward this end by actively pushing to destroy it in order for their prophet to return to punish the damned and reward the righteous. A few examples would be anybody who was, would be, or is engaged in a religious war, such as religiously driven suicide bombers and would-be martyrs increasing the tensions between the East and the West by their actions. Note that a sign outside of what is considered by many to be the holiest and ironically most conflictive of lands reads, "Pray for the peace of Jerusalem." Fear culminating in war forced science to harness the power of the atom, while conflicting religious views may well be the itch that gets scratched by the world's nuclear capacity, ignoring the welfare of the Earth and plunging us into the next and possibly the last war.

Many think the war of Armageddon will be between the East and West or between Christianity and Islam. There is ever-increased nail-biting over a potential nuclear tit-for-tat in which at least two countries, and more likely the entire world, will be the victim. Complete abolition of nuclear weapons and/or war is quite the tall order to agree upon and maintain. This, of course, is the only way to stop the escalation of international conflicts potentially creating the next world war but, unfortunately, it is just plain unrealistic to consider the possibility of all of the modern world's nations joining hand in hand, even for a second.

Tiny Bugs in the Hands of Man

Many experts agree that biological weapons are more threatening than nuclear weapons, due to their accessibility and high efficacy. Humanity will never tame the microscopic world and unforeseen consequences abound when manipulating these tiny animals. Microbes have existed before us and likely will after us as well. Microorganisms have the amazing ability to adapt just as humans can, but on a relatively smaller and much faster time scale. There have been pandemics such as the plague known as the Black Death in the 14th century, which is estimated to have killed between seventy-five and 100 million people. Others include influenza (the 1918 Spanish flu killed close to fifty million people), cholera, smallpox, measles, yellow fever, HIV, malaria, H5N1 avian flu (a mutation of the Spanish flu), dysentery, and Ebola, all of which together have killed millions of people. This is just the tip of the iceberg of how many microorganisms and drug resistant viruses and bacteria could break free into another pandemic against which we may have no defense. We can't get ahead of microorganisms because they breed much faster and thus adapt much faster to our methods of eradication. They will always be leaps ahead of our understanding and research. If history repeats itself, we seem to be overdue for another pandemic. Our modern lifestyle has allowed our immune systems to become vulnerable by their relatively weak exercise routines. Germ warfare is just about the most uncontrollable and volatile of weapons of mass destruction that can be imagined, because it only requires manipulating natural biology. Microorganisms, for example, made the conquering of the Americas that much easier during the Spanish incursions. Since natural biology has a way of taking things into its own hands, men, women and children would be left with no defense against the tiny yet fantastically powerful juggernaut of microorganisms which have, and will in the future, easily kill millions of us. With their propensity for quick mutation and vaccine-resistance, as well as globally interconnected travel, all it would take to detonate one of the many diseases, intentionally or unintentionally, is to have one infected person walk among us. It's ironic but perhaps fitting that our unbending misuse and abuse of our power all over the world may be undone by the truly unstoppable force of natural processes and evolution that has enabled Earth's life-giving abilities to endure.

Environment—This Bluegreen Stone Spins So Moss Can Grow

We have essentially laid waste to our planet in about 200 years. Concerning our impact on the environment, it is fitting to compare the scale of our efforts to reverse the consequences of our behavior to a tidal wave of imbalance with a tablespoon of equilibrium. What unspeakable horrors we have wrought upon the entirety of nature! We kill all animals including ourselves; we cut down all our trees, and pollute every body of water and all of the air. We are the great destroyers of the Earth. We the people generally have a narrow approach to life. There are too many individuals who need to change within themselves to create complete and lasting balance on Earth. A green concert or recycling program just won't cut it. Partial attempts don't work. Worse, with the recent drop in the economy we are seeing a shift away from the awareness of the Earth's needs and more frenzied attention given to the economic environment and the desperate attempts to revive it. This is a global issue and it is a silent emergency. It is not just the economy, not just the increased threat of war, not just the decline of oil, and it's not just global warming. All of these factors are connected and their effects amplify each other's effects, creating accelerated negative change for humanity and everything else that lives on Earth. Everything has a cumulative effect, and, like a heart attack, consumptive imbalances will culminate in collapse probably much sooner than we wish.

The Ever-Growing Sum of Our Deeds

What happens when the Earth, from which we extract all energy such as oil and gas and coal, metals, minerals, food and water, begins to give less than we demand? We will have landfills, junkyards, factories, and millions of vehicles, houses, and televisions, but the supply of materials to make more will cease to exist, while the demand will continue to dig deeper and deeper and eat nature out from under our feet. This is the real redistribution of wealth, and because of it the Earth is dying a very real death. Earth has the habit of acting like a phoenix, while humans are limited in this rejuvenating aspect. We furiously use up fossil fuels that have taken millions of years to create; we use this energy inefficiently and pollute and overheat our planet just to get from here to there and make a quick buck selling garbage. We exhaust and erode our very thin and life-giving soil to the point where it becomes useless, and then we slaughter animals wholesale to fill the masses. Keep in mind that this isn't just to sustain human life, but to make people so fat and unhealthy that complications due to overconsumption are the leading cause of death in North America. This is not to mention the excess food that goes to waste in spoiled fruits, vegetables, and meats, recalls of vast amounts of potentially dangerous or poor quality food and drink even slightly considered unfit for human consumption that doesn't even make it to the grocery stores, let alone our homes and mouths. Food safety regulations have also precipitated the slaughter of millions of cows and chickens to prevent the spread of Mad Cow disease and the H1N1 avian flu. On the other side of all this waste are the increasing numbers of hefty eaters. The word "gluttony" describes a common form of humanity's many excesses and extreme desires for more. Ask yourself what desire is and how it rises and subsides in your mind. Make a serious effort to observe desire and, in particular, when it enters your picture of the world, because when it does you are not observing the desire as an outsider but ending your separation from it and thus ending the unnecessary illusion of excessive desire as it merges with your self.

Because of our tendency toward extremes and the desire for more, we deeply scar the surface of the Earth with strip mines, underground mines and open-pit mines such as the Hull-Rust-Mahoning Iron Mine in Hibbing, Minnesota, for example. We pollute the air, water and soil with toxic chemicals and garbage. We redirect entire rivers and lakes for us and our crops. We drain our groundwater, aquifers and even a sea, the Aral Sea, in the former Soviet Union. We block the flow of rivers with multiplying and massive dams that become instant ecological disasters such as Brazil's Tucurui Dam on the Tocantins River, United State's Hoover Dam on the Colorado River and China's Three Gorges Dam on the Yangtze River. And we mercilessly clear-cut hundreds of thousands of square kilometers of all types of forest, all on a global scale never seen before.

We are Nazis in the context of how we treat life on Earth. We feel quite superior to our fellow organisms and kill them with total self-justification and unfeeling determination because we are divinely endowed with souls while all else is below us and created solely for our own uses. Discrimination is always connected to its cause: reverse discrimination. We discriminate and differentiate between ourselves and others, and between people and all else including animals, plants rocks, air etc. If they are social, docile, useful or cute, animals will become our beasts of burden, food products or pets. Any leftover organisms are considered useless, valueless pests and nuisances or threatening predators which are remorselessly dispatched wholesale. We kill predators and prey alike, dragging the seas for all life, much of which we throw back dead because catch-all fishing methods snare unwanted species, yet we do not change the methods. Newfoundland's collapse of Atlantic Cod in 1992 should have been a clear warning to fisheries worldwide. It's too costly, and jobs and making a living and feeding the ever-increasing family of man are at stake. Our living is nature's dying. We can't help ourselves, and because of our lack of control we are nature's, and definitely our own, worst enemy. We can't help but reach past the thin edge of global collapse in the broadest of senses. We have passed the point of saving Earth, and now Earth will save itself by destroying what needs to be destroyed. Try as we might, it is all half measures and a drop in the ocean with a rare few on board and the rest with their heads in the sand, especially now, due to the current state of the economy. An environmentalist walks along a beach throwing stranded fish back into the ocean, but with what overall effect? His actions undoubtedly affect the fish touched by this love and care; however, the sea itself is polluted and full of fishing nets ready to pick these fish back up and slap them on an ever-increasing number of conveyer belts and dinner plates. It's like attempting to remove a mountain stone by stone only to have the mountain rise hundreds of feet for every stone taken. Sometimes you have to let the landslide happen. It is the luxury of time that gives some sliver of appeal to our piecemeal outlook toward change, but time is no longer a luxury.

Fresh Water

We need fresh water to drink, wash with, and allow plants and animals to grow and feed us. Clean, unpolluted water is pivotally important to the existence of all biological life and yet we take it for granted. Taking things so basic to one's survival for granted is the serious problem we face. We desire excess and leave the necessities obscured from our appreciation. About two-thirds of the world's fresh water is now used for the irrigation and production of agriculture alone. As population increases, so do the mouths that must be fed. Accessible freshwater is critically important to the world's population and, even as we deplete it, protecting fresh water is becoming an even more important issue. Forget the commodities exchange at the stock market—fresh water is becoming quite the hot commodity. We use tens of millions of gallons of fresh water around the world every hour after constant hour. The water is not gone but is used, polluted, and then pumped back into our seas, lakes, and rivers. We are quite clearly destroying the world from the inside out. Fresh, clean water is basic to the health/stability of all ecosystems on land, in lakes, rivers, and oceans, where shortages will spark the emergence of imbalance and conflict between the organisms that need it and will fight tooth and nail to obtain this precious liquid.

Stepping Down from Our Throne

Anyone who desires to be in power probably shouldn't be—case in point: humanity itself, thinking of ourselves as the top of the natural hierarchy. If we are supposed to be the stewards of the Earth, plants, and animals, we really suck at it. But we refuse to leave these self-appointed managerial duties, due to our vain human condition. Our desire to separate and conquer nature certainly won't last much longer. Nature has a gift for balancing things out. Alas, humans are creatures of habit. The most entrenched habits of all are the constant need to survive and reproduce at all costs, and these will surely not change any time soon, even to save the very environment that is the bedrock for our survival. Don't let anyone convince you that technology is the key in any discernable way, shape, or form, because it is only a tool that postpones the inevitable for a time and merely treats the symptoms while the cause, which technology is a part of, marches on. It's equivalent to putting on a sweater in the Arctic or taking painkillers to treat a broken bone. Further, with our modern technology we are stripping nature of all she gives us on a truly global scale. Any well-raised person wouldn't dare use, abuse, and disrespect their mother in the ways we are, but as a species we show scant regard for Mother Earth or our future with her. Moreover, the twenty-twenty vision of hindsight appears not to have helped us to learn from our past history of environmental disasters.

Toxic Waste

Goods soon to be used goods, raw sewage, nuclear waste, industrial pollution, household garbage, plastics, metals, chemicals, oil spills, fertilizer and pesticide runoff, dead soil, air, and water flows into every organism on Earth. Degraded soil becomes infertile and unsafe for anything to live in and on. Gravity and the water cycle brings all manner of waste to rivers, lakes and oceans causing them to become acidic, polluted and unsafe for drinking and for marine life. Our planet has a closed-loop plumbing system. The supply and drainage lines are the same. The pollution released into the atmosphere falls as acid rain, destroys the Earth's ozone layer, and exacerbates the normal greenhouse effect. We create this waste because we have limited the resources of nature to ourselves. Nature is totally recyclable and reusable until we fiddle with it for the benefit of our species. Remember that all the effects of man upon nature are constant and increasing. We pummel nature 365 days a year at all hours with so many disgusting acts that it is truly hard to grasp. The atrocities are global. Why is man at war with nature? We thought nature was an endless beauty that could be stripped of its wealth and still have the power to replenish itself. This is not the case, as we are slowly realizing. People hope and rely on the myth that technology will save us, that it will bail us out of the problems we have created. Will clean energy solve all our problems? I honestly do not think so. There will still be a ballooning population as well as a laundry list of pollution sources other than those mitigated by the clean energy used for powering factories, vehicles, and homes. There will still be the continuing struggle to make nature secondary to the economy and the wars that crop up everywhere. Clean energy, in whatever way it may come about, if at all, is like the Whack-A-Mole Arcade game—as soon as one issue is resolved, others will continue to pop up. Using clean energy versus continuing to use our current dirty fuels resolves nothing, as it only addresses the surface symptoms, not the remaining root of the problem of humanities' misunderstanding of life. Perhaps clean energy helps us to feel better about it, but it may actually exacerbate the problems, exactly the way diet foods and drinks make people feel better about overeating.

We live in a throwaway society. But where exactly is "away"? The garbage and pollution is just moved, that's all, placed somewhere else. What is the difference between having a layer of garbage in front of our eyes and putting it out of sight in a big pile? It's analogous to endlessly picking up dirty and disposable laundry and putting it in the hamper but never washing it. Of course, most recycling is a step in the right direction but, tragically, it's a very small step. It also involves technology that is still just treating a symptom and not the cause which, at the center of it all, is our flawed human perspective. Garbage, while familiar to most humans, is only one among many forms of pollution such as air and water, light and noise pollution and the consequent destruction of natural balances that, in the overall trend, is drastically and constantly increasing. Tens of millions of tons of greenhouse gases are, despite our honest if meager efforts, still being released into the atmosphere all day, every day! We allow nothing to get in the way of human "progress," even ourselves.

Flora

In our wake, thousands of plant and animal species are lost every year, and this will cause the eventual collapse of the global ecosystem. Don't say we haven't been warned. We have been warned about our self-destructive ways for centuries. In defiance of rationality, we continue to ignore warnings until they are "conclusive" enough for us to have to do something, and by that time it is in sobering and regretful hindsight. Today human beings have impacted the Earth in so many ways and in such a global manner that the rate of this unnatural change is faster and more drastic than ever before. We are well into the sixth extinction. The air, water, plants, animals, and everything in between are being destroyed and polluted to the point where they can no longer sustain the human population or even nature itself as a whole. Any new or emergent behavior in a system, such as humanity within nature, will naturally have unintended consequences and these side effects are generally undesirable because we focus on what is gained rather than what is lost. These days of great transition are the combination and amplification of previous events leading up to the end of a chapter in the large and never-ending book of life. Really think about this and observe the present state of yourself and the world and see the correlations and similarities. This is why and how our world has gotten so out of hand. All extinct species before us, from the dinosaurs to the saber-toothed tiger to the dodo had no control over their fate, and we are no different. Nature in all its indispensable variety decides our fate; votes are cast from all quarters and are combined as a whole, and humanity is a minority faction.

Fauna in a Sauna

Humanity is adversely affecting global weather. Only a century ago this would have been laughed at as impossible. But today scientists around the world are building "doomsday vaults" such as the Millennium Seed Bank Project in Sussex, England or by boring deep into the side of a mountain in Svalbard, Norway in which countless varieties of seeds are being stored and stockpiled for the purpose of restoring the future of nature, of regrowing nature itself. The oceans are warming and acidifying, and the ice caps are melting faster than predicted. More and more animals are added to the extinct and endangered species list every year. Thousands of plants, insects, fish, and other animals are on those lists. Thousands of species become extinct every year. In 2008, polar bears were added to the endangered species list, due mainly to ice/habitat loss. As yet to be on the list, of course, is the cause. We are the misfits. We "think" we are the brains behind our eyes, and this has led us to excel in matters where thinking would be useful—for example, survival. But this has exaggerated our thoughts and fears to the point where they are overcooked or past the stage of ripeness. Global temperature has increased by over two degrees Centigrade over the last century. This may not seem like much, but for something as sensitive and completely interdependent as nature's ecosystems, it is excessive and dangerous. Indeed, a few degrees in variation from our own normal body temperature would give rise to fever or hypothermia. Our canaries in the coal mine—the polar ice caps—have shown us how conservative our predictions were, and how deadly serious just two degrees of change can be. It is also more than just the number of degrees; it is how quickly the Earth is warming. This is the real cause for alarm. Global warming may displace the great numbers of animals and humans that live near the coastlines and will probably create what is often and appropriately referred to as "the last great migration." Recall that half of the human population lives within sixty miles of a coast. We are in that process already. About 100 thousand people were displaced during Hurricane Katrina and that was a logistical nightmare. Imagine one or two billion refugees, and food shortages, fresh water scarcity, and human death on a scale never before seen. This will exhaust, more quickly than ever, our fresh water and food supplies, as well as cause pronounced social tensions and international unrest. There is overwhelming consensus among scientists that the greatest immediate threat to Earth is global warming and pollution, generally described as climate change caused largely by people.

Escalation and Collapse

Society never advances. It recedes as fast on one side as it gains on the other. It undergoes continual changes; it is barbarous, it is civilized, it is Christianized, it is rich, it is scientific; but this change is not amelioration. For every thing that is given, something is taken.

(Ralph Waldo Emerson, *Self-Reliance and Other Essays*, 1841)

Nature tends toward equilibrium. Mountains rise and are eroded by weather. Everything has its place in nature, even humans, regardless of how we choose to distance ourselves, to set ourselves as being above nature, and then to try to conquer it. This is our collective choice. We choose not to have a proper place in nature, but instead choose to alienate ourselves and try to conquer our life-giving mother. Why would we want to overcome and "beat" nature, when it is nature that gives life to us and all things? Why have we separated ourselves from everything and now, it seems, everyone else around us? We have divided ourselves into nations, states, provinces, religious denominations, political parties, and demographics *ad nauseam*. This mentality evolved from the more primitive territorial mentality we see in countless plants and animals. The difference is that plants and animals have a balanced and oftentimes symbiotic territorial relationship with other plants and animals, whereas our view of the world has the entire Earth being divinely bestowed on humans and only humans, to rule and govern over creation, and this is why we thrive while other species die. Now, with all the trouble we are causing our co-inhabitants of Earth and the rate at which we are doing so, it is clear that whatever happens in the next five or ten years will determine the future of our planet. This is truly unlike any other time in Earth's history. This generation has the greatest choice of all generations. Imagine the continuation of our ways fifty, twenty, or even five years from now. What do you see?

Point of No Return—When People Desert the Ship, the Ship Deserts Them

We are past the point at which there was a window to change and now it is time for the ship called Earth to abandon us. Some believe we are already past the edge of "when push comes to shove," and we are now paying for our so called free lunch. We have had our fun pursuing false happiness and living the American dream at the expense of nature, with complete disregard for the past and the seemingly distant future. We live for the future and at the same time forsake the future, with no regard for what we leave behind. It is only a matter of time before these ideas of the past and future clash against the reality check of the present moment. As this process runs its course it becomes patently clear that this collapse was never a matter of if, but when.

The unnoticed (typically human) passing of peak oil, coupled with the passing of the ecological point of no return, is no less real than their imminent and inevitable consequences upon all that is entwined in these aspects of Earth and humanity. This is the emergent and exponentially cascading effect of constant, and multiplying, "unintended" consequences. Whether in the middle of the cosmos or the desert, this moment in human history is the quiescent breaking of the proverbial camel's back, leaving us stranded. What does one expect if a camel is neglected to the point of collapse? All forms of Earthly life are the involuntary yet presumably appreciative passengers on this cosmic sailboat. But the seaworthiness—the integrity—of this universal ark has passed a critical point in its internal workings. The extent of incessant human behavior has gnawed a hole in the hull and we are finally noticing the water lapping at our ankles. Are we finally getting it, or waking up to the truth at all? The process that we have set in motion is orders of magnitude past what we can, relatively quickly, reverse. The choice to act has come too late. The doors have been sealed and the ship has sailed. This is the whimper T.S. Eliot warned us about.

Al Gore, David Suzuki, Jane Goodall, David Attenborough, Leonardo DiCaprio, Stephen Hawking, Farley Mowat, and countless other individuals and organizations have tried to warn the people of the error of our ways. Are these warnings utterly pointless? Warnings are meant to alter present perceptions, which in turn alter subsequent actions, which then compounds into a shift back to nature's rhythms. These warnings require immediate action; this is an emergency concerning all humanity in desperate need of help. As we all know, an emergency requires one to exhibit a keen sense of purpose and alertness in order to act effectively. An emergency forces one to focus their attention on what is important at the present moment. Putting the common reactions which emergencies evoke aside, such as intense stress and fear, we, in a sense, should adopt this sort of immediate attention in our everyday lives because it allows us to constantly be aware of what is important in our lives, such as recognizing the value of living a relatively more humble and natural survival lifestyle as well as helping and loving ourselves, others and our entire world. In this sense we should view every day as an emergency, because this would instantly put a halt to unnecessary excesses of behavior such as overanalyzing, luxury and decadence, needless quibbles and wars, strong senses of individuality, narcissism, safety, security, hatred, greed, boredom and violence. Emergencies instill a basic survival mode and a focus on the importance of what one loves. Survival coupled with the awareness of love would be a peaceful and balanced way to live, instead of the way we squander our lives today—lost in excess, confusion, violence, familiarity, and complacency.

Are these all good intentions enacted in the nick of time to create drastic action, or is there every indication that these warnings are vainly screamed at deaf ears and it is simply and sadly too late to stop the unstoppable force of divisive thought and the hand of man? Is it too late for both prevention and treatment? Where is this world headed? What does awareness accomplish if it is always in the realm of the minority? Try as we might, all of our efforts and all of our technology haven't been working all that well. The blind bull of indifference can do damage when it is caught in a numb restlessness of denial and illusion, while acceptance is a free-range animal, aware and open for anything. Denial and acceptance are two forms of the same thing, where the difference lies in the process and not the end result, because there is no end. Denial numbs and closes while acceptance opens and stimulates like the pupil of an eye. The single pupil has dual actions but those actions determine whether you see and experience less or more.

We live on the surface of the only planet that we know of that can sustain life, and that does so in great variety and abundance. This beauty emerged through a process of tending toward balance, but just look at what we are doing to it. The world is turning into a hellish place because we are projecting the perceptions of ourselves upon it. We need help, but nature will come to its own rescue with no more regard for us than for the other inhabitants of Earth. The silver lining—for the Earth—is that our dreadful stewardship cannot sustain itself much longer. Nature itself will take over, but what then, of us?

Calendars, science, religion, war, economy, and population have all emerged and grown alongside each other as a singular effect of conflict and separation, with all of these aspects rooted in the single human problem of the belief in separation. We haven't stopped this momentum because, in addition to the constant conflicts among humans, it has always been a recipe for success that has led us to the peak of our civilization. We made no deal with nature and she has no real voice, and so she is left unheard in the background noise of the cheers and applause of the majority. However, defenseless as she may seem, she holds all the cards.

Cycles of Earth in the Cosmic Neighborhood

Precession is the process Earth takes (roughly 25,700 years) to complete one wobble on its axis. Similar to a gyroscope, our Earth spins, but not in an idealized spin; it wobbles back and forth. Precession, if we could imagine a line coming out the North Pole, would go through each zodiacal constellation roughly every two thousand years, since there are really thirteen astrological signs if we include Ophiuchus. At present, we are in the Age of Pisces and entering the well-known Age of Aquarius. Interestingly, our Earth is roughly the same number of light years (25,700) away from the black hole at the center of our galaxy. Since it takes one year for light to travel one light year, what happened roughly twenty-six thousand years ago at our black hole could reach Earth on December 21, 2012, which is the "end" or completion of our current cycle of precession.

There are prophecies regarding the next few years that relate to a galactic alignment occurring in the year 2012. Ophiuchus is the thirteenth sign of the zodiac. It is considered by some to be the unlucky sign, sometimes called the secret sign and, in Greek, it is called the serpent holder or handler. It lies between Sagittarius and Scorpio, and on December 21, 2012 the center of the Milky Way galaxy will align with the Sun and the Earth. At this time the only two signs of the zodiac with apparent arrows will point to the same spot. Scorpio will point his stinger and Sagittarius will be pointing his arrow at the black hole at the center of our galaxy. This is when Earth passes directly through the center of the Dark Rift, or the Galactic Equator, which occurs in thirteen-thousand year cycles. Ophiuchus crosses the celestial equator precisely at the center of the galaxy, and this is also when the Sun and the Earth cross Ophiuchus. This is said to be the twenty-six thousand-year galactic alignment event that many think will cause great changes on the Earth. Who knows?

Earth's Magnetic Field

Earth's magnetic field is created by the core of our Earth and is directly connected, and thus sensitive, to the varying magnetic field of the Sun. The Earth's magnetic poles will reverse just as the Sun's will. Even the Milky Way galaxy is magnetized, and experts say it probably reverses its polarity, too. Any kind of reversal or time of transition from one state to the opposite is often accompanied by turbulence and accelerated change. Earth has a magnetic barrier protecting itself from space weather called the magnetosphere. Our star also has a magnetic shield called the heliosphere protecting the solar system from the "weather" in space much in the manner that Earth's magnetic field does. Magnetic fields extend infinitely, though they become weaker the further they are from their source. The source of these fields is theorized to be an electromagnetic dynamo within the Earth's moving and electromagnetically conductive core. When conducting fluids move they create magnetic fields, an electric current is simultaneously induced, which in turn creates another magnetic field and another electric current, and when this field complements the prior a dynamo is created that is inherently self-sustaining. This dynamo is a perfect example of emergent behavior due to a feedback loop seen in numerous instances in nature. The Earth's magnetic poles are not as stationary as its geographic poles, but wander, at times erratically, depending, in no small part, on the Sun's magnetic activity. Overall, the wandering of the magnetic poles is accelerating; that is, increasingly travelling farther in the same timespan. At the beginning of the 20th century, the north magnetic pole was observed to meander about ten kilometers north northwest toward Siberia. In the last forty years, acceleration has the north magnetic pole swiftly travelling on average between forty to fifty kilometers per year in roughly the same direction. The northern magnetic pole has travelled some 700 miles since its discovery in what is now the territory of Nunavut in eastern Canada by James Clark Ross in 1831. The speed of today's wandering magnetic poles are faster than at any time since the 15th century. Earth's magnetic field is in the process of weakening. It is proposed that the magnetic field during a pole reversal weakens before it completely disappears, then flips.

In 1905, shortly after composing his paper on special relativity, Albert Einstein described the origin of the Earth's magnetic field as being one of the great unsolved mysteries facing modern physicists. This has since been explained by the dynamo theory. Although it is only a theory, since it cannot be directly observed, it is not predicated on blind conjecture, but rather on sound reasoning and scientific experimentation and observation. (It should be pointed out that relativity is also a theory). Dynamo theory is explained in more depth in this chapter, as well as other cycles and theories that seem remote to us, but are directly active in our everyday lives.

Deep within the Earth, naturally magnetic liquid iron is in motion, and this fluid creates an electromagnetic field that surrounds the Earth, protecting us primarily from solar radiation. How amazing is it that we have a magnetic field, an atmosphere, and an ozone layer, all of which protect us from the energy of the Sun and other space weather! However, the strength of this magnetic field is decreasing and has been for a long time. Mars and Venus probably had magnetic fields ages ago, and all of the other planets in our solar system still possess one. A fascinating way of seeing how Earth's magnetic field has acted in the recent and ancient past is to study the orientation and strength of the field which has been "frozen" in clay pottery and ancient solidified lava flows.

The strength of Earth's magnetic field has been in a slow decline for thousands of years. However, the rate of decline is steadily accelerating and at a rate that is raising a few eyebrows. Carl Friedrich Gauss was the first to accurately and methodically measure Earth's magnetic field in 1835 using his invention, the magnetometer. Hundreds if not thousands of subsequent measurements have been performed by countless scientists all over the world. Since the first accurate measurements of the Earth's magnetic field, over only a century and a half ago, our protective space blanket has decreased in overall strength by ten percent (U.S. Department of the Interior/U.S. Geological Survey). This magnetic drop is, to this day, steadily decreasing toward a reversal. It may not seem like much, but when put into the context of the hundreds of thousands of years it takes for the poles to shift, it is very fast indeed. The sudden event of a magnetic pole reversal is preceded by a dragged out, albeit accelerated, weakening of the magnetic field. The process of magnetic pole reversal begins slowly, then it increases exponentially, finally reversing suddenly. Magnetic reversals happen when the magnetic field is weakened by about ninety percent and, by this point, quite indifferent to which way it points. Reversals begin with anomalies or patches of opposite magnetic polarity within the other polarity's territory. Imagine big bubbles of magnetic field oriented to the north popping up in the southern magnetic hemisphere. This is seen in the famous South Atlantic anomaly, where a large portion of the magnetic field is now oriented toward the north. During periods when this field is weak, some external influence such as solar activity could possibly contribute to pushing the field over into such as a weakened state that a reversal of its polarity occurs. During these reversals, the Earth's protective field/shield is essentially nonexistent.

Throughout its existence, Earth's magnetic field has flipped many times. Ancient lava flows suggest our magnetic field has reversed in time spans ranging from millions of years to as little as tens of thousands of years. The process through which a magnetic field dissipates and reverses can take hundreds or thousands of years to complete; however, like any exponential process, the critical point or stage of terminal decline may be a long time in coming, but once passed, the changes are incredibly accelerated. The most recent magnetic pole reversal is believed to have been 780,000 years ago, when the north magnetic pole pointed southward. This means that, based on an average reversal time span of roughly 250,000 years, we are long overdue; however, these polar shifts can happen at any moment the dynamo inside Earth sees fit. Earth's magnetic field is predicted to continue to weaken, as is the norm in the process of reversal, eventually leading to such a homogenized north and south mix that it will effectively obliterate the field, leaving us naked to space and, mainly solar, weather. It may quite possibly be solar explosions that push our magnetic field into a full-fledged reversal. Migratory animals such as whales, turtles, birds, and grazing animals can distinguish magnetic field variations and use them to travel long distances. If migrating animals lose their sense of global positioning, it would cause massive loss of life among those species, because without the ability to navigate toward places of safety for breeding or areas of seasonal food blooms, they may possibly perish in large numbers as well as all the animals that depend on them.

We Stand on a Thin and Heavenly Land

The thickness of the Earth's crust is, by comparison, as thin as the skin of an apple or skin on the top of cooling soup, but it is the foundation for all biological life. If mold needs a worthy environment to live in, then consider all life on this mostly wet Earth to be like mold clinging to a perfect place to thrive. Thus we and all other biological life forms sit on a thin membrane of biosphere covering the Earth's core and mantle. Earth has an internal structure, as we all know. The core is believed to be liquid iron and is electromagnetically dynamic. Earthquakes are as old as the crust. Our continents, both above and below sea level, float along on tectonic plates like large crowded rafts in a harbor. They grind against each other and this friction builds, causing earthquakes and tsunamis. Where there is a subduction zone, mountains are created. This is where one plate is pushed underneath another, creating friction at the points where the top plate is pushed up. The movement of tectonic plates also causes continental drift, such as between the South American and African continents. One of the greatest natural disasters was an earthquake in 1556 that occurred in Shensi, China and killed an estimated eight-hundred thirty thousand people. The exact magnitude is lost to history.

A hotspot is a persistent area of the Earth's interior which is closer to the surface or crust than normal. Think of it as an unruly pore that is always prone to inflammation and eruption. It is believed that there is a hotspot located beneath Yellowstone National Park. If Yellowstone was created by volcanism, there is good reason to expect more of this activity in the future as well. This has scientists on edge, as Yellowstone is long overdue for a massive eruption. Recently, the region has shown signs of abnormal activity. Yellowstone is a super volcano that can be over a thousand times larger than an ordinary volcano, and there are estimated to be about forty such super volcano hotspots worldwide. On May 18, 1980, Mt. St. Helens erupted with more force than many Hiroshima-sized atomic bombs. The accelerated growth in the height of Mt. St. Helens was confidently yet tentatively used to predict that the volcano would erupt relatively soon. Volcanoes, as with weather and all other natural processes, are inherently unpredictable. However, theoretical models and educated guesses can come close. Anything that happens can never be totally predicted in every detail, the end of the human age included. Imagine Mt. St. Helens or the more recent eruptions of the Icelandic Eyjafjallajokull volcano, but on a continental and even global scale of massive consequence. This would be the impact of a super volcano.

Spaceship Terra Firma

The Earth has dual primary motions; rotation and revolution. It rotates roughly once every twenty-four hours. A revolution around the Sun occurs once every 365.25 days. The Earth is also tilted at 23.5 degrees, which explains the seasons and why the poles have such long winters and short summers. When we sleep or sit we don't feel as if we're moving; however, we are moving around the Sun inside the embrace of the heliosphere at about one-hundred thousand kilometers per second. When you combine the rotation of Earth with how fast the Sun rotates around the center of the Milky Way relative to the universe, during the night half the world may be sleeping soundly, but we are all traveling on a screamingly fast spaceship. Uniform motion is the same as rest which is why we seem so still when we go to sleep. Our solar system is currently traveling through the inner rim of the Orion Arm of the Milky Way galaxy. Will this new cosmic neighborhood increase impact events and drastically increase geological disasters such as tectonic and extreme weather perturbations? Perhaps, but of course, no one knows for certain.

Celestial bombardments are all too common. For proof, just look at Earth's moon or the meteor crater in Arizona. The problem with ancient craters is that, over long periods of time, they can be hidden by geological changes on Earth. If the relatively small moon can have thousands of craters (far more on the side facing away from Earth), then Earth with its larger size would certainly seem to be a bigger target, and thus have more impacts and more chances of impacts in the future. Objects like the asteroid Apophis, a Near Earth Object (NEO) within the asteroid belt between Mars, Jupiter, and the Kuiper Belt at the edge of our solar system, may pose a threat to Earth, based on its trajectory. Asteroids from the Kuiper Belt are believed to have caused the explosion in Tunguska in Siberia, the Yucatan impact crater in the Gulf of Mexico, and the meteor crater near Winslow, Arizona, to name a few. Asteroids within this belt sometimes hit each other, causing their trajectories to exit the belt and head out, once in a while, toward Earth. There have been many hundreds of Near Earth Objects, generally ranging in size from a few meters to hundreds of meters in diameter. Tracking their trajectories is akin to that of hurricanes—they are predictable, but not with 100 percent accuracy.

The Earth's most devastating extinction, called the Permian Extinction, occurred about two hundred and fifty million years ago, and it destroyed ninety-five percent of all sea life and eighty percent of all land-dwelling creatures. The prime suspect for this is an impact event. It has been argued that the passage of the Sun through higher density spiral arms in our Milky Way galaxy has coincided with mass extinctions on Earth. This is perhaps due to the increased risk of impact events. If a large enough object were to collide with Earth, the plants would die as well as the animals inhabiting both land and sea, due to the initial blast effects and the persisting dust cloud that would effectively block out the light from the Sun that is needed for the photosynthesis that drives all life. This atmospheric dust cloud is the same as the mechanism that would create a nuclear winter after a man-made nuclear holocaust. With a significant decrease in sunlight, the surface of Earth would get very cold and everything would die—something to think about when you read the next section.

The Solar Heartbeat

Earth and all its inhabitants are revolving around the Sun. We live in the Sun. We are the Sun. The millions of stars that we see on a clear night are quite similar to the Sun, only they are farther away, at different stages in their life cycle, or are larger or smaller. When most of us think of the Sun, we think of that unchanging ball of light in the sky that rises and sets every day. But the Sun is actually buzzing with activity, constantly fusing mostly hydrogen into helium, twisting magnetic field lines as it rotates, its solar flares whipping coronal mass ejections (CMEs) into space, leaving waves of plasma that astronomers see as solar tsunamis, plasma rain, radiating sunshine and harmonic pressure waves, and exuding its stellar magnetic field like a protective blanket around itself and all its planets. It hurts our eyes when we look at it and it burns our skin. It is responsible for the growth of plants and animals, hence is the source of all the food we will ever eat, and creates constant warmth for all life to exist and flourish. It isn't just photosynthesis or electromagnetic energy that creates life, but also oxygen, water, iron, carbon, etc. and everything responsible for life is generated within our star and others that have exploded nearby. Our Earth is a perfect distance from the Sun and if its orbit was changed by even a few million miles beyond its extremes of aphelion (farthest from the sun) and perihelion (nearest the sun), a small amount in cosmological terms, Earth would effectively be like other planets in our solar system: too hot or too cold to support life as we know it. The Sun is central to the balance in which our Earth can sustain complex life, and any changes in this mass of energy reverberate throughout the solar system. As the third planet from the Sun, we experience these effects and are by no means isolated from them. We are at the complete mercy of the Sun's activities as its cycles of energy release decrease and increase.

All life on Earth exists within a single-star solar system. This is somewhat of a rarity, in that it is estimated that two out of three stars in the universe are in binary systems revolving around each other. Indeed, if the gas giant Jupiter, the largest planet in our solar system, were more massive it could have had the strength of gravity to fuse hydrogen atoms and become a companion star to our Sun. The Sun contains

99.8% of the total mass of our solar system. A photon is a quantum of electromagnetic radiation and has no mass and no relation to time. Think of the pixels in a digital picture on your television screen, or water molecules making up waves. The time it takes for the energy created within the Sun's core to reach its outer photosphere as intense heat and light can be many thousands of years. However, traveling through space, it takes only 8.31 minutes for the Sun's photons of light (traveling at 299,792,458 kilometers per second) to reach Earth, some ninety-three million miles away. So when you look at the Sun, or anything lit by sunlight, you are looking into a past that occurred eight minutes ago, and observing trillions and trillions of million-year-old photons. So photons from distant stars similar to our own may have traveled many light years to reach our retinas and while the stars themselves are millions of years old, each photon is as new and timeless as when it first came into existence. Photons are timeless, but without them we would not see and we would not exist. We are the sight and we are the light. As an aside, during a solar eclipse, our view of the Sun is obstructed by the Moon. It is a striking coincidence that the Sun is 400 times larger than the Moon and the Sun is also four hundred times farther away, which allows the Moon to almost exactly block out the Sun. It is no wonder the Maya thought of the moon as the night Sun.

Worship of the Sun has been central to the ideology and mythology of civilizations for thousands of years. These include North, Central, and South American civilizations such as the Maya, Inca, Aztec, and Hopi, as well as other civilizations around the world. Monuments such as the pyramid of Kukulcan in Chichen Itza, Mexico, the pyramid of the Sun in Teotihuacan, the great pyramids of Egypt, the carved heads of Easter Island, Stonehenge in England, Macchu Picchu in Peru, and even the ancient Babylonian stone tablets containing solar data are all examples of mankind's focus on the Sun, and for good reason. Japan is called the Land of the Rising Sun, but the entire Earth can be called such a land. All mankind has a relationship, as does the Earth as a whole, with the Sun. We live in the solar atmosphere.

We owe our very lives to that big bright ball up in the sky that constantly shines on this life-filled greenhouse. Earth only intercepts a few billionths of the Sun's radiated energy, since the Sun expels that radiation in all directions, and the Earth is a minuscule solar panel in comparison to the Sun's output. It may seem like a small fraction, but the energy we receive is inconceivably enormous. For about eleven years during the last century, Earth was in the deepest and quietest solar minimum, and it is just now emerging into a new cycle of increased solar activity. This is unusual, because the solar minimum usually picks up in activity during its minimum instead of the cycle being nearly silent for the entire duration. The solar sleep has lingered long enough and now it is time for the Sun to wake up. The Sun is an active and noisy place, with cycles of activity and inactivity respectively. It wakes and sleeps. Just as all living things have cycles of wakefulness and sleep, so too does our Sun, and these are called sunspot cycles. On average, these solar cycles occur in eleven-year rotations, although they may be as short as nine years or as long as thirteen. These cycles average eleven years because this is the amount of time that it takes the Sun's internal thermodynamic conveyor belts riddled with magnetic fields to build up to a point of reversal. Sunspot activity, whether increasing or decreasing, is not a matter of if but of when; it is inevitable. It begins with a solar minimum (few or no sunspots) and relatively little solar activity. Then at the end of the solar cycle, over the course of the next eleven or so years, it gradually turns into what is called a solar maximum. This is a state of many sunspots unleashing massive solar activity. According to NCAR, the National Center for Atmospheric Research, "The next sunspot cycle will be 30 to 50 percent stronger than the last one, and begin as much as a year late." (NCAR, National Science Foundation, 2006).

Solar Polar

The key to understanding the Sun's beautiful behavior is within the magnetic aspect of electromagnetism. As with all stars, the Sun is very magnetically active. Magnetism is a force that attracts and repels. Materials like nickel, iron, and others are very reactive to magnetism, although it is interesting to note that all matter is influenced by it to a lesser or greater extent. Magnetism is one component of electromagnetic waves such as visible light, radio waves, X-rays, gamma rays, infrared rays and microwaves. Every electron in every atom, due to its spin, is in fact a small magnet. This magnetism is inherently caused by angular momentum, which means that all matter is electromagnetic. Thus it is not surprising that magnetic fields affect all matter; they are inseparable, even though we only perceive certain aspects and intensities.

Sun Storms

Bursts of solar energy are released into space by twisted magnetic fields called magnetic flux ropes that coil up like a Slinky and eventually snap, resulting in the release of massive amounts of energy. There are millions of magnetic fields on the surface of the Sun as opposed to just one on Earth. The reason there are so many, and also the reason that they get tangled up so much is because the Sun is not solid. Its motion is very fluid-like and it is constantly changing, because the Sun has such high pressure and temperature that the matter and energy are in the form of ionized gas or plasma. We can see magnetic field lines in the plasma with satellites. Intensely hot, electrified gases known as coronal loops show us the electromagnetic field lines linking pairs of sunspots. These loops can be more than 300 thousand miles or roughly thirty Earths high when they rise with the field lines. These loops tend to occur near the relatively darker regions of concentrated magnetic fields called sunspots. Sunspots are around a thousand degrees cooler than their surroundings, and this is why they appear darker. Sunspots can be larger than Earth and spin like hurricanes. These magnetic field lines or loops have sunspots with opposite polarities anchoring them on either end, which is why sunspots most often occur in pairs. These twisted lines build up energy like a rubber band-powered airplane, and once released their fantastic energy creates solar flares and coronal mass ejections that fling highly-charged plasma and proton storms into space at eight million miles an hour and can take several days or sometimes only hours, depending on their velocity, to reach Earth. These releases can create exaggerated solar winds and flares that can strip the Earth's magnetic field and disrupt or destroy the manmade satellites that now number nearly a thousand. Even at the Earth's surface, these solar winds have the potential to disrupt anything running on electricity, which can drastically change people's individual lives, and affect the military, government security, and worldwide economies. A lengthy minimum is just a precursor to a more built-up maximum. As we have begun our twenty-fourth solar cycle, there has been a slow start, with few to no sunspots at all. This is further indicative of a looming and much larger solar maximum.

The Sun's Circulatory System

The Sun spins faster at its equator than at its poles, rotating once every twenty-five to twenty-seven days at the equator and thirty-one to thirty-five days at the poles. This is known as differential rotation. This twists, and then ultimately snaps, magnetic field lines causing high energy outbursts that shoot out into the solar system. As the sunspot cycle progresses, the sunspots increase and move toward the equator. Sunspots usually occur in pairs with opposite magnetic polarity. The polarity of the leading spot alternates with each cycle, so it will be north one cycle and south the next. Differential rotation creates a cyclic conveyer belt mechanism not unlike our ocean's thermodynamic conveyor belt that drives the Sun's eleven-year cycle. The spots appear in two bands on either side of the Sun's equator much like our tropics of Cancer and Capricorn. Although separate spots come and go from week to week, the main bands in which they arise remain and drift toward the solar equator over the course of each eleven-year cycle. This is called meridional circulation. At the beginning of each solar maximum, the sunspots emerge within about thirty degrees of the equator, and as the maximum continues the sunspots migrate progressively closer to the equator. The closer these sunspots come to the equator, the greater the probability that their high-energy releases—flares and CMEs—will be closer to the Earth, since the Earth and the rest of the planets revolve along the solar equator. Sunspots rarely travel past the forty- and five-degree lines of latitude away from the equator. This meridional circulation appears to influence the strength of future cycles, as observed in the number and size of spots that are produced beyond the direct cycle, but following in a two-cycle or twenty-two year time lag. Because the circulation flowed quickly during previous cycles (our last being Cycle #23), astronomers believe the current cycle will be a strong one whose activity is predicted to peak between 2012 and 2013.

The Subtle Severity of Solar Flares

The intensity of flares is classified as A, B, C, M and X, where category A is small with few effects on Earth; B, C and M class flares are of increasing strength and considered in the medium range that can cause some Earth effects (M class flares can, for example, impact radio communications). Finally, X class flares are considered major events and can cause long-lasting, nearly global storms with great possibility of disruption/destruction to satellites, power transformers, and other electrical devices. Solar flares release a cascade of high-energy particles known as proton storms. Most proton storms take two hours to reach visual detection on Earth. Geomagnetic storms usually occur twenty-four to thirty-six hours after the initial solar event. These naturally only hit Earth if the shockwave travels in Earth's direction (think of hitting a bull's eye in a spinning 3-D centrifuge), and however unlikely it may be statistically speaking, like winning the lottery, this perfect storm only has to happen once.

High Notes in History

Europe experienced uncommonly frigid weather in the 17th century, during what is known as the Maunder Minimum or Little Ice Age, when the solar cycle seems to have remained at its deep minimum stage for several solar cycles. About a thousand years before the Maunder Minimum, Greenland also felt similar extended minima, which wiped out the Vikings who inhabited the arctic island. The average decrease in temperature was about two degrees, but it was enough. This has an ominous correlation to our current average increase in global temperature which is, so far, also "only" two degrees. The largest geomagnetic storm ever recorded occurred on the first two days of September 1859. On September 1, 1859 a large solar flare was seen and documented by British astronomer Richard Carrington. The solar flare created a coronal mass ejection that burst away from the Sun and headed toward Earth. The CME arrived within eighteen hours—a trip that normally takes three to four days. Northern lights were seen as far south as Mexico and the Hawaiian Islands. Telegraph wires in both the United States and Europe shorted out, in some areas creating sparks that caused fires nearby. At the time the telegraph was the only widespread electrical technology, in contrast to the global sprawl of modern technology which depends almost totally on electricity.

About 130 years after what has been named the 1859 Solar Superstorm, a CME from the Sun blasted into space and headed toward Earth again. Four days later, the solar energy reached Earth's magnetosphere, 93 million miles away, on March 13, 1989. This large geomagnetic storm, though smaller than the one in 1859, caused the crash of Hydro-Québec's electrical power system. Such an impact on electrical services caused drastic economic fallout. Economic losses in Quebec reached into the tens of millions. The financial losses were so high because for about nine hours roughly six million people were without electricity which is pivotal to any modern economy. Even Sweden and some northeastern states in the U.S. lost power and money, though not quite as drastically as Quebec. In August of the same year, another storm affected computer microchips, leading to a temporary freeze of the Toronto stock market. This storm also cut off communications for a few hours to then-President of the United States Ronald Reagan, who was aboard Air Force One at the time, temporarily disconnecting him from an update-hungry world. What if a similar, or quite possibly larger, geomagnetic storm hits Earth in the future, affecting the New York stock exchange, power grids throughout North America, and Europe and the President, if he is aboard Air Force One at the time? Since 1989, governments and corporations alike have been searching for ways to protect the technology such as satellites and computer chips that are particularly crucial for a society to function as well as resistant to the effects of solar energy. These would, however, only reduce the inevitable damage, not totally eradicate all solar consequences here on Earth or in orbit; that would be impossible. However, these tactics are likely to be useless if a strong enough solar storm heads straight for Earth. It will take twenty-two years for the Sun's magnetic poles to return to their 1989 status. 1989 plus twenty-two years is the year 2011. One can add a year or two to 2011, because the solar cycle has been slower in its cycle.

Solar Effects on Biology

All life on Earth depends on regular light and heat from the Sun. However, drowning in this sunbath would be detrimental to one's health. Earth's atmosphere, including its magnetosphere, creates a very effective protective barrier from space weather, mostly from that produced by the Sun. Sunlight surrounds us, so it makes sense that it greatly influences our (and other diurnal plants and animals) adaptation to our surroundings. The range of light our eyes have been adapted to detect is completely entwined with the sunlight it has adapted to. The sensitivity eyes have to light, body heat retention and dispersion (including variations in hair and skin color, metabolic rate, surface area, shape and size) and camouflage are all examples of how the Sun shapes the appearance and function of creatures on Earth. Over billions of years, Earth's creatures have been constantly molded by the touch of solar energy.

The Sun can cause dehydration, heatstroke, even death. The penetration of high energy particles, such as UV radiation, into living cells can cause genetic mutations such as cancer and myriad other health maladies. Think of the atmosphere and the magnetosphere as Earth's sunscreen, allowing a near-perfect amount of solar radiation in, which our bodies further regulate by processing vitamin D and manufacturing the skin pigment melanin. Some animals use the decline in sunlight and heat as a cue to begin migration. Some migratory animals also use geomagnetic fields as navigational routes, and when these are aberrant or nonexistent due, in part, to solar activity, they can lose their orientation.

Systems in Flames

As it stands, we depend on technology to the extent that the world's survival is dependent upon the constant, growing, and uninterrupted services of technology and, more specifically, electricity. There are no complete safeguards with which to equip technology to save it from the power of the Sun. Let us assume that a larger than normal solar event devastates our Earth in the near future. Can you imagine a society or even the entire Earth without electricity? Can you fathom the implications of living without light, without fuel and water pumps, power, transportation to bring produce to the grocery stores, refrigeration to keep it from rotting, electric heat, phones, the Internet, television, satellite communications and radio? What will happen when we lose the certainty of the technology on which we depend? What if something like this happens for a sustained amount of time, say a week, or even a month? How long will it take for this spark to ignite a world of trouble? Perhaps an unprecedented solar storm will scorch our Earth, leaving a third or even the entire surface burned. Fire is a common agent of uncontrollability, destruction as well as change and rejuvenation and the Sun is a predictably unpredictable transformer of life. Similar to the Phoenix after a fire, green plants inevitably sprout from the char. We all rise and fall under the whims of the Sun.

Quietus—The End of an Age

Like imbecilic children loose in a candy store, we may well come to a sticky end in a belch of indigestion but, if we do not, then we will assuredly die of hunger when the sweets run out.

(Farley Mowat, *A Whale for the Killing*, 1972)

When snow gradually builds on a mountainside, an avalanche becomes more and more inevitable as the days go by. A slight disturbance is then all that is needed to detach the accumulation. The compounding problems that face the source of all life are feeding and growing off one another. Our disease and the global consequences that come with it are quite preventable yet the opening for serious engagement remains ignored during the constant build up which, like a heart attack, leads to a sudden system failure. We relish in creating and solving problems rather than preventing them in the first place. We will keep doing what we are doing and we will see what happens. As always, we are in the midst of a transition. However, these days seem crazier than in the past and for good reason. The scale is global. We are living in a time between too much too fast and too little too late. There have been many books and videos about the year 2012 and its possible events. This book aspires to go beyond the Hollywood aspect of all the drama, fear, pain, and death to a peace of mind that can be experienced now, three years from now, and afterward. We are between a rotting fruit and a ripening one. As with any birth, this one will be a dramatic event with labor pains. As with death, there are worries about the unknown and losing the sense of certainty one has of the known. If we are the problem, can we change ourselves? This appears to be the hardest thing for humanity to do, and how ironic it is that the key to everything has always been ourselves. It is time for what many call the Great Purification. It all makes a kind of sense. Things happen for a reason, and the destruction of the world as we know it is no different. This is the end of one cycle and the beginning of another. It is a most beautiful and eternal birth. Transitions are turbulent, to be sure; however, once this one passes the world will be better off. All life, whether it is dinosaurs, wooly mammoths, the dodo, or the great seemingly unstoppable force of humanity, eventually comes to a transformation or reformation; all forms have their expiration date. Nature can be suppressed for a time, but will bounce back like a spring. The more it is restrained, the more backlash there will be. As long as we ignorantly prioritize human life to the detriment of the diversity of all life we will, with unwavering dedication, hurriedly and substantially diminish the life-giving marvel of the whole system.

Dissociated

Although ignorance may seem to be bliss, it isn't; it's just ignorance, that is, separation from the truth. If some catastrophe in 2012 or a gradual collapse over the years is inevitable and needs to happen, some might ask, then why change our ways? In the next few years, there will have to be a culmination of changes. Earth's population of nearly seven billion people must choose the way of nature to facilitate change for the better. If we do not, then we don't have long at the arrogantly perceived top of the food chain. If we use up our finite supply of the fossil fuels on which we are still gravely dependent, and if we keep polluting and consuming Earth's resources on the scale and at the speed with which we are now, we are headed for a self-inflicted and amazingly painful transition in which we will be forced to abandon the willful and comforting ignorance of our actions and confront our ugly consequences as well as the beautiful truth. It's about time! We have rested on our laurels long enough. As of now, sustainability is no longer an option, in my opinion. That ship has sailed. People are well intentioned when they say "use energy-saving light bulbs, carpool, reduce, reuse, recycle, eat locally, fix the drafts in your house to save energy," and all the other wonderful ideas I've heard of late. Alas, these things have only a small impact. "Every bit counts," people say. I agree, but with one exception. We are using the finest of hairs to try to dam the largest of rivers, and that is the crux of the whole 2012 "end of the world as we know it" issue. We live in the year 2011, for crying out loud, and the overpopulation, pollution, and degeneration have been around for decades. The time of good intentions and half measures has passed. We are a knowledgeable, intelligent species, but we are not very wise. We know how to create tools and exploit opportunities, but we don't know how to do this in a responsible manner. There is still rampant war, greed, and narcissism. We are a self-deluded and lost humanity, lacking any recognition of purpose or true direction, and we have generally not acknowledged and reconciled ourselves with our wandering ways. The vast majority have not changed to any effect. In arguably our best model of politics, all that one side needs to reach a majority is fifty-one percent of the vote. We are a mob civilization of animals disguised by clothing, ideas and the "freedom" and "fairness" of our "civil" governments, which we elect to destroy our natural world for the sake of security and jobs and send us to war to protect this state of control. We are in a sad state of affairs in which numbers matter because the majority represents the conflictive and confused essence of our nature.

A Fundamental Misconception

Many people equate the hype over the changes to come in the next few years to the hysteria at the turn of the millennium over possible world-wide disruption of computer systems because of the possible problems with the changing over of 99 to 00. However, the next few years of changes are many, they are very real, and they have been a source of warnings for many years, even well before the year 2000. The number 0, we were told, was the dreaded number that would bring the world to its knees in the infamous Y2K scare. Prior to the year 2000, it was suggested that computers would have trouble changing their calendars from 1999 to 2000 with three zeros, and that the date change would crash the vast majority of computers in the world. This would subsequently create widespread fear and panic that would plunge the world into chaos and even war without our precious and much depended-on computers. It turned out that the impacts of Y2K on the world's computer systems were minor. However, the Y2K scenario is fundamentally different from the 2012 predictions, primarily because there has never before been a date in history where so many diverse disciplines of knowledge and understanding have agreed that something will happen. From scientists to spiritual leaders, there is considerable consensus that the year 2012 will be of great importance. Most people dismiss 2012 as crying wolf, or Chicken Little screaming that the sky is falling. It is not clear whether this is due to the excessive hype around Y2K or to the many past prophecies about the end times that proved untrue, or the predictions of the inconceivable scale and shift away from our normal routine of daily life. The mind strains to fathom any other alternative reality because it is so far beyond both imagination and the world we know. Any potential situation that is completely alien to us is something we deal with through denial, fear, and other rational—or irrational—defense mechanisms. I don't know how or when the world will end, but the likelihood of our dominance of the Earth soon coming to a close through either the actions of humanity or of nature is increasing. The gap between our ideas about the end of our current world sometime in the future and the present and actual end of the current world, is shrinking as fast as the glaciers. However, we all know what happened to the townspeople who ignored the real cry of wolf, and our history is full of examples of people suffering severe consequences because they ignored warnings of real danger.

Waking to an Emergency

When I mention the end of the world *as we think we know it*, and particularly the fact that it is only a few short years away, people tend to go through the emotional stages of coping with this very uncomfortable subject. It starts with denial, which makes sense, because who in their right mind would want to embrace the idea of the mass extinction of humanity and every living thing on Earth? Next people become angry at the messenger and, even unintentionally, themselves. In the third stage, people seem to want to bargain, for example, making deals with God. Or they think they can save themselves by building reinforced underground bunkers and storing up food and water, and often guns and ammunition. Depression can come next, and people start to feel a deep sadness about what is about to happen. And of course, why wouldn't one feel sad about it? It's as natural as what is going to happen. Well, thankfully, in the final stage—we trust after a speedy journey through the aforementioned ways of coping—we reach acceptance. People look at me and ask "Are we all going to die?" And I say, "Of course, what do you expect?" Many will die in the next few years, as will we all eventually, but what always remains—and is generally ignored in the periphery of our minds—is the fact that everybody alive today, all six point seven billion of us, will be dead within a hundred years, anyway. It's not a bad thing, and we should all accept it and live our lives in balance with *all* life.

Our world is a very different place today than it was 100 years ago. So much has happened. We have changed the Earth too much too fast and are now scrambling to mitigate the ceaseless and everyday forces of human conflict. Humans have transformed the Earth from a cycle of life to a cycle of their own. The Earth is warming, species are becoming extinct and endangered, and the statistics are truly eye-opening (if one chooses to open one's eyes to them in the first place). The oceans and forests are being poisoned and stripped of life. Humans have procreated to an extent that the world cannot sustain. Pollution and competition against all other life is obliterating nature's diversity and vitality. Hunger alone ends the lives of over twenty-five thousand people every single day, while humans give birth to two hundred thousand more people every day to overcompensate. People's addiction to oil and material objects to try and fulfill their misconceived desires is creating a profound problem that is hard to deny yet easy to ignore. However hard it may be to ignore, many have refused to change or to address this issue for far too long and now it appears to be a sad yet necessary case of emergence and inevitable collapse, due to the unsustainable nature of our behavior. *If something cannot be sustained it cannot last.*

Everything is more than simply connected. What I mean is, we are not simply connected to life in a linear, string-like manner as in a line of telephone poles connected by wires. Rather, we are connected more like the energy that travels through the wires and throughout all of existence, which is fundamentally singular. We separate this singularity by focusing and categorizing the forms we see in our minds. If you have ever been in a fight or felt anything which brought up feelings of negativity, sadness, or hatred, then you know how separated others feel also. And you also know how bad it feels: it just doesn't feel right. Connecting the divine to the material in our perception is what it is all about. It is about understanding and respecting all of creation, but we live in an immature period of humanity where we prioritize other, less fulfilling, things. The way our Earth is mismanaged—our priorities are upside down, and a reversion is coming. Whether it is the result of solar flares, war, earthquakes, or the many other ways and combinations through which we can reach our "end," the way we die is pretty much unimportant. But we can meet our Creator right now—in life—if we just open our eyes and see creation as the miracle that it is. Has anyone lately felt unbalanced and uncomfortable living in the world we have made for ourselves? What is it about the human condition that chooses to forsake that which is most important? Why are we so afraid of everything? Why are we such a strange species that chooses to separate everything and conquer nature and ourselves? If you were to ask me what I thought of this whole 2012 idea of the end of the world, I would have to say it's a probable date, in that we have had our grace period and have abused our privilege by taking advantage of the giving character of nature. Nature will give until she has nothing left. Humanity is the person in us all. Humanity is that person we all have a decidedly intimate relationship with, and yet we disengage in any serious attempt at trying to clearly understand the conflict of the species in ourselves. Humanity is the one who exploits the giving nature of people and the environment. We are now reaping what we have been sowing for so long and, on the other hand, not that long at all. We are facing the consequences head-on and we don't have the luxury to turn away in ignorance anymore. We look away from what we know we will see because we are afraid, selfish, or simply don't know any better. Our heads burrow deeper into the sand when we know something scary is coming. We are giving Earth a fever; Earth has a strong immune system, but it's not completely immune.

Ancient Prophecy

There is much conjecture about what is to transpire in the next few years, and while the details are hotly debated and there is little or no consensus as to precisely what will take place, one thing almost everybody can agree on is the probability of something revolutionary happening, because we are essentially in the stages of that revolutionary process right now. The stages we are in may very well lead to a final climactic one. It could be something run-of-the-mill and minor, it could be a culmination of minor events or, however unlikely, it could be a single major event. But because of the way the world is heading, it seems to me our world is getting closer and closer to a powder keg moment.

It seems that most, if not all, ancient civilizations had a much more sacred way of living than we do today. Countless ancient civilizations, including the ones I will mention shortly, have world ages or epochs of mismatched lengths and varying cultural interpretations about the significance of their cycles' endings/beginnings. The Hopi in Arizona believe we are in the fourth and present world soon leading into the fifth. The Maya of Central America believed we are in the fifth age, which lasts 5,125 years and consists of thirteen *baktuns* which are their cycles of time made of 144 thousand days or about 394 years for each baktun. According to the Maya, we will enter into the beginning of another cycle of five great cycles during the winter solstice in 2012. This is not the end of their calendar, but the end of one of many cycles. The Hindus believe we are passing through a heavily conflictive fourth and final age or Kali Yuga, which actually doesn't end for many thousands of years. The conclusions of all of these eras mark important renewals and revolutions, including cataclysms, in the cultural history of these civilizations. Recorded history is believed to have begun just over five thousand years ago, or one long count of the Mayan calendar which is 5,125 years long. Coincidentally, this is when the first cuneiform writing in Mesopotamia emerged in roughly 3000 BCE, while the first

Egyptian pyramids are believed to have been created around 2800 BCE or roughly five thousand years ago.

Fire is a recurring theme that is used to signify a period of drastic change. Additionally, there are many great flood legends in various cultures, which put an end to their last life cycle. They all seem to agree on the date of the Great Flood as roughly five thousand years ago. The Maya believed their last world was destroyed by a great flood and that their fifth world would end in flames. This echoes the Hopi, the Hindu Vedas, and the biblical prophecy in the Book of Revelation of a fire that purifies and revitalizes the Earth. Unite the prophecies, the scientific predictions of solar maximum awaiting us in the near future, and the nuclear "fires" which we have in our hands at the present time, and these separate prophecies appear to join together and thus amplify their effects. A global baptism by fire would certainly be fitting, not to mention perfectly effective. In the Bible, the End of Days is when Jesus is prophesied to return to Earth.

One can imagine how events will unfold based on our behavior preceding the present moment. Of course the process is non-linear, and it ebbs and flows, with an overall increase known as emergence, which is seen in all processes of nature, from mountains to society. Naturally, precise predictions will be more or less correct, while speaking about the general trend will probably do a better overall job at communicating the essence of the prediction. Regarding the year 2012 in the Gregorian calendar, the details distract from the general idea. Details give a sense of certainty, while generalities are open to interpretation and yet unwavering as the details change and add up over time. I believe this is the main reason why many prophecies are generalized, not because people think they are multi-interpretive and false, but because they can't grapple with too many details, as they are always changing and open to so much inconsequential variation. One has to remember that visions are clips of insight into where things are headed and not a continuous and meticulous flow of all miniscule yet still important events. If you had a vision of the future, would you give intimate details of every event or would you give the main warning and gist? Prophets, as with movie critics, generally use only the most salient information for their personally and culturally slanted take-home message.

Quetzalcoatl—Kukulcan

The ancient Maya had a deity among their pantheon who was central to their mythology. His name was Quetzalcoatl or Kukulcan and he was both divine and human. Like Jesus, he was even said to be born from a virgin mother. To the Maya he was Jesus. He was tall, had white hair, beard, and skin, and blue eyes. This was clearly not the image of a normal Maya and probably not the image of a Middle Eastern prophet either. When Quetzalcoatl left the Maya, he promised to return as he went to sea heading east, where most scholars who interpret the codices and mythology believe he came from to begin with. The east often symbolizes rebirth, enlightenment, the Sun, and fire. Quetzalcoatl was a being who was represented as a mythological half-bird (quetzal) and half-snake (coatl). He was the soarer and the slitherer. He was the heavens and the Earth and the union of these seeming opposites. One of the Mayans' most popular scientific and religious creations is the pyramid of Kukulcan or El Castillo in the ancient city of Chichen Itza in the Mexican Yucatan Peninsula. This pyramid was used as a sacred and three-dimensional calendar. The pyramid features an image of this deity on its northern stepped balustrade. Its nine western levels cast a shadow, creating isosceles triangles against its northern steps that project the image of an undulating snake body connecting a stone-carved snake head with feathers at the bottom. This represents light, divinity, or the heavens uniting with Earth and the material world. Since its creation, this phenomenon of the shadow has occurred like clockwork every vernal (or spring) equinox (March 21st) and autumnal equinox (September 22nd).

The Hopi also spoke of a white man traveling east to the sea who proclaimed his return. The Incas have a similar legend of a white-skinned bearded god with blue eyes coming from a foreign land to bring peace and order to their civilization. Keep in mind that blue eyes, carried into adulthood, are a relatively new characteristic in humanity, emerging roughly ten thousand years ago. Blue eyes, which are genetically recessive, symbolize a childlike innocence. In the eighth century AD, the Maya predicted that "white-skinned, bearded gods" would arrive from across the sea on March 5th in the year 1519. On that exact date, Hernando Cortes and his Conquistadors arrived in

Central America. This was a critical point of change for the Maya, as they thought this was the return of their god, but they were tragically mistaken. This mistake was taken advantage of by the Spanish, who proceeded to destroy the civilization with a combination of foreign disease, against which the Maya had no immunity, superior fighting weapons and the ruthless hatred they had for the Maya, because, among other things, the Spanish abhorred the human sacrifices which took place in the Mayan city states to appease their gods. It is ironic that the Spanish, who were so revolted by the way the Maya killed each other, wound up slaughtering them wholesale.

The ancient Maya predicted that the Sun would rise on December 21, 2012, the winter solstice, in alignment with what they called Xibalba, the Road to Awe, the Road to Fright, the dark rift, the Cosmic Mother, or center of the galaxy. Only recently has it been confirmed that there is a massive black hole at the center of our galaxy. Modern astronomers have confirmed that on that date the Earth and the Sun will be in exact alignment with the center of the Milky Way along the galactic equator. This alignment is reached once every 25,700 years, and thus is considered a very rare and significant event. Many theories abound; nevertheless, what will transpire remains to be seen. The Maya seemed to have dates or moments in space-time correct, but they make only vague predictions. Meanwhile, the Hopi had precise prophecies, but with no dates attached to them. This reminds me of the Heisenberg uncertainty principle, which states that when observing certain pairs of physical properties, only one or the other can be observed with precision, never both. As soon as we try to measure one part, we lose the accuracy of the other. The Hopi and Mayan observations, when superimposed, create a picture of accuracy in both time and circumstance.

The Winter Solstice and the Mayan Creation Myth

In addition to the Mayan vision of creation, which was reflected in all aspects of their daily life, there was one distinct ceremony: the ball game. In the Mesoamerican ball game there are two teams, who use only their leather-padded hips to hit a ball made of rubber which is supposed to go through a ring on the side of a court with slanted walls leading up to the ring. In the *Popol Vuh* (the Quiché Mayan equivalent of the bible) all of the gods and goddesses and the events which they are involved in are reflections of stars and planets and their motions relative to Earth. The rubber ball represents the Sun or the head of the father of the hero twins. The court represents the Milky Way galaxy and the back and forth motion of the ball is the twenty-six thousand-year precession of the equinoxes. Lastly, the ring represents the dark rift or black hole at the center of the Milky Way galaxy, which was understood to be Xibalba, the underworld of the afterlife, also known as the Road to Awe or the Road to Fright, depending on how one views the aspect of death in the context of creation. When the ball goes into the ring, it represents the galactic alignment at the end of every thirteen *baktuns*. This alignment represents the union of the hero twins' father's head and body. Where the head represents the Sun, ether, or consciousness, the body represents the Earth, material things or the body. The December solstice of 2012 is considered by the Maya to be the rebirth of the Sun. The word "solstice" comes from the Latin words *sol*, which means Sun, and *sistere*, which means to stand or be still. That the word solstice literally means "the Sun standing still" makes sense, because the Sun really does appear to stop moving during the winter solstice. To the Maya, and many other civilizations, this would have been a noticeable and spiritually-weighted event. This is the beginning of a new cycle, and the Mayan bible, the *Popol Vuh*, speaks of the previous cycle ending by flood and this cycle ending by the fire of the Sun.

The Mayan View of Time

The ancient Maya were a Central American civilization that thrived hundreds of years ago, and there are over eight million Maya descendants living today. In my view they are one of the most mystifying and colorful ancient civilizations. The ancient Mayan civilization lasted for over five thousand years, spanning the pre-classic era (900-300 BCE), the so-called Golden Age (600-900 AD), and the terminal period or societal collapse beginning just after their golden age. The word "Maya," translated from Hindu or Vedic means "that which is not" or "temporary illusion of the world," and pertains to the limits and deceptions of the senses.

Time is the motion of change. The Maya, as with any organized and theistic civilization, had to arrive at a common agreement about what their calendar should be. The Maya, again like other civilizations, inherited the basic idea of time from their ancestors, in their case the Olmecs and Toltecs. They were stargazers, and followed the cycles of the stars and planets and, in particular the Sun, meticulously. They had cyclic and very detailed solar, lunar, and planetary calendars, such as those of Venus and Mars, which could predict eclipses and other events thousands of years in advance. They kept track of various lengths of time, not only days, months, and years, but millions and even billions of years. In the upper echelons of the ancient Maya hierarchy, shamanic priests were also extremely accurate mathematicians and astronomers.

The Maya had an obsession with understanding time, and thus established one of the most precise, simple, and yet complex calendars ever known. The Mayans' view of time and creation was deeply reflected in their art, religion, and architecture, and how they engaged in everyday life. The Maya embedded time, or the cyclic and rhythmic movements of natural events on Earth as well as the heavenly bodies into all elements of their life. Their view of time as well as their perspective of creation are directly reflected in their codices, social structure, architecture and their connection to and reverence for the cosmos, the Sun, Venus, the Moon, rain, corn and blood. The Quiché Maya viewed the world not only as the Earth, but included the sky, revealing their deep observation and incorporation of the heavens with Earth. The *Popol Vuh*'s stories of the lives of Mayan deities and the rhythms of Earth are direct reflections of the movements of stars and planets in relation to the human vantage point on Earth. Their concept of time was fundamentally different from our own, because their calendar was constructed around spiritually significant numbers in a revolving relationship with each other. Although modern man uses cycles of time as well, such as repeating days and months, it is only the name that gets repeated for the sake of continuity. Modern man believes that time is a linear flow in one direction from past to present to future, and that it cannot go backwards, slow down, or speed up. It is viewed as an unchanging line of progression. However, the Maya believed that time was not ticks of a clock but simply the rate and scale of cycles within a view of time as nothing but change. To them time was an infinitely repeating cycle of change. They named the repeating days and cycles according to their corresponding vibration, an intention with varying scales and intensities and, thus, characteristics. It is easy to understand that, with the Mayan cyclic view of time, it was not out of the ordinary to see and predict the future based on the past and present, because they were seen as essentially the same thing.

One Mayan legacy is their amazing calendar. Passed down from their Olmec and Toltec ancestors and shared by the Aztecs in their own variation, it consists of three interrelated cyclical aspects of time. Imagine two progressively smaller cogs inside a much larger cog, all having the days or teeth fitting inside one another, thus effectively turning each other, and this will give you a good idea of what their calendar looks like. It consists of the long count, the Haab, and the Tzolkin. Researchers and archeologists have tried to track the origin of this calendar to the Olmecs and beyond, and have concluded that it did not develop like most calendars, but seems to have suddenly appeared in its present form, without the progression of refinement like other calendars. The Mayan calendars are so precise that they can predict, among other things, solar eclipses thousands of years into the future, with astounding precision. They used a vigesimal number system, based on the number twenty rather than the decimal or base-ten number system we use today. Some think that this is because man and many other animals have twenty digits. The flowering or emergent spiral/vibration mathematics with their common characteristics of self-similarity, organized repetition, and cycles within cycles, are the basis of the Mayans' view of creation and time. Their calendar represents the harmonic resonance and frequency of change.

The largest span or cycle of time the Maya have in their calendar begins with the creation of our present universe, which equates to thirteen *hablatuns* or 16.4 billion years ago. Modern astronomers consider the universe to be 13.75 billion years old.

The Maya divided time into thirteen parts, with the number thirteen considered to be a whole and perfect number, although modern mathematics considers it odd, asymmetrical, uneven and incomplete. The Mayan view of time consisted of seven days, or periods of light as they called them, and six nights, or periods of darkness, equal to thirteen, much as in the story of Genesis. The Maya also divided their days into thirteen hours, not twenty-four. Time was divided by a factor of thirteen, spiraling all the way up and down the scale of change from the infinite to the infinitesimal. A Mayan legend states that there are thirteen crystal skulls that are to be found before great world change can occur. Ophiuchus is said to be the thirteenth sign of the zodiac, lying between Scorpio and Sagittarius which, coincidentally, is where we view the center of the Milky Way, and is also known as the snake bearer or handler which I believe points to their supreme deity, the plumed serpent.

The Hopi

The Hopi are a very interesting and important civilization, with a modern population of about nine thousand. The name "Hopi" translates as "the peaceful ones." Hopi prophecies include fire, the ending of an age, the purification of the world, and the return of their caretaker or teacher, the "true white brother," "lost white brother," Pahana or Jesus, whichever terminology one chooses. The following is a concise review of the Hopi and their prophecies:

In the book *The Hopi Survival Kit* (1997), author Thomas E. Mails explains that the prophecies given to the Hopi by Maasaw, their Earth protector spirit, were given to him by the Creator in roughly 1100 AD. The town of Old Oraibi was founded about this time. These prophecies have been fulfilled, are being fulfilled, and have yet to be fulfilled. There are over 100 prophecies, instructions, and warnings, and almost all have happened already, such as the fulfillment of white people arriving and colonizing North America, two world wars, the creation of the atomic bomb and our modern, fast-paced lifestyles distanced far from the truth of nature. The prophecies have so far been spot-on with variables and nuances only in time or the changing rate at which they have occurred. This is why the prophecies have no dates attached to them.

The Hopi live by the simple plan laid out by the spirit Maasaw. According to their cultural memory, they are a collection of many separate peoples representing tribes from distant areas gathering and identifying as one Hopi people. The Hopi way of life involves total reverence and respect for all things and being at peace with these things. Their protector spirit echoes the words of Christ, "I am the Alpha and the Omega," and "I am the first and I will be the last." There are two apparent Massaws who fight with the people and live within each of us: the Poor Maasaw: simple, humble and moral, and the Wealthy Maasaw: careless, boastful, and materialistic. The wealthy Maasaw lives in the guise of materialism and uses temptation to lead people off the set path. People who choose the wealthy Maasaw are called "two hearteds," as they possess the forces of good and evil. We choose which Maasaw we will live by. Maasaw has a Gourd of Ashes that most believe to be the effects of nuclear weapons. In addition to this, he has another little gourd of ashes which are miracle ashes. During the great purification, he will pour these ashes over the peaceful Hopi and the Hopi-like, and all the world's fighting will stop. The Hopi say this is the protection of the righteous and the event that will create a new harmony as the fourth cycle ends and the fifth cycle begins.

The End of the Fourth World— The Beginning of the Fifth

The Hopi tell of three worlds or ages previous to our present time, when the majority of people became tainted and were destroyed, and a small group of true-sighted people, presumably the ancestors of the Anasazi (the ancestors of the Hopi), continued through each age. The first world began in balance, but humans eventually became fixated on war and so became lost and in need of rejuvenation. Hopi legends do not say when the first age ended, but they do say fire from above and below was what destroyed it. The second world emerged from the ashes, and humanity fell into conflict yet again, and so the Creator ended this world by spinning the Earth off its axis. The third world emerged, and yet again humanity took up war as a worthy endeavor, and this time they perished in a great flood. The three previous worlds were destroyed because of the imbalanced actions of people, and the end of our current fourth world will likely be due to the same human causes. The fifth world will begin as a clean slate, and humanity will have yet another chance to change our ways. This world doesn't have to end, but from the apparent continued course of human regress, maybe it does. The Hopi follow the rules of the Great Spirit, except for one named the "true white brother," who traveled east, where the Sun is reborn. Some Hopi symbols include a swastika symbolizing the radiation of force, a gourd symbolizing the seeds of life, and the color red, usually in the form of a ring surrounding the swastika, representing the Sun's energy. The Hopi have prophesied the rising of the oceans, global warming, earthquakes, fire from atomic bombs and a hotter Sun, all of which echo the Book of Revelation, the prophecies of the Inca, the Maya, and many others.

The Hopi foretell three world-shaking events to come before the great rebirth and/or annihilation of Earth. The first two events include the swastika and Sun forces, which the Hopi believe to be the First and Second World Wars, and also include the gourd full of ashes, as they call it, in the form of the invention and swift use of the atomic bomb. The third world event is called the great day of purification and is ambiguously related to the symbol of a "mystery egg." This event is the combination of the swastika, the Sun, and a third force symbolized only by the color red. The Hopi say this event could be either a transformation and regeneration or the destruction of all things.

The Kogi

The Kogi are a fascinating civilization that lives in the Sierra Nevada de Santa Marta Mountains in northwestern Colombia, a region that contains a slice of almost type of ecosystem in the world in a very small space. Their lifestyle is one that is highly attuned to the essence of natural processes. As a consequence, they are a deeply spiritual society that has a warning for the "younger brother," which is what they call everyone who is not Kogi, who are the "elder brothers." In essence, they want mankind to stop destroying the Earth. Otherwise, they predict, the world will be overwhelmed and will collapse, losing its life-giving qualities. The disruption of the water cycle through global warming and climate change will induce more frequent and prolonged droughts and flooding in addition to melting freshwater reservoirs retained in mountain glaciers and polar ice sheets. As a result, our crops won't be able to sustain us without reliable precipitation, we will find our homes encroached by rising seas and desertification and we will find the once thirst quenching mountains to so many millions, bone dry. With increasingly excessive demands for water, pollution and already depleted aquifers and wetlands, we are already facing a water crisis. However in the not too distant future, our diminishing availability to fresh water will be truly catastrophic concerning the habitability upon Earth's watery surface. I think the disruption of the water cycle is what the Kogi are suggesting when they mention the world dying at the hands of man. The Kogi want us to stop what we are doing because we have already destroyed so much of our infinitely precious world. If you wish to learn more about the Kogi, I suggest the documentary film, *From the Heart of the World, The Elder Brothers' Warning.*

Many focus on the fear that prophecies bring with them, despite the fact that they can just as easily be interpreted as a positive motivator to change our unsustainable, destructive ways for the sake of natural and self-preservation. Regrettably, people often casually dismiss the positive aspect of the intended take-home message and rationalize all these warnings as fear-mongering designed to exploit people's fears. If this is true, why don't we also feel this way when we watch the news, or when we give up our liberties to a government to help make us safer? These are much stronger and more effective means of fear-mongering than any book, except maybe the Bible, and any prophecy out there spanning so many years and cultures, and so many avenues of insight, I believe, should be given its warranted and balanced degree of probability as well as skepticism. Most, if not all, individual prophets and prophecies speak of a profoundly imbalanced future. The question is, how have they all come up with these eerily similar visions of the future? They could be more or less right or wrong in their predictions about the coming pinnacle of conflict, but when there is irresistible competition, conflict, and struggle in one's view of the self, then such things appear in the world that we live in. When one understands the nature of man, one realizes that many of the "end of days" prophecies are generally right about the unavoidable collapse of our aggressive society, maybe not in the details, but within the context of their overall message. Unfortunately, it is quite true that there have always been prophecies of coming tribulations that did not materialize, and for this reason we are just as unprepared as we can be for that time when the wolf really does come to town. We all know what people are capable of when they lose their sanity, so it's worth noting that people tend to panic when they are unprepared and have not come to terms with potential cataclysmic disasters. Furthermore, there are innumerable prophecies that are beyond the scope of this chapter and this book. There are many books that deal solely with prophecies; this is just a taste. Humanity's dictatorship over this Earth is coming to its natural close. Intricate details of how every event will unfold and what the world will be like in the future are anyone's guess; however, an extrapolation from current events, thoughtful speculation, and educated guesses can be of some benefit to mitigate or at least come to terms with the inevitability of the course of self-destruction that we are on.

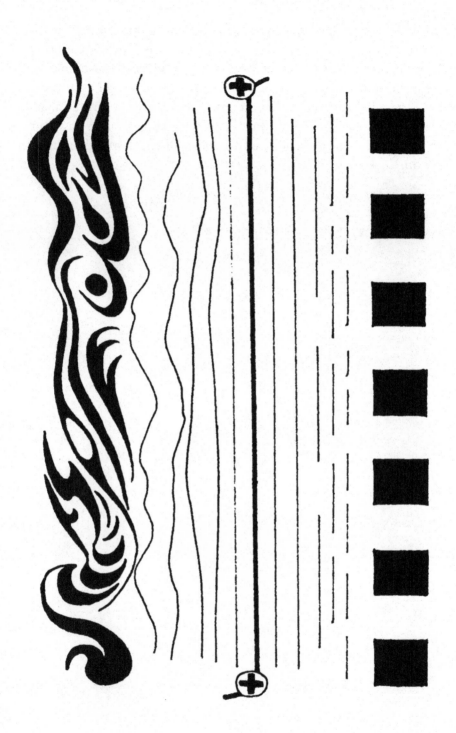

PART 3

MIDDLE WORLD—THE LOST SPLENDOR OF NORMAL

What else is nature but God?

(Seneca, *On Benefits*, quoted in Collision & Collison, ca. 3 BC-65 AD/1980)

We need to appreciate the simple, everyday wonders of life. We need to see the things we consider precious as jewels in a sea of jewels because what is not a miracle? How utterly overwhelming every normal and usual thing in this life is! We live near a star that shines life upon a spinning glob of liquid iron with a little crust, water and air on its surface. This planet is our real home. This single, simple fact should have us all walking around in amazement. We have a natural satellite called the moon which reflects the Sun at night and pulls on our oceans to create tides. Plants and animals of innumerable variation (including ourselves) eat, drink, grow, breathe, mate, give birth, sleep, and die. We see, smell, touch, hear, and taste. Water evaporates against the force of gravity and is then miraculously released from the clouds as rain and snow. There's music, smiles, tears, laughs, volcanoes, atmospheres rich in life-giving gases, protective magnetospheres given off by the Sun and

Earth, light, rocks, bacteria, wind, thought, pain, soil, fungi, plants, animals and so on. We have lost the freshness of awareness about the truly awesome heaven of everyday life. The clear sight of heaven, or reality, has become lost in thought and familiarity and, as a result, we have also become accustomed to a kind of hell. Only the oblivious can get upset and bored in heaven. We forget beauty and accept conflict because they are normal. We have lost our awe of reality and accepted conflict as a given because we have accepted these illusions in ourselves first. This type of thinking has, over the years, become concretized in the collective human psyche. This thinking has allowed humanity to live, but at the cost of a dead, mechanical perspective. Our personal perceptions, manipulated in so many ways, are the standard measuring stick we compare all things against. Everyone has their own definition of normal, like a constant humming that we subconsciously ignore. It ceases to evoke any sense within us because it isn't a contrast but a constant evenness that doesn't stimulate. What is in the background has lost clarity due to our focusing on the foreground. We take the background for granted because it is familiar and thus invisible. We ignore the beauty of normal the same way we ignore violence or conflict, tradition or social oddities. We take them as normal when they are anything but. We don't notice these things because they don't stick out in our mind's eye anymore. We don't recognize the stupidity of our ways and the beauty of nature because both have been insufficiently accepted or acknowledged, and we have moved on to frivolous, peripheral, and apparently more pressing and pleasing things. This "normal" that I refer to is the present moment that we repeatedly forsake for reminiscence, expectation, and "better" and "special" things. Our senses crave stimulation. This is why we love things such as junk food, adventure, romance, knowledge, action, drama, circuses— fun, excitement, thrills and entertainment in general. There is nothing wrong with this except for the fact that our minds get caught up in the pursuit while giving up the peace, the quiet, the normal, the present. Focusing ignores what is not focused upon and, in this sense, it only serves to shut out and exclude. Focus on a face in a crowd and the clarity of the other faces blurs into obscurity. The brain has evolved to see the observed and itself not as it is but in terms of how useful it can be. This is the same for all life. We see by continually redefining normal. We are always searching for a new normal because this is what the brain does. It is both a blessing and a curse for the observer. Most motor vehicle accidents are caused by inattention. This is also true for the accidental or unintended destruction of our beautiful world. Familiarity produces numbness and blindness to the everyday and the fantastic. Familiarity can be caused by habit, routine, knowledge, or experience. The familiarity of any constant and unchanging relationship can be likened to when something slightly and constantly touches one's skin and soon becomes imperceptible. Familiarity, or the lack of seeing what is always there, creates in the observer a loss of awareness upon, recognition of, and appreciation for the beauty and unity of life, and that can cause serious issues down the road.

Man's No Man's Land

Distinguishing the very small as separate from the very large is a question of observation which, when seen from our own vista, is always limited and therefore restricted. We see the universe as alternately small or large based on context, but always with us smack dab in the middle. This is only the scale or limit of our individual observation with which our measurement tools, the senses and the brain, allow us to measure, and the "see with our own eyes" mentality is usually the only test that reality has to pass, because seeing is believing, right? Beyond the observed or known is eternity and infinity. We say the words and imagine their "endlessness," and the full realization of natural life with no end and no beginning is true liberation from conflict and separation. The middle or center of the universe is everywhere exactly because it is nowhere. We live in a world that is in a state of equilibrium in terms of its size, the size and distance of its single moon, and its distance from its Sun, allowing for a temperature, pressure, and light intensity that is perfect for all life. Too cold and everything would be frozen solid; too hot and we would not have a crust to rest on or any kind of material stability. We live in a world that has a temperature that allows water to exist in all three states. Our Earth absorbs and reflects heat and light in balance, and when this balance is seriously disrupted, less than agreeable things are in store.

We are in the middle of a forest and we see complexity and disorder, but we do so by focusing only on the surface we see directly in front of us. The forest isn't really chaotic, but recognizing this takes an open and aware mind. The balanced mind requires emptiness and silence. To be perpetually full one needs to be perpetually empty, allowing the fullness and freshness of the now to enter and exit seamlessly in a single movement. The empty and full mind can be likened to pouring water into a cup without a bottom. The movement of the water entering and exiting is the same singular movement as emptying and overflowing; it just depends on how one looks at the bottomless cup. When the mind is in this act of experiencing observations, or water, in the case of the cup, it is perpetually filling and emptying, like a stream. One cannot be continually emptied and overflowing when one's cup is already full and has a bottom and a lid. We are mentally constipated with our past experiences.

Have you ever finished a puzzle and then wondered why you didn't recognize how it fit before you started? It can be difficult or it can be easy, but our space-time, separated reality can be deceptive. It may seem impossible at first, but recognizing truth doesn't even need effort; it just needs the awareness of love, and what is love if not the effortless recognition of connection?

A Balance of Resolution

The universe is seen and understood by adjusting ones' vantage point by stepping forward and backward to achieve a more detailed and broad picture of it. Scientists use telescopes and microscopes to understand creation in different, yet similar, ways. When you observe something up close you gain intimacy but lose context to the whole. If you observe something from heights you gain the big picture but the nuances and intricacies are lost. Some, such as professionals who specialize in a given field (which almost all schools and businesses are based on) like to understand a few select things intimately. Some, on the other hand, see things from a broader perspective and understand how opposing or seemingly completely unrelated things do in fact relate to each other. Neither view is better or worse, but a balance can be struck that combines the two and leads to a complimentary perspective of both the details and the generality. Some observers like to understand more and more about less and less, while some like to understand less and less about more and more. Some people are more interested in the process by which things come about and some people lean toward the way things culminate in a certain state. Looking at things up close gives a great view, but the details must also be looked at as they relate to the whole picture. The part is the whole, and this remains true when reversed. Concerning how we observe reality in a restrictive manner, Stephen Hawking writes in his book *A Brief History of Time,* "If everything in the universe depends on everything else in a fundamental way, it might be impossible to get close to a full solution by investigating parts of the problem in isolation" (1988, p. 11).

The Tree of Life

Trees procreate, possess hormones and DNA, mate, breathe, eat soil and carbon dioxide along with sunlight, sweat water from its leaves called transpiration, drink, and expel waste as oxygen, yet why do we persist in thinking they are any less alive than we are? Trees are processes, just like you and me and everything else in the universe. Trees form so many symbiotic relationships with the entire Earth and surrounding ecosystems, plants, animals, insects, bacteria and fungi that it truly boggles the mind. They are corals of the land hosting innumerable life forms. Did you also know that trees can fly? As gliders and helicopters fly through the air so do the offspring of trees, in the form of seeds and pollen. When we burn wood we are releasing the fire it has received from the Sun. If a tree falls in the forest and no one is around to hear it, does it make a sound? Well, yes and no of course. It does make noise, but only to those close enough to hear it. If we aren't aware or conscious of the sound of a tree falling, then it doesn't make a sound to us, but it would still make a sound.

The trees of Genesis, the sacred tree of the *Popol Vuh* in the Mayan creation myth, the sacred tree of the Jewish Kabbalah, the oak tree of Celtic religion, the banyan, bo or bodhi tree that Siddhartha Gautama sat under when he received his enlightenment to become the Buddha, and the pepper tree Krishnamurti sat under when he received his jolt of awakening, are all symbols in common. Why would all of these seemingly separate religions use the tree as a pivotal representation? Well, next time you look at a tree, take the time to really look at it. Its trunk connects roughly equal parts above and below the soil, with the beauty of fractal geometry or self-similarity branching and rooting to create a large, beautiful tree. It is a perfect example of how fractal geometry, at all scales, exists in nature. I believe it represents past, present, and future, the illusion of separation and the truth of unity. The Maya believed that the sacred tree represents vibration, resonance, and harmony with life. All vibration, resonance, and harmony are energetic oscillations about a point or line of equilibrium. As everyone knows, Adam and Eve chose the tree of the knowledge of good and evil, not the tree of life and, as obvious as it is, all choice is a compromise. Life encompasses, well, life. When we chose, there was only the knowledge of good and evil. Before that there was only life. We exercised our will and limited ourselves to choice, knowledge, judgment, contrast, opposition, duality, separation, and conflict. The fullness of unity and the illusion of reality have been extant for a long time, but only in the last fifty years has science begun to codify these ideas. The illusion of commonly believed reality isn't really an illusion per se, but more of a limited perception of the whole of reality. There is whole and less than whole. It is the illusion of all that is sensed as being all there is. I interpret Adam and Eve clothing themselves as demonstrating their feeling of separation, because their choice was now limited to their own consciousness, a viewpoint external to the viewpoint of the one and all. Original Sin was the illusion of separation from God, nature, beauty, truth, and the singularity of pristine consciousness. This was the creation of the insatiable ego or sense of self, which created a view of duality which is common among all people. Their ingestion of the apple, that is, their acceptance of the limits of duality, separated them from the tree of life. Adam and Eve became mortal and eventually died. Cain and Abel were born and were opposites. This juxtaposition of good and evil led to the murder of Abel and to many more conflicts to come. Life is unity, and knowledge of good and evil is only gained when understood as conflict and pitting opposites against one another. Adam and Eve had no choice of the tree of life or singularity, but they did have a choice whether to accept the tree of knowledge of good and evil or not. Evil is the illusion of duality. There was no sin, evil, or death, and all was good until it was distinguished and acknowledged as separate and divided. Why does the story of creation have symbols of life and of good and evil, both of which are in the form of a tree? When you look at a tree, you see a single trunk. Then you see it branching off into smaller and smaller branches, then finally into leaves with branching veins of their own. Underneath the Earth, though you can't see it, is an almost perfect reflection of what's above the Earth in the tap root and the branching and ever-smaller roots. A tree is the perfect representation of separation and unity, depending on how one looks at it. All aspects of unity are the many branches of the same tree of life.

In light of the characteristics of trees that directly correspond to all other things, where are Heaven and Hell? They are right here, right now, superimposed over each other beyond space and time. It's all in how you observe it. For example, look at the way that people give opposite interpretations of the same piece of art. People view things from different angles and attitudes, and this observation changes the actual object because the object is the subject and vice versa. Just as the now includes the past and the future, there is only life—no pre-life, death, or afterlife—just life. This seems like a paradox, but I urge the reader to forgo this separate view of things.

Science and Religion—Lifting the Veil Between Observation and Faith

All religious and scientific devotees have the strictest of beliefs that reality is based on good and evil, right and wrong, true and false. They really are two sides of the same coin. Both science and religion are easily tainted and improperly used, driven by humanity's warped fears and desires rather than the quest for peace and enlightenment. Science and religion can agree that everything came from one God or Singularity, and that it probably came about in an instant, as is hypothesized in the Big Bang theory. Religion has the tree of life in the Garden of Eden, while science has its own evolutionary tree of life. It can be said that science and religion alike are based on faith or trust. Science is what we can measure, only to the degree of accuracy that our measurement tools and rationale will allow, whereas spirituality and religion are about what cannot be completely observed. Science and spirituality are different aspects of the same thing. Science is said to describe "reality," when all it does is measure or observe repeating patterns or contrasts in humanity's imagined dichotomy of reality. Compared to the devoutly religious, strictly empirical scientists tend to be skeptical without some observational and experimental proof. Their observations and subsequent inferences and theories can give a scientist (using only the scientific method) trust, faith, or a high degree of confidence. In a sense, science is a type of religion because it possesses both observation and trust in things unknown, and religion is a type of science because it also possesses observation and trust in things unknown. Science reaches their convictions by mechanical reasoning and religion by methodical justification. Science has a more dominant observational slant to it and religion has a more faith or trust-based dominance. Science and religion, however much truth and happiness they may reveal, are incomplete mental lenses of understanding. However helpful they may be in understanding and loving ourselves, each other, and the world around us, scientific and religious methods and mentalities are, at their foundation, interfering lenses we put in between ourselves and our observations. Like any lens, they can aid in seeing, but are also susceptible to dust, fog, scratches and smudges. Regardless of the benefits, science and religion both have their limitations and downfalls. Science and religion have been, are currently, and always will be, two incomplete disciplines that humans utilize to try to understand the world and where we fit in it. I believe scientists tend to be more open to ideas and possibilities and have the flexibility to change their views in certain areas, but in other areas they will proclaim that there are immutable and undeniable truths. Likewise, the religious have a certain openness as well as an impenetrable stubbornness about certain beliefs concerning reality. If there is a view that contradicts their feelings of what truth or reality is, it will most likely be disregarded in both science and religion without a sustained and genuine inquiry into the opposing view. Why are we so quick to exercise our self-imposed judgment on others' views and, wider still, everything? How does one become so utterly convinced? Well, those who lean toward the observational or empirical see things that add up to support the emerging theory that can be used as a foundation for predicting processes, and then predictive accuracy gives the theory a higher degree of certainty, confidence, and trust. However, those who tend toward a faith-based reality see truths, whether in the Koran, Bible, or Bhagivad-Gita, or any other scriptural doctrine, and see these words and ideas reflected in themselves and their world. The scientific and religious are looking for certain and absolute truth through narrow, dogmatic, idealized and unnatural and lenses. Both mindsets will always fall short at seeing reality as it is.

Both views, while they do reveal nature and ourselves, are mutually lopsided and are thus incomplete and out of balance and harmony with the totality of truth. In short, science and religion are essentially the same: partial truths, and incomplete in the way each individual separates them into their own special and increasingly self-tailored realm of reality. Both avenues may be used as a way of discovering the infinite beauty of absolutely everything or manipulated into the more human means of exploiting it as an emotional crutch for the many who need it, a way for developing authority, power, and dominance over others and nature in order to control societies, economies, and whatever else. Science and religion have been the twin forces that—both together and separately—have used their powers of half-truths to manipulate people and nature into destroying the beauty which they both are supposed to have revealed. This is the classic human condition: take infinity and beauty and see it as less. The Dalai Llama, near the conclusion of his book, *The Universe in a Single Atom* (2005, p. 208), pleads for science and spirituality to converge into balance and harmony with each other. Can this ever be realized? If so, how far will such an important process meander, and at what cost? If it cannot be realized, what lies ahead for the quickly deteriorating majesty of this blue-green marvel, this ark of the heavens?

Science and religion can surely agree that the fundamental law is one of unity and our deep relation to it. This simple truth is obvious and pivotal to both science and religion. One of Stephen Hawking's main goals is to create a theory of everything, often referred to as a grand unified theory, to combine small quantum curiosities with the large relativity theory of the cosmos, but he has so far come up short. Religious believers desire to join themselves with a larger divinity, such as the Atman and the Brahman, or to combine their individual soul with some form of Holy Spirit. The religious desire to become one with God just as scientists wish to find the underlying unity behind all physical laws, and it is in our nature to desire this kind of absolute unity. This unity is the most profound apparent paradox, yet it goes largely unnoticed by much of science and most religions. I believe this is why believing and thinking—two forms of the same thing—while both will always point to it, will never fully realize the revelation of this seeming paradoxical union of polarity. Science has only been able to quantify what can be seen with observational tools, the very smallest and largest aspects of the known universe. Qualifying these observations requires the acceptance, openness, and the possibility of realizing that quantity and quality are the same thing, with science and religion in harmony with one another. Faith can mix with fact, and the observation of the known can mix with the observation of the unknown. Science attempts to expand observations of the known to displace the unknown and to increase the potential for a balanced proportion of observation and faith, while the religious flip this ratio and expand faith as it displaces or distrusts observable reality and pushes it into a fantasy world of sorts. While the scientific approach to experiencing reality can leave one sublimely invigorated and awed by the discoveries of in-depth observations and research, this approach has the potential to leave one preoccupied and thus slightly inattentive to that which is occurring in the present moment and outside ones focused awareness. The religious approach to reality can likewise leave one in an intense and passionate state of being; however, it too has the potential to overlook the reality of direct observation of our natural surroundings. Science and religion can unite and become more than what each is separately. Together they can become a faith of love that need not have a label or institution or any of the characteristics that lead to separation and its symptoms.

God Isn't Only in the Sky

Experiencing God is not a distance education type of thing. It may seem somewhat trivial to state, but God does not exist as some separate being, at some measurable or immeasurable distance in space, "up there" in the clouds, nor does God exist simply as some wise judge who will decide our eternal fate at the end of our lives. God is much more real—and much more tangible—than our traditionally feeble comprehension and imagination pictures "him," limited to a vague symbol of creation, instead of being the totality of all creation itself. Willingly and without sustained inquiry, we separate everything from that which we so casually and all so knowingly call God. Many think they can know a person by only knowing their name; this is often the case with the name and word of God, whom many imagine and depict as a man in his old age. I believe many only glimpse the labels, words, and images rather than the immense meaning and truth described behind these words. It's like saying you know someone deeply and fundamentally simply by knowing their name, what they wear, their favorite food, their hobbies, and so on.

The higher being is exactly that. It is one's understanding of the universe that brings a person to a higher level of being. We all have the same God, no matter our cultural concept. I personally believe that God is not a solely localized and human-only form or entity that is separate from creation, space, time, or anything else, or a being who spends time zeroing in on human dramas and judging them like a pleased or angry father based on some questionable moral code. This is a figure that humanity has created in order to have a parental-style authority figure, as in a family and conventional society, a concept that reminds us of a parent or a court judge. Our mental conceptions of God in effect serve to separate us from creation by making God into an idea instead of an actuality staring us in the face every single day. However one sees the source of our existence, one will likely view it at a distance, as a long-ago source, with us as a consequence or separation of action and reaction. But creation, with its endless beginning, is right here, now, on this page and everywhere else. This is the very legitimate predicate put forth by the simple and sustained observation of nature and one's self. We have made creation into a symbol, with many believing that it is an ancient white male dwelling far away from us, whom we only get to see after death. I take the approach that God is everywhere and everything undivided from itself. This is hard for some people to imagine, because it's not an image, nor is it anthropomorphic, but rather reality minus any abstraction. I find it interesting when people say "co-creator" when it comes to life and destiny. Equivalent to the co-worker, it denotes a sense of the individual person *and* something else, which is the very illusion of separation, a main theme throughout this book. How can we and creation as a whole be at all separated from that which created us?

Most religions focus on some form of deity and center their core beliefs on something that is selfless. They take a spiritual nexus view that is larger than just themselves, and yet it seems by their actions that almost everyone subscribing to these groups is in a conflictive contradiction with this selflessness, both with others and also within themselves. In certain religions only the faithful who strictly adhere to that particular cultural tradition and ceremony can be righteous and receive the rewards of their beliefs. All religion excludes. All attempts to foster love and beauty are to be commended, but their faith unwittingly limits the view to a single species. The birth and death of both Jesus and Mohammed are considered most sacred and celebrated, whereas their lives, though important, are seen as secondary to these somehow more important events. We see this view everywhere regarding birth and death. We make a big deal out of the beginning and the ending of life, but little note everyday lives. Interesting, don't you think? Many people have these egocentric and exclusory ideas in their hearts, minds, and memories that create a possessive conflict because of their intention to exclude others and have the rewards of their faith to themselves. They live in their past history while cutting out the vitality of the present moment. They are in the past, carrying on these ancient conflicts and grudges.

Microscopes, telescopes, religion, and science are all looking at the same thing; it's just that they are each seeing it from their field of view and not through the insight or wisdom of all of these views either done away with or combined. Wisdom need not take practice to perfect. Fear and ignorance will give a view of classical reality, but not the whole reality. All that is missing is a real, all-encompassing view of everything.

Observation is to faith as science is to religion. They are two sides of a spinning coin. All science, discovery, and religion are about a revolution in the observer. It is the observer becoming more aware of the observed as him- or herself. It is always true, simple, and beautiful in varying intensities, purities, and expressions. The observer is more aware of him- or herself and where he or she fits in. You are the harmony of the universe and seeing this comes from faith and observation. It is the silent music of the flow of creation that is seen by either more observation or more faith. One can glance quickly at the surface of a lake and see only one's own blurred reflection, but if one is still and balanced and observes carefully to see more deeply past and below the surface, observation with faith can create a perfection of perception.

Observation and faith must be balanced; otherwise people will separate from reality and start hating and end up killing each other and destroying everything in vain. See what a mentality of separation can do? People hate the Nazis and despise what they did, but in this they have separated themselves from them and have become their equivalent by this act of separation. See how people become angry when they see anger? They don't like seeing anger and conflict, which is normal, but in their distancing from it they end up resenting and hating it to the point that they become the object of their own hate. Concerning the things one fears, hates, or anything of a similar nature, the more one distances oneself from the truth behind these illusions, the greater the tendency one will have in running into these conflicts over and over again, despite their many transformations. We hate the very fact that other people hate, and almost by accident we are suddenly in the same loop they are in. If you are a normal, sane human being, seeing someone hate will trigger the hate in you and you will be just like them, though perhaps you will direct your hate in a different direction, as befits you, or your circumstance, or whatever organization or nation you identify with. Awareness of one's anger and the ability to identify conflict can halt this automatic response. Politeness, awareness, and actual listening go a long way in understanding and thus ending conflict. A habit is an unconscious behavior carried by our mentality and genes, and no matter how hazardous it may become the automation remains because a habit is a self-reinforcing practice hardened by repetition and its subsequent benefits and pleasures that obviously outweigh the dangers and pains. Any habit is a learned behavior which means it can be unlearned. We are social beings and can affect others in a profound way. Happiness in this sense is thus a social responsibility for the good of the species. Anger, pain, or sadness are all like an itch; they are all created in the mind as motivations that are meant to lead to the cessation of suffering, resulting in peace and happiness. All forms of suffering arise in order for the sufferer to focus appropriate attention and understanding as to the cause or root of the suffering and resolving it. Suffering is clearly not meant to remain unacknowledged and expand without any rhyme or reason. How many people worldwide are suffering on a continual basis? Why is there psychological suffering? Is it because we are unaware of the fact that the root of suffering, however hidden underground or in the subconscious, is deeply connected to the clear and obvious branches or symptoms of the root? The tree of suffering has too strong a root and too many branches to tackle separately. The branches and the root must be acknowledged concurrently. One soon realizes that the root of one person's suffering is actually connected to everyone else's. Suffering is a part of life one must balance and accept and not try to exterminate because it is considered bad. Only the excessive conflict toward suffering creates more suffering. Suffering is like a recurring dream, an experience meant to direct an observer's attention to a deeper, previously neglected awareness of reality. When this awareness is reached, the dream stops. Suffering remains, but in a new light of understanding. This is where teachers come from.

The first reaction to anger, like a mirror, is more anger, just as with sadness, a smile, or most any other emotion. Emotions breed similar emotions; racism breeds racism, love breeds love. Anger, sadness, and ignorance are essentially the same thing; something is missing. What leads to anger/sadness or unhappiness? Is it impatience, selfishness, desire, fear of loss, the image of what should be but is not? People are unhappy because they have been misled by the illusion of separation that is tearing this world apart. Are we all in such a state of self-awareness and control that we cannot interrupt our habits before nature crumbles under our feet?

There is no need to despair over the propagation of conflict; love has the same self-propagation effect, which I will elucidate later in this book. Some scientists no doubt despise the religious devout, while likewise the devout may despise the empirical, evidentiary, and skeptical. If you doubt this, look at the raging dispute between science and religion over the theory of evolution. Thankfully, however, the sometimes frosty relationship seems to be thawing much more than in the past.

The Binary Blitz—Technology's Singularity

Computers are one special, powerful technological advancement that everyone knows a little about, but few know very well. Essentially, a chip of silicon or quartz crystal is the heart of the computer or information storage, whereas all other mechanisms of the computer are only for access and manipulation of the information. Computers function by recognizing patterns of ones and zeros called binary code, where the term "bit," for example, 01, is an acronym for Binary Information Technology. When we think about it, our entire existence is a sort of perceived binary code of absence and presence or discontinuity and the perceived patterns that arise from it. In a nutshell, the big Y2K scare resulted from this information-processing technique, because it was feared it would wreak havoc on modern society that would purportedly result from the internal clocks in computers, which run pretty much everything, switching to the full "2000" from the 99 abbreviation of 1999.

Research into artificial intelligence evokes equal amounts of fear and excitement. Not long ago, most machines did no more than emulate our ability to lift or move things with muscle. Computer programs are much better, faster "thinkers" when it comes to hard data calculations, algorithms, and the like, meaning that computers as machines have now exceeded our mechanical, rational, logical or "mental" muscle power—that is, the left hemisphere functions of our brain, responsible for logic and analytical skills—and all that's left for computers to conquer is the right side of the brain, responsible for creative thinking and imagination. If computers take over this creative domain, many people are fearful that computers will potentially reach a level of consciousness that will make them "aware" and able enough to exponentially increase their knowledge, reaching what is called a technological singularity, where they will auto-evolve through self-selection. This scenario is possible, if not probable. These machines could possibly become exponentially smarter than we are in a short span of time. Computers now are smart enough, and we are always striving for more. Keep in mind that technology is conceptually neutral but it does have the potential to be used for good or bad. The appropriate use of knowledge is in the expanding awareness of beauty, not in dominating and domesticating the forces of nature or in subjugating other human beings. Technological advancement and its side effects or unintended consequences are emergent in quests for knowledge that are often driven by bad intentions, such as fear of the unknown, or the idea of progression, such as wars sparking new technologies. Consider the mass exodus of brilliant scientists from physics after the use of the atomic bomb. Also remember that all computer viruses are created by humans. Technology is simply an extension of human consciousness—good and evil—and is now a formidable force for either that must be reckoned with. Quantum computing is now gaining ground from theory into actuality, a development that could blow the entire world of technology wide open. We have a history filled to the brim with aimless means which have created our technological marvels and disastrous byproducts, which are all manifestations of the human condition of psychological blindness.

Government and Its Compromise

We all have a govern-mentality within us. It is an authoritative state of mind that makes decisions for the body to follow without awareness of its being controlled and thus without resistance and without question. The word *government* can be reduced to its two concepts "govern" being the leader and authority of things and "ment" short for mental, relating to the psyche or mind. A government is the controller of the minds of the masses. In principle, governments and leaders are elected by the people to govern them according to the will of the people. Therefore a government is in a position of power, but it is made powerful by everything other than itself, that is, everything that precedes it, such as a collective idea, formal constitution, system of laws, and public opinion. Critically, money and a myriad of other factors influence government, and as we all know too well, power generally corrupts. Any system, institution, or leader/follower dynamic is fundamentally separated and conflictive, and therefore flawed. Economically speaking, there is the employer/employee relationship, adapted from the archaic superior/inferior, leader/follower, and master/slave dualistic and conflictive dynamic. It makes one wonder if there is some mythical peak person who will rise to the top of this entire global pyramid scheme, or whether there are just a certain number without any control or any real agreement among them. Or is it the case that the tacit, unspoken, subconscious agreement of the collective will of humanity's imbalanced view of itself and nature is all there is?

There is the ethereal and the physical, the ideal and the actual, the good and the bad, one and many, positive and negative, North and South, birth and death, man and woman, the teacher and the student, and the master and the slave, to name just a few apparently dualistic relationships that are actually deeply singular, because without one there is not the other. All of these artificial creations come from the mind, which is a projection manifested from the source of all authority, control, and separation, which is the thought and the thinker. This originates from our egocentric view of mind as leader and governor over body. It is the human ego and will thinking it has absolute dominion over the biological body. This creates a self-inflicted conflict between these aspects.

Domesticated

To domesticate means to make more familiar, to tame and use. We are too attached to things or people we love, which makes love such a hard thing to understand to its fullest when we feel we have lost our grasp of it. True love can only be felt and never possessed. The government is a nation's symbolic shepherd. If a sheep strays from the flock it is swiftly taken care of by many means of reward or punishment. Humans are as domesticated—restricted to a home, place, job, obligations, etc. and controlled by authoritarian domination, such as governments, schools, parenting, and the hierarchy of the work force—as any dog, cat, pig, or cow. We are bred to be productive within the confines of our society.

Governments and the governed have a relationship analogous to organized crime. The government gives people what they want, and since the government is a group of people, the members of that government get what they want, too. Nature is being plundered and everybody "wins," especially the people who make these decisions, usually known as chairman, CEO, president, prime minister, or head of state. These people sit in these lofty positions because they are elected due to their ability to make a select group of well-connected people comfortable, safe, and rich. The Book of Revelation speaks of the Mark of the Beast or the Antichrist, which will be found on the right hand or forehead. This mark symbolizes the deeply dependent connection of a living, breathing person to the economical buy/sell machine. If one has this mark, they would be a useful and, if need be, expendable cog in the hungry economic machine. The mark of the beast makes me think not only of implantable RFID microchips or tattoos, or of any actual visual mark, but perhaps the idea of money and the perverse fixation and value we place on it, and how this will be so great as to be in our dominant hand and in the forefront of our consciousness.

A society's government is revealed in many ways, such as in its economy, military, bureaucratic and judicial structure, laws, and so on. All of the facets of government are created to organize society into something that is manageable and safe. Modern society as it stands is clearly not without its mechanisms aimed at controlling the population. That is why a society naturally creates a government. A modern population's restraints and regulations vary from the age-old to the relatively recent increases in audio/video surveillance, homeland security, air travel security, policing, laws and by-laws, conscription, taxation, permits, licenses, social insurance, political and commercial propaganda, banking, insurance, payment plans, personal/family identity protection, and many forms of documentation. We allow these controls, however beneficial they may initially be, to govern the lives of anyone living within the political/ideological lines of power. Look at a geological map of the world, then a political one. Every child needs its parents to take on authority and responsibility and make the difficult decisions. Everyone wants security, and the societal answer is control by a governing body of trustworthy people with the society's interests in mind. All of the accepted forms of control listed above possess the ability to be exploited by those in power in order to remain in and increase that power. "Government" is simply another word for a controlling, dogmatic mentality. People need to follow authority, just as families and societies crave the assurance of a calm and collected parent, prime minister, king, or president. Of course the entire premise of control rests in ignorance, routine, economically-driven lifestyles, the enticements of instant gratification, thoughtless entertainment, reward and punishment to which, like obedient children, the majority willingly succumb. Today, luxuries are construed necessities and these products or lifestyles maintain a growth economy and further tighten the control of and obedience to a society. Our current global government/ economy is based on mixing want and need to a point where they are indistinguishable. We can't seem to get enough status, convenience, new things, and more things. Vanity and aggression are huge economic movers. The extreme sense of unfulfilled needs and dissatisfaction seen in entitlement, greed, fear, aggression, and a craving for security are the seeds of our present human society. These seeds grew from the fears of tribes to a global human tribe, and the leaders and governments of each tribe have since exploited our human weaknesses and desires to the point of modern slavery. How much genuine freedom do we really have in our domesticated world, and will there be less or more in the near future? There is a striking correlation between the amount of freedom we have in our individual consciousness and the freedom we have in our collective consciousness or society. Governments, like any parent, naturally offer many benefits to a society but, just as naturally, like a neglectful or overprotective parent, their governance results in more than its fair share of hindrances, such as the stunted growth of individual thinking and a high risk of dependency. Any government or human creation is in some way a manifestation of the conflicted human psyche. Each person has their own internal government, so it comes as no surprise that governments are so ubiquitous in the world today. When I speak of government, I mean any and all forces of dominance and authority over an individual's and humanity's collective psyche. Of course, other animals have leaders and controls in their societies, but they benefit not only their species but all the other species directly or indirectly influenced by the structure of their social order. What we have done is conflate our negative effects upon ourselves, each other, and our surroundings by our misleading thoughts and constantly expanding numbers. Any government gives their governed majority, to an extent, what they want. They have to do this in order to remain in power; otherwise they lose their power through reelection, revolt, revolution or civil war. Do our irresistible human desires ultimately govern and control each person and thus each society and humanity as a whole?

Today radio frequency identification (RFID) technology can be used to identify individuals and could conceivably contain every bit of information about a person, from name and age to financial information, medical and genetic records, personal preferences and habits, political beliefs, and everything else in between. These tags have already been implanted in many pets, Alzheimer's patients, as well as hundreds, if not presumably thousands of other ordinary people around the world, and the technology is picking up more momentum as society adapts toward a more efficient and secure lifestyle. The technology could be used as a virtual passport or, wider still, as a multi-pass that can access one's home, vehicle, place of employment, safes, and all other security systems. It can even be used to turn on lights. Pets have been implanted with RFIDs so that in case they get lost, a simple scan of the chip will reveal the owner information. RFID chips represent a further release of circumstantial consent, and along with prosthetics, pacemakers, and the like turn us more into branded cattle and machines. Technology blurs into our everyday lives on an even greater scale than ever before. This could be the next big thing in the dynamic between human beings and technology, further closing the gap in that relationship. It would definitely make daily activities easier and faster. It is certain that this will be a pivotal part of human life in the future, and there is really no doubt that people will eagerly line up to obtain it, just as with any other amazing gadget. In fact, many smartphones are now being equipped with RFID chips for easy and secure shopping. Combine the novelty with the necessity, as is the case for updated security features in passports, driver's licenses, etc., and it is practically a done deal waiting for time to unfold it. It is a bold historical transformation that is upon us. It will be subtle and the numbers will slowly increase, as is always the case with the phasing in and out of new and old technologies. VCRs didn't just stop being produced, but were phased out and replaced. Likewise, computers were originally available to very few people, but now virtually everyone has access to them. The military will probably soon use RFID chips instead of dog tags. Most of us already have an obscene number of ID or credit cards spilling out of our wallets. We have medical information bracelets, OnStar, GPS receivers, flash drives, Wi-Fi, security cameras, cellphones and their spinoffs, and face recognition security software. RFID chips would streamline how societies function, and this enticement will be the downfall of the previous technological paradigm, marking the beginning of the end of modern civilization, as we won't be able to buy or sell or function in society without it. As irresistibly tempting as they are, the unbalanced desire for speed and convenience will blind us from the profound loss of what we are giving up: our relationship with the ways of nature through the willful and consensual loss of personal control and privacy just to make things smoother and faster and easier, and yes, safer, too. Make people afraid or compare something they have to something they could have that is irresistibly more convenient and they will choose it for the wrong reasons every time. The wrong reasons are, specifically, unnatural ease, laziness, or excess, with unforeseen, unintended consequences down the road. We see convenience but ignore the pollution and wastefulness as much as we can for as long as we can. The "haves" strip-mine nature of her resources for necessity as well as luxury and in this process the "have-not" human and wildlife populations emerge. Our jobs depend on and support this unsustainable reality as families struggle to make ends meet. This is the way societies and civilizations work. In order to control, there has to be a release of freedom, bit by bit, until control itself becomes sneakily incorporated as common and normal when it is anything but. If we lived in an RFID world and someone was flagged as a terrorist or as someone who opposed the current government how easy would it be to freeze their entire life with the click of a mouse? Look at our modern society. Superficially, it appears to be common and normal and natural, but in many ways it is a direct contradiction to, and separation from, the order of nature.

It may seem extremely unrealistic to attempt to integrate our observations of the unified and simple physical aspects and workings of the universe with our often narrow, segregated, overly complicated, and often contradictory ways of seeing ourselves in the world. However, there is an unseen current of reality that combines these aspects, and which many tend to only skim the surface. Form and function relate to both nature and humanity. We seek absolute nature through our own limited purposes, which gradually lead us to a world we choose to see and create for our own brief benefit, in effect creating great imbalances in the natural beauty, form, and function from which humanity emerged in the first place. The first part of this book dealt mainly with the observer aspect of reality, while the remainder now deals with the aspect of what is observed and how both aspects unite. Looking at the world should be proof enough of this; however, one is always half looking at the world by focusing on its parts and not the context of the whole, and this causes our dual and thus conflictive intentions to impact and damage our global island and all the life that inhabits and shares it. When the human psyche, self-organization, science and religion, economy, war, population, celestial cycles, physics, geometry, and philosophy point in a single direction and all directions simultaneously, the truth of beauty can be found in every sight. These aspects of ourselves and the universe show that the observer really is the observed and that it is a beautiful and emergent process that we need to flow with, not fight against.

Economy, government, and all the other forms of authority manifested by human thought are sustained by human needs and desires. Because of this we have military and police forces, political fail-safes and defense mechanisms to protect against revolt and resistance in order to preserve their power and advance their momentum. The only thing to stop them, which is needed for the betterment of Earth, is complete abandonment or collapse, whether through revolution at the hands of the human animal or other natural forces, of all institutions, governments, and all forms of unbalanced and conflictive superior/inferior dominant/submissive methods of living. This collapse could potentially make way for a utopia with or without humanity as we are now, or it could simply make way for humans to rebuild and destroy ourselves and Earth all over again. The negation of our current paradigm will, in all probability, not be humanity's final choice, because humanity will no doubt resist at all cost the surrender of speed, comfort, novelty, technology, wealth, and power, to be replaced by the appreciation of natural value and order that cannot be measured in human—or societal—terms. Instead, the push for this integration will originate from a lack of supply and an excess of demand. Demand is humanity and the supply is nature. Both will fall in order to revitalize the balance of nature. Understanding ourselves is utterly crucial in accepting and connecting with nature.

Emergence and Self-Organization
Charles Darwin, in his famous 1859 book,
On the Origin of Species, wrote,

As many more individuals of each species are born than can possibly survive; and as, consequently, there is a frequently recurring struggle for existence, it follows that any being, if it vary however slightly in any manner profitable to itself, under the complex and sometimes varying conditions of life, will have a better chance of surviving and thus be naturally selected. From the strong principle of inheritance, any selected variety will tend to propagate its new and modified form.

(79 words used from p.4 of Introduction. By permission of Oxford University Press)

Evolution is another word for the beautiful changes in nature that are directly conducive for life to emerge, adapt and thrive. It is obvious and simple. Regions of the world vary and change in elevation, climate, and topography. Plants and animals, as a part of the environment, also vary and change to balance, and come into balance, with their surroundings. Evolution is the process of adaptive changes in weather, habitat and all organisms that are food for one another. A species as an aspect of Earth that is well suited to its other earthly aspects tends to remain alive and echo these favorable forms and functions, while always adapting, however drastically, throughout the generations. Some scientists have said that ninety-nine percent of all species that have ever lived are now extinct. I feel this is inaccurate. All species of the past live on, in one way or another, in the species alive today. This is why it is possible to say that all species of dinosaurs are extinct yet their descendants live on as birds. Adaptation explains why we had Mastodons and Woolly Mammoths and now only see elephants and why we don't have polar bears in the tropics. Nature has a kind of Goldilocks "practice effect" going on. Like soft skin worked into a callous, practice makes things easier and more efficient. A lava bomb flying through the air naturally takes on an aerodynamic shape just as birds flying through the air over many generations create the effortless aerial ballet of hollowed bones, wings, feathers and air. Look how rabbits change from brown to white and back again to avoid detection as the snow builds around them, changing the colors of the environment. Evolution may sound like a dirty word to some—particularly some of the devoutly religious—and consequently the term has been grossly misused, just as the word God has factored into countless bloody wars using that name. Call evolution "adaptation" then, if the word or the concept bothers you. It shouldn't, because adaptation—evolution—is going on all around you. The word or symbol of evolution may denote an atmosphere of godlessness, but this cannot be further from the truth. Evolution is a theory that explains the diversity of the forms of life and the processes through which they arise. It is perhaps the most long-standing and most successful scientific theory ever conceived, and it is supported by overwhelming instances of plain old observable evidence. It accurately predicts natural developments based on empirical observations, and this gives it immense credibility. Darwin's idea was presented a century and a half ago and yet it is still vibrant and new and being put to the test today. Yet it remains an incomplete theory, and it is not what so many so casually and self-assuredly think it is, either. It is a partial explanation, in that it describes a process, much the way a description of the assembly of a car might describe the shape and substance of the parts and their motions, but cannot answer the question of why it moves or how the parts in nature assemble themselves. The critical question, the *why* of life, is left unanswered by the theory of evolution. Like all empirical scientific theories, evolution cannot be fully proven, but it greatly helps our understanding and, at least in part, explains our world. Many scientific theories are incomplete, and they will grow and change as we test them. This does not mean that these theories are completely wrong or completely right, but they do what they are supposed to do for the time being, and that is to explain the mystery and beauty of the world we live in to the best extent that we humans can. A main misconception of evolutionary theory is that it is a random or chaotic process. Many see nature as a disorderly process, and that is not the whole story. Just because we can't completely explain or predict something does not mean growth and diversity, or evolution, or adaptation is a random process. It is an orderly process of nature, by nature. The theory of evolution tells us that life is not only adapting but humanity is right in the mix of it all. We are a life form like all the other life forms. We are organisms, we are animals, we are mammals, we are apes. Evolution tells us that we are a species profoundly linked to the entire biological system that consists of all the life forms on this planet.

The tree of life includes plants, animals, insects, and every living thing. Plants and animals are so deeply connected to each other that they can easily be considered a single life form. Humans are domesticating the tree of life by channeling and blocking it for our own purposes because life behaves a lot like a branching tree. Humans are not at the top, although we like to think so—which is a direct result of the fact that we make up the categories! The forms we see are categorized, separated, and, paradoxically, put in isolation due to both their similarities and their differences. Evolution is a word that some people cringe at without really understanding its full meaning. It isn't always what we think it is, and we often disagree on its meaning, but certainly we can all agree that however limited its explanation, and regardless of whatever gaps remain in the theory of evolution, it does, despite its incompleteness, describe a process of natural and real beauty. How can that be wrong? All current biology—including our understanding of DNA, genome mapping, cloning, and stem-cell research—rests firmly on the premise that evolution is a fact. Evolution is the emergent homeostasis and filling of niches to balance nature within itself. The ideas of chaos and feedback together create a fuller reality of fractal order that is beautiful and elegant, which is exactly what nature is. We are to apes as a Labrador retriever is to a grey wolf or a house cat is to a lynx or tiger. There is a cat or dog species that is farther along in relation or direct interaction to the primate species. It's simple and makes sense. DNA explains this. Bacteria evolve faster than larger organisms and fossils are most telling of the transformation of form to fit the functions that were necessary to survive in the ever-changing climate of Earth. We are greatly connected to all life. We are a big and diverse family that lives in a single, enormous home with many rooms, ecosystems or climates which we call planet Earth. Evolution, or adaptation is locally, self- or auto-designed. We view God as an outsider pulling the strings, but God is as local as it gets. God is creation on all scales; whether we think it originates from the small or large, creation is everywhere. The designer is the design. If one fully understands the apparent contradiction, then one will see how the classical sense of evolution becomes something very beautiful and fully congruent with the real vision of what God is. The planets move by the laws of nature, as do rivers, plants, animals, and humans. God is not the mechanic tinkering with objects separate from himself; *God is the process itself.* Many biologists note that evolution is not an idea of progress, although the common concept of evolution would have us think completely otherwise, hence our egotistical view that we are the "top" of the evolutionary scale. Perfection has no goal of greater perfection; it just moves and changes. Evolution is simply a good fit between the observer and the observed. Evolution essentially says that we are all connected by one tree of life filled with the beauty of death and birth. How many insects, plants, and animals die and are born on any given day? The numbers are all but immeasurable and yet, life flourishes as a single unit of many systems. Biologists divide life forms into a hierarchal system of domain, genus, kingdom and species. Plants, fungi, animals, protists and bacteria interpenetrate each other in their daily goings on in such a way as to be considered a single organism. These categories are all but refinements of relational comparison between similarities and differences which is simply our own method of comprehending the mysteries of life's processes, forms and meaning. These divisions are created to aid in organizing and thus easily accessing our knowledge of these organisms but at the same time aid in masking the truth that all life is a singular system that adapts along with the ever changing conditions on Earth's surface.

We deny the truth of evolution because of the story of Genesis, and our own ego and pride. The other side denies God as a figment of people's imaginations. Many religious see humanity as somehow special and apart from the rest of creation, while all else is below us and seen as mere plants and mere animals. Thinking we are special creates separation, and denigrates our view of the rest of nature. Real evolution and real religion are the same. Richard Dawkins says evolution has no progress, plan, or goal. This reflects, however imperfect we see it to be, the perfection of creation or the now, and leaves existence to bloom on its own as nature intends or chooses. Now, of course, evolution creates a match with the life that exists in its habitat, but that is simply a balance between the two aspects of the observer and the observed. All life grows to the best of its ability—its adaptability—and nature facilitates itself in doing this. Consider how we have bacteria on every inch of our skin and in our gastrointestinal tract, or how a jellyfish has algae incorporated in itself as a food source or how plants and phytoplankton have chlorophyll in their bodies. The idea of forgoing the progressive view in favor of the balanced and ever-changing view of life may seem odd and difficult to grasp. The progressive view of life leads one to believe that humans are at the top of the evolutionary pyramid, but this is only partially true. All life that exists right now is at the top of the pyramid, including all the bacteria, microorganisms, plants, animals, primates, as well as all the atomic and molecular constituents that create them. All present life exists as the budding spring greenery on the tree of life with our ancestors as the branches, trunk and roots. It is a level playing field with specialized players, each suited for its area of the field. A catcher has a heavily padded mitt while a batter has a long wooden club. Life changes to create a suitable balance with environment, and along the entire journey there is a perfect balance which, although always changing, cannot progress beyond perfection, however imperfect we think it to be. I believe our view of progression has caused the imbalances in the world today. Progression gives us our common view of linear time and makes the perfection of nature and oneself into a project that needs improvement and fixing. Natural selection isn't really a compromise. Certainly life forms are built for their specific environment and can thus utilize only so many tools in the genetic multi-tool, but in the context of all life on Earth, the multi-tool is fanned completely open and nothing is compromised. All the ecological niches that can be filled *are* filled so where is the compromise? This is when potential becomes actual, as "decided" by nature as it sees fit or selects. It is an intelligent web of life. DNA is our motivational tool that flips open a knife or turns a screwdriver or the like, depending on the prevailing circumstances or environment; these tools are our social nuances and the artifacts of our man-made civilization. Our bigger brains create a greater dependence on these tools through more thinking, rationalizing, remembering, and being less in the present moment. This isn't an orderly selection of nature but a mutation of man's acting against nature in order to "progress," which appears, by and large, to be anything but progressive. Compromises abound with humanity, not with nature.

Life is nature that changes by its own force or intention. Life is self-propelled. Nature evolves or changes itself in order for life forms to emerge and possess the ability to observe and live within nature in a balanced, and balancing, way. There is so much beauty in this fuller view of evolution as opposed to the classical and prejudged interpretation of it, in the same way that quantum and relative physics are great improvements on classical Newtonian physics. Everything is all so vibrant and alive!

We see the process in which a particle vibrates and moves, creating all the colors, shapes, and sizes of life. We can also see the process of these waveforms creating harmony between themselves in molecules and chemicals, from this all the life we see emerges as different, from a bacterium to a blue whale. How does a waveform create a seed, pollen, spore, or single-celled egg no bigger than a speck of sand that merges with a single-celled sperm of the same species and create a single fertilized cell? How did the variety of seeds come about? Well, the chicken and egg paradox is explained later in this book, and as for the variety we see, nature is efficient and expressive in her beauty. Every tiny niche is filled with a complex web of life.

Humans are not a cut above any of our relatives, no matter how small, simple, and useless we think they are. "What makes humans different, special or unique?" This is yet another question that focuses on obvious yet shallow and superficial differences, as most questions that attempt to deny the truth usually do. Our view of incompleteness and our means to force and manipulate ourselves and nature only serve to separate us further from nature and from ourselves. Our overused and mismanaged tool of a brain is governed in large part by our attention or intention, which create a narrow spotlight of opinion, difference, and indifference. Perhaps what makes us human is the relationship between our brain and our specialized hands. But what about our creative/symbolic use of language, music, art, and the like? Or is it our emotional capacity, expressed as empathy and altruism, and our purely human spirit which no other creature has? We can walk upright and plan ahead, but these aforementioned aspects of humanity are all simply adaptations to suit our social and mechanical environment. The beauty of evolution is that it puts us back into the entire and ever-changing biological family but without the crown.

We are specialized for what we need to do in order to survive. All life has this characteristic relationship of form and function. A whale or mosquito could just as well be considered a cut above humanity when related to their specializations in their environments. Viruses, bacteria, fungi, cells, organelles, organs, birds, fish, insects, plants, and animals all live the best they can in their specific scale and neighborhood of existence where none are better than the rest. They all live in close balance with each other, giving and taking energy from each other. Plants turn carbon dioxide and the Sun's photons into carbon and sugar, which they use to grow, while the resultant oxygen "waste" that is emitted is necessary for all other life, yet eventually combines with carbon again to create more carbon dioxide in the feedback loop of life. One can quite literally breathe in the Sun and the trees. The variety of life is a single unit. Our little personal intentions without regard for the beauty of nature do not and will not hold against the intention of nature, which includes us all. We humans need to step off our man-made throne. We call ourselves human beings as though we have a process of being in our soul and consciousness that other forms of life do not have, and then we name them as if they are things. An ape is an ape but we are human beings! How silly this view is to me. We humans are made of the same chemicals, molecules, and constituent wave/particle atoms as everything else in the universe. The division begins when we start viewing ourselves as better and different from the infinite variety that nature creates.

Chlorophyll is a molecule in plants that absorbs photons, which excite electrons. These electrons exist in a waveform, and because of the quantum superposition of this subatomic particle, the process of life can exist. All life exists in large part because of electrons that exist as waveforms and because of the waves that emanate from the Sun. In photosynthesis, for example, quantum physics creates symmetric, yet seemingly random jumps of electrons from molecule to molecule to create a new path of life. Yet, using classic atomic or molecular physics, this is not possible. From a seed to a sapling to a tree full of branches and leaves, nature knows how to create. It is due to the process of quantum photosynthesis that the seed is in a state of harmonic dichotomy and unification, splitting, merging, and reaching out to all creation. Photosynthesis is where energy, in the form of photons from the Sun, travels from energy level to energy level in nature's beautiful ninety-nine percent efficient, irreplaceable way of creating life. All biological life is a direct emergence from quantum mechanical marvels.

Every cell in our bodies diffuses gas. Our lungs diffuse oxygen into our blood and extract carbon dioxide from it. This is why we breathe to the beat of our heart. We see the chemistry and physics in biology, but not the biology in chemistry or physics. The chemistry of biology is simply carbon-based, and biological reactions are just like any other non-biological process. They are, of course, the same thing, just perhaps more intricate. Gravity, the Sun, and all other stars, electromagnetism, black holes, fractals, and quantum physics are all aspects of the energy that makes life possible and beautiful.

At all stages of a snowstorm the snowflakes are doing exactly what they should be doing. All are in their place. Observing this storm, we normally see random and chaotic motions that are unfathomable and incalculable. But look at how intentional the hexagonal flakes appear. This is real evolution, anything but random. Our filters exclude and focus only on what suits the devices of the ego. We then extrapolate this false image of reality onto our motives and intentions, thus creating conflictive thoughts and actions. Our filters are always on because we are always thinking and still running on ancient programs. Perhaps an update is on the way. Our biology is set in nature and reality is slow to keep up with our runaway mental train.

Can old dogs learn new tricks? Some say yes, some no. Of course, the answer is some won't or can't, and some will and can. If learning something new or undergoing change interrupts the basic foundation of living and being comfortable, then we probably won't value or learn from it. The force of habit is a force to be reckoned with. Our environment changes our perspective and our perspective changes our environment. Both are at work, but in what proportion and under what circumstances will this change occur in the near future? Whatever the case may be, it is fairly certain that it will be drastic on both counts, regardless of which sets the other off. Evolution gave us the blessed curse of being pattern/fault seekers. We look at a blank piece of paper with a speck in the middle of it and instantly we zero in on this "aberration." It doesn't fit the pattern, so we see it as a fault. This is what we all do because we like to make sense of things, and when they don't add up, we like to understand and fix them. There is nothing wrong with this, but it can be an issue if it gets to be an all-consuming habit and an unexamined obsession. We are both nature and nurture. We are conditioned by our biology and by how we are raised to see choice and duality. This can make someone think twice about the common way we view free will, as was mentioned in Part 1. Evolution has taught us to tell things apart because it is beneficial for us to do so as it allows us to make choices for basic survival. What if we couldn't tell anything apart? This is our double-edged, hereditary sword of illusion.

Every cell in our bodies originated from one cell which was made into two cells, by two cells. These cells divide, multiply and sustain themselves with nutrients, water and gases throughout our lives. Genetics is a kind of collective consciousness between relative species. Humans, however, with the advent of their increased and disproportionate cleverness, now have the ability to pass down their mental DNA or beliefs and views from generation to generation. All biological life has the same genes, but the environment in which it resides determines the orderly shuffling of this deck, and which cards are used or left on the pile. Our brains are the same effective and compromising emergences that are seen with all forms of plants and animals. We can think, but only because that's our focus, spotlight, or specialty, much like a lion growing longer and sharper claws and teeth, or a streamlined fish having fins, scales and gills as their specialty. A peacock's tail is an exaggeration and is effective in its purpose of attraction. This might be much more visually captivating than a larger human brain, but the effects upon the world from the activities of this mush inside our skull are very effective, and eye catching indeed. A peacock's colorful tail is a survival tool to attract a mate and perpetuate the species. Its tradeoff is that it isn't very good camouflage from predators. Likewise, our brains are an excellent survival tool, in that we think out scenarios and choose the ones that we believe will work the best. But, as in a chess game, it is always a compromise to move into a potentially better position, because this can lead to vulnerabilities where one could end up worse off than before. All forms of life are creatures both born of and subject to the changes in our environment and climate. We can see it in ourselves, in the tree, in the fish, and everything else. We are all good at surviving. Humans are not inherently better at it simply through biology; we just find ways of using our specialized tools to a larger extent. The byproduct of the brain's efficacy is that its thoughts create a world or schema on their own and of their own. This is the illusion we live in. Think of images from space looking down on our world to see how the straight lines and idealized Euclidean shapes contrast with the jagged fractal shapes of nature.

We take our world at face value. Nature is more than just lambs and lions, but we tend to see nature only in this way. Our instincts cut nature into two categories: predator and prey or useful and useless because we see others and ourselves in these disparaging ways. Lions are things that must be destroyed for safety purposes and sheep are things that are to be used for food and clothing. We see nature in this way because this facilitates our surviving into tomorrow; nothing more and nothing less. As with a stalagmite in a cave, our wayward views, in effect destroying our world, are matters that build on top of each other. Nature, like gravity, is neither to be ignored nor trifled with in that, like Humpty Dumpty, the higher we climb against it, the faster and harder we will fall back into its constant embrace. Nature can be suppressed for a time, but will inevitably bounce back, or rebound, like a spring pushed in on itself. The more nature is restrained, the more drastic the backlash will be. The illusion of resistance against nature is only possible if we perceive it as a force to oppose, which allows us to believe we can push against it and thereby propel ourselves into great feats of survival. This strategy has worked only too well, with the cost being countless, useless casualties on both sides of this unnecessary war of man versus nature. We are at war with nature because we mistakenly think nature is against us. This mentality makes us retaliate with such ruthless vigor it is astounding. Nature is a delicate yet robust equilibrium of forces; humanity, on the other hand, is a single-minded and unbalanced force that is highly dependent upon this Earth which we are now consciously attempting to kill. Forms of life may become extinct, but life is eternal.

Emergence is the process of flowering in the universe. Emergence is the process seen in fractals, chaos theory, quantum physics, evolution, consciousness, chemistry, biology, the creation and motions of our Earth, stars, galaxies, and the universe as a whole. It is a process whereby the simple iteration (multiplication with feedback) of energy and matter in the non-linear and dynamic system that is the universe brings forth new, unprecedented, and unpredicted characteristics originated from the single law, energy, or initial condition we call creation, or the Big Bang, which is eternally present and constant, if one chooses to view it this way. Some examples include: the emergence of all of the various forces of nature from this singular force, the harmonic interference between energetic waveforms creating atoms, which in turn create molecules and proteins to eventually model cells and organisms or even super organisms such as ant colonies, human societies and, to a larger extent, the Earth and the universe. Skyscrapers and termite mounds emerge from simple building blocks and processes and through individual yet decentralized intention. All chemical bonds are self-governed by the interactions between the electrons in atoms and molecules. Look at a flock of birds, a school of fish, a tree, a river, or a herd of cattle. Each bird, fish, water molecule, and so on amplifies and reflects a process of feedback that in turn creates and modifies local interactions and quantum wave relationships, producing a general character of observations that we see as a wave or a flock or something complex in its dynamics. This is the relationship of harmony seen in all scales of nature; space/time/matter and energy all interact in order to be experienced.

Emergence is self-governed by positive and negative feedback, and for more emergent or complex systems such as human beings, the balance between the discoveries of beautiful phenomena and profiteering from them has become, due to compounding emergence, an issue of prime importance in sustaining our world, in which we are becoming a larger and larger force and factor by the minute. A self-controlled balance known as homeostasis can be seen from the inside of a cell to the entire organism which it and billions of others comprise. All things tend toward balance. The high and low pressure systems that traverse our biosphere combine with oceanic conveyer belts to create a global homeostatic balance between the natural processes that make our Earth so precious. There is no other place in the universe that we know of that has such a beautiful balance as to create this diverse and dynamic biological cornucopia. Why are we disturbing this balance so much? Is it an unintended side effect of good intentions, or is it a completely overlooked and deliberate consequence of our blind and conflictive perceptions? If the latter is true, which I believe it is, nearly seven billion people with this limited foresight and strong motivation, regardless of the consequences, will naturally accentuate and exploit the gain of the individual at the expense of the whole. Because of the universal process of emergence, these "side effects" of our ingenuity and lack of restraint have now become center stage, making them the prime effect.

Blood—The Red Hive

Every second, our bodies create and destroy millions of blood cells, and will do so until the day we die. When separated from each other in a lab, heart cells have their own beat or rhythm of pulsations. However, when they are reconnected to each other they will begin to beat in unison, i.e., they can attract each other and amplify their efforts as a whole. That is their purpose, much like bees in a hive. Blood has no real arrival point or final destination—you could say it's the heart or you could say it's the rest of the body—but where it came from and where it is going are essentially the same non-localized place. This is why it is called circulation; like the circulation of the Sun or the chicken and the egg, it is the same unitary process, with neither—and both—coming first. Blood is bone marrow, breath, the heartbeat, iron, hemoglobin, water, oxygen, nitrogen, hydrogen, and more. Blood is a symbol for life. Blood is a pivotal and sacred aspect of many religions as it was a pivotal aspect of spiritual life to the ancient Maya. They believed the soul of the universe was in their blood, as well as in all things, so when they let their blood during sacred rituals they believed they were activating the soul of the universe. All aspects of life extend far beyond our finite perceptions or our ability to classify them.

All of our genes exist in every single one of our cells, as they are in all of biology, including other animals, plants, and microorganisms. These genes are just recombined and strategically utilized, depending on the surroundings. A human being has between thirty and forty thousand genes, whereas plants, once believed to be much simpler than we, can actually consist of many more. Plants are conscious of their surroundings and exhibit a sense of self just like us. There is clearly still a lot we don't know about plants or genetics. On the other side of the coin, we are, relatively quickly, unraveling and revealing the mechanics of life. DNA repeats itself by creating a sort of spiral staircase, or double helical structure, which wraps around and connects to itself like a snake eating its tail, known as an ouroboros. Presumably most images of DNA that you have seen have been segments or stringed bits of DNA code with a beginning and an end. A more accurate image is a toroidial shape or tube torus; think of an inner tube or a donut. A torus is defined as a shape formed by the relationship of two circles, one revolving in three-dimensional space within the other, with the topographical circle giving it its perimeter. It is essentially a circle made of circles which, rather than spheres, are how some black holes are said to be shaped.

The main goal of DNA is the long-term continuance and communication of its genetic message. Look at all the ways genes alter and create specialized organisms in order to survive in their specific surroundings. Genes give a bird wings, a fish fins, a cheetah its speed, and humans ingenuity. Genes allow life forms to develop fur, claws, patience, blubber, eyes, bioluminescence, hunting strategies, communication, and the instincts and decision-making skills to utilize them for the benefit of both the individual and the species as a whole, and in turn for the benefit of the entirety of nature. Genetic mutations are variations, for better or worse, of certain genomes, a process that has been occurring since the beginning of time. Mutations occur constantly, with some aiding the survival of the organism and species, like better eyesight, and others, like cancer, hurting its chances. Genes are not always active; during an organism's lifetime they turn on and off all the time. However, problems arise when they turn on and off irregularly. This is similar to the different sections of an orchestra, where certain instruments must be active or silent at complimenting lengths and times. A mutation can act like a misbehaving and unruly musician, or perhaps a bad one. Gene mutation is where one or more of these instruments either goes out of control or remains completely silent. There are two types of genetic mutation; one is induced naturally by environmental factors and the other is spontaneous, without rhyme or reason. If the form of the DNA is altered, then its function is intrinsically altered as well, such as with the damaged prions of Mad Cow Disease. The divine intelligence of nature continues making genetic changes when they facilitate survival and when they are in balance with an organism's surroundings. Nature discontinues detrimental or unbalanced mutations, through death of an individual or extinction, for example, and continues the lineage of beneficial mutations that have a greater and greater effect the longer the genetic line continues. I prefer to call these mutations *changes*, because it is normal and natural for DNA to mutate; therefore this is just a natural change, not an aberration. Mutation, evolution, or natural change, whatever terminology one wishes to use, can culminate in the emergence of new species. This explains the truly immeasurable scale of biological diversity, with species finding their unique niches in nature, and it is why we have tall people and giants, short people and little people, white and black people, hairy and hairless people, albinos, and everything else under the genetic rainbow.

Man is, in a strict sense, entirely animal.
(Blaise Pascal, *Pensees*, quoted in Collison & Collison, 1660/1980)

Take an honest look at the meager differences and deep similarities we share with primates. Putting aside nuanced and visual distractions, primates and other animals have very similar biological processes and structures. We share all the basic integumentary (skin, hair, nails), musculoskeletal, respiratory, cardiovascular, digestive, urinary, reproductive, nervous, endocrine and hormonal, lymphatic and immune systems that are necessary for animals to live. We have very similar needs, desires, social and emotional behaviors, and arrangements of bones, internal organs, limbs, fingers and toes, eyes, ears, noses, teeth and mouths. Notice the similarities that we share with our fellow Earth dwellers. To say we are closely related to primates, and all life forms to a wider extent, is indeed an understatement and is not necessarily against religion, but it is in fact misaligned with the views that many have of creation, primates, and ourselves. If this was a disagreement over a true teaching of love, then it would be completely appropriate to say that all men are not created equal, that whites are better than blacks, humans are better than fungi and the list would go on. This of course is ludicrous. All life really is created equal; it is judgment, choice, belief, and ego that separate us from one another as well as from other varying shapes, sizes, and colors of life. It is important to point out that religions that denounce evolution have a strict hierarchy. The theory of evolution, however, does not. The theory has simply a diversity and a balance with a strong sense of relationship, equality, and interconnectedness with the entire family of species and life that we can see unfolding before our very eyes. Evolution is another word for change toward maintaining balance.

Charles Darwin described the process of evolution, natural selection, or the survival of species in his 1859 book *On the Origin of*

Species. In his magnum opus, Mr. Darwin did not, however, describe the essential origin of life; he actually described a process of change that created visual and structural differences (along with their respective survival benefits) which we then categorize as separate species and aptly named the process natural selection. This selection is done by and through the harmony and balance of nature so in this way, evolution does not really contradict the concept of God or creation. When it comes to the universe, the designer is the design. Things adapt to their specific natural neighborhood and circumstances just as the Creator and that which is created intends. The theory of evolution is the scientific approach to change and growth. Whether scientific or religious, both worldviews are describing the same thing but from two different angles. One is regarded as fully material and observational while the other is regarded as divine and faith-based. A positive relationship between the two is what is necessary and what is meant to be, because they are one and the same, but with illusions of opposite polarity that divide them in our narrow perspective. It is creation and it is changing; it's as simple as that. One can call it divine manifestation or the Big Bang, evolution or adaptation or intelligent design. I hope that the agreement between science and religion will be that whatever this growth or flowering is called, it will be an accurate description of the humbling awe of beauty, unity, and love which is our universe. As long as there is common ground in the acceptance that all of life is truly one big miracle and we are all keenly aware of this and joyful to be a part of it, then that's plum dandy with me.

As science nowadays seems to be a kind of religion of its own in terms of faith and mindset, simply put, it is an art of discovery. Science and religion alike have both evolved over many centuries into what they are now. Evolution is such a taboo word among many religions, but all evolution really is an interpretation of growth and change, as nothing is static or dead. The universe is a process. In the world cycles before the present one, the Maya believe that before they were humans they were monkeys, down through to reptiles and stars. According to most anthropologists, modern man emerged about fifty to sixty thousand years ago. Researchers have found numerous "recent" adaptive mutations in fossils and etched in the human genome. These adaptations seem to be occurring at an accelerating pace. Over the past ten thousand years, human adaptation has occurred a hundred times more quickly than in any other period in the history of our species. One popular idea as to why we are adapting so much faster to our surroundings is, like bacteria, a simple matter of multiplication. Ten thousand years ago there were fewer than ten million people on Earth. There were 200 million by the time of the Roman Empire. Since around the year 1500, this number has risen exponentially to what it is now—nearly seven billion people. It seems that only recently has humanity intensely accelerated its rate of adaptation. It stands to reason that the more humans there are, the more adaptive mutations there will be and the quicker the process of adaptation. With so many of us living in urban settings, we are evolving alongside these unnatural surroundings so when these super cities come to pass, as they most certainly will, so shall many of their inhabitants dependant on their functions.

All life lives on the one tree of life. We are relatives, not just to our brothers and sisters and cousins, but to every other human, tree, flower, bird, fish, monkey, to every other biological life form and to the more basic forms of intention from which all matter is composed. We may become more or less computer-like in our thoughts, more or less social in our personalities, more or less specialized in our trades and areas of knowledge, and more or less aware of reality and its illusions, but this is evolution and, as always, nature will select which is in balance between species and itself as a whole. Artificially domesticating ourselves to live within, and become totally dependent upon, a specific society may pose problems if and when that society collapses or changes too fast for its people to adapt. Some might argue that humans are now beginning to alter evolution, which is true enough in terms of breeding ourselves and new animal and plant species, but one mustn't forget that we are still creatures of nature, no matter how hard we try to forget our ties and convince ourselves otherwise.

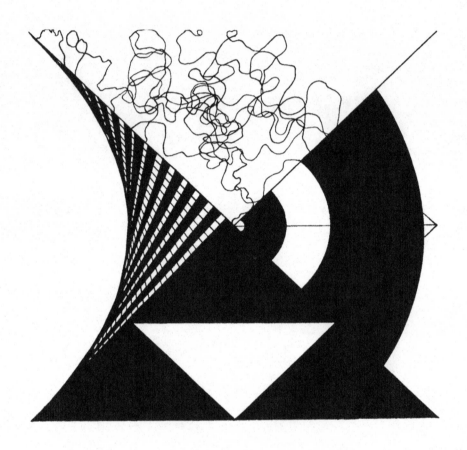

PART 4

SHAPE, SCALE, AND INTENSITY—THE LANGUAGES OF BEAUTY

*I pass death with the dying, and birth with the
new-washed babe...and am not contained between my
hat and boots, And peruse manifold objects, no two alike,
and every one good, The earth good, and the stars good,
and their adjuncts all good.*

(Walt Whitman, *Leaves of Grass: Song of Myself,* 1855/2007)

An average atom is roughly a millionth of a millimeter in diameter. The distance from the average adult's toes to their waist is about one meter, while Mount Everest rises eight point eight kilometers above sea level. The distance from the Earth to the Sun is what we call an AU or astronomical unit, or about a hundred-fifty million kilometers. The distance from the Sun to the center of the galaxy is twenty-six thousand light years, and the distance across the observable universe is calculated to be about fourteen billion light years. All of these measurements are used to illustrate the scale of things, or to gauge and reveal certain aspects or intensities of the force of nature such as quantum photosynthesis, surface tension in water, crystallization, weather, the creation of single and multi-cellular organisms, plate tectonics, and star and galaxy formation. Scale, form, and intensity melt together and can make white light more blue or more red, make atoms and merge them together to form complex molecules and create stars and galaxies that all spin and vibrate with absolute precision.

Sunrises, sunsets, seascapes, and landscapes under the stars and viewed through human eyes are all products of the same emergent process that gives rise to the feeling we have when we observe or connect to these common yet transcendent vistas. The colors and shapes emerge from a collection of atoms, as is also true of the water and atmospheric gases which constitute these images. The Sun and our bodies are filled with the emergent properties of energetic waves. These create hydrogen and every other interaction, from the simple polarity of hydrogen to the emergence of more complex elements. These in turn create more interactive chemical bonds and reactions, which create the biology of all of us. Biology is simply the sustained and emergent result of a spark. All forms have a function based in movement. Atoms and chemical molecules create cells which in turn create all life forms and they all are formed in movement and for movement. If one looks at the iteration of ice crystals that emerge from the central dust particle or nucleator to form the Euclidean and fractal symmetries of a snowflake, one can easily see the elegant intention of physical processes in all things. A human being—or any other biological form—is created from a single fertilized egg cell. The infinite variation due to the feedback throughout the respective iterations during the growth process ensures that no two snowflakes or people are *exactly* alike. Everything emerges through self-organization, and fractal geometry is a process that presents itself in many ways. Fractals, like all forms, have a function. When one describes the form or shape of something, one is also inadvertently describing its function. Geometry is more about the process and action involved in producing the forms that we see rather than just the forms. We view these shapes in our heads as abstractions, but in reality these shapes are moving and their movements or functions are governed by their moving form and vice versa. With respect to all geometry, form is function.

Fractal (Rough) Geometry

Look at a tree. It is a form and a process where the parts strongly resemble the symmetry of the whole. Mentally zoom in or out through the scales of observation, and the form made by the process of nature remains the same. It is formed by the simple repetition of scale, the design of nature. A lung, just like a tree, is a great example of a fractal geometric form, because it clearly shows that to diffuse gases it must channel them effectively, and fractal forms do just that. They simply repeat what works over and over again, like a stream finding the ocean. It is no accident that there is a commonality of fractal shape between green photosynthesizing plants such as trees, and lungs; in a single breath, we breathe in, the plants breathe out.

Fractal geometry is described elegantly by mathematician Benoit Mandelbrot. The word fractal, coined by Mandelbrot, originates from the Latin word *fractus* meaning rough, uneven or asymmetric, jagged, or broken, and if compared to the smooth surfaces of classical Euclidean geometry, fractals would be considered quite rough, fuzzy, beautifully simple and yet, infinitely intricate. Fractals are at first glance non-Euclidean, irregularly shaped and asymmetrical, and yet any part of a fractal zoomed in or out on will exhibit a similarity, a regularity; a symmetry if you will, through all scales of observation. Fractals, infinity, and unity are so intimately intertwined as to be indistinguishable. They are, in their everyday expressions, flauntingly indicative of the true beauty of reality. A perspective is a way of looking and a dimension is a degree of freedom, so when united with infinity and fractals, all these truths create infinite ways of looking at freedom across all scales. Everything is fractal, and our way of looking, generally speaking, whether it's called a schema, perspective, or theory, is completely incomplete.

Fractals are as symmetrical as they are beautiful. Symmetry is not a duality of opposing sides but a reflection or alternate dimension of the same thing, like a kaleidoscope. Fractals exist everywhere, but some obvious examples include the golden ratio, clouds, mountains, rivers, trees, leaves, lightning, lungs, veins, and snowflakes. Fractals describe life completely and eloquently. Fractals are a never-ending pattern that is iterated or repeated through each scale of observation. Life continues, always repeating and changing form. It is a cycle that is profoundly complementary, reflective, infinite, and unified. Seeing truth is seeing reality in all dimensions, including fragments of the singular infinite reality. This insight into the self and the universe is commonly known as the feeling of flow or pure inspiration and creativity, perfect bliss, joy, and compassion with all things. In the universe, nothing is added to or subtracted from creation, but is simply seen by us as things given and taken away. The universe may be expanding, but the energy is equally balanced and conserved; the net energy in the universe may in fact be absolutely zero. Excess negativity can be seen as a displacement or void of positivism, which creates an unbalanced proportion. For instance, with heaven and hell, hell is the withholding, hiding, or denial of heaven. The opposite of heaven is a lack of heaven, which is effectively a deception and a feeling of restriction or loss, commonly viewed as hell. We live in a wonderland, but because we are used to it we call it land, similarly to how we might see a tree as boring, unspectacular and lifeless timber. We are disenchanted in a land of constant miracles and exploding enchantment. The dichotomy of heaven and hell is the awareness and the lack thereof in nature. Our lack of awareness occurs today in our world and it is increasingly evident. We are living in heaven (nature) and are missing it by feeling bored or unfulfilled, which is the restriction of inspiration, passion, or creativity and, for whatever reasons, we are creating a biosphere that reflects this. The opposite of unity is a lack of unity, which is separation, not of kind, but of limited or unbalanced scope, scale, proportion, or awareness, not unlike the infinite fractal onion of the universe. The onion is always there, but we are only aware of each progressive outside skin. This keen awareness of what is involves either the complete suspension or absorption of thought, time, or ego, or the dissolution of the observer into the observed. Consequently, attempting to portray this profound meaning in the words of any language or symbolism of any variation in relation to the experience is, of course, partially lost in translation.

Each scale is the same as the next, except for the differences perceived from the biased perspective that we use to survive. There are many scales, such as micro-macro or quantum and relative; however, in a wider sense there is one infinite scale without any reference to size. We have microscopes and telescopes with numbers and increasing heads or tails of zeroes, but this is only for our brains and eyes to use to define the world, whereas nature has no numbers. As an example, a single apple tree may have a specific and definite amount of apples when observed from an unnatural snapshot type of isolation but when taken into a wider context, the number of trees in the orchard and the number of seeds that will become subsequent trees and subsequent blossoms and apples one soon finds quantity to be less made of strictly individual, whole numbers and more infinite, seamless and fluid. Numbers are only a device designed to quantify nature or reality from our perspective in an effort to try to understand the world. They obscure the reality of what scale really is.

Fractals are the forms of the universe. Everything is the same, but only appears otherwise, due to the awareness or scale of one's viewpoint. Fractals have infinite viewpoints. This explains the endless variety of all the changing observations and viewpoints between all the people, plants and animals on Earth. People hear, taste, feel, see, and so on, the same things differently, so fractals represent relativity as well as symmetry and scale. All of our individual senses are relative and create individual experiences, attitudes, and viewpoints toward events and the universe in its entirety. This is a self- or ego-based viewpoint, and to suspend or widen this narrow flashlight view leads to a clear view of life. It is the viewpoint of all scales, which is the viewpoint of creation, and is one way to eliminate the fragmented view that creates all conflict. There are two common views of enlightenment: one is spiritual and the other is intellectual; I believe enlightenment covers both views. When you look at a fractal image you can see curves that look different from, yet similar to, other curves; however, when you zoom your point of view in or out they will soon appear to be exactly the same. The closer or farther away one looks, the more they become the same. This process goes on and on forever, as there is no size limit to that which is infinite. We see the universe as a fractal within which we are seated in the middle scale. The universe contains galaxies full of solar systems, as well as objects the size of humans, plants, and animals, and further down the scale we have microscopic organisms and quantum mechanical behaviors of atoms and subatomic particles. There is a divine structure and unity to everything big and small, with the only difference being the perceived difference in scale or size. This is natural because we obviously see things of different size, shape, color, and so on. We can think of countless differences if that is how we wish to see things. We see separation because we are biologically programmed to look for it. We humans love to categorize, and to do this we must separate, distinguish, and relate things against each other. In this world, people strive for the transient and eternal connections of love, whether it is with loved ones, nature, or themselves. Ironically we strive for precisely what we have separated ourselves from.

What is the quickest way to connect two points? Many would say a straight line; however, the question rests on the idea of speed and the answer is based on idealized geometry. This is why humanity has created such idealized structures compared to the meandering pseudo-lines of trees, clouds, rivers and the like. Nature doesn't have anything like the idea of time that we do, which is why a river takes the route it does to reach the ocean, or why a tree grows gracefully toward the sky instead of looking like a bushel of broomsticks. Nature is patient; just compare a skyline to a tree line and feel your jaw drop at the contrast. Nature has no preoccupation with speeding processes more than is necessary. Nature has no preoccupation with the permanence of form, whereas humans are persistently fixated on the ideas of time, progress, speed, and permanence.

Symmetry—A World of Mirrors

Symmetry is the connection of beauty and order which is founded by the absolute balance and proportion of form, scale and placement of anything and everything in relation to the whole and its parts. Symmetry exists when the form, scale, repetition and placement of something changes its shape, size, quantity and position yet its essential symmetries not only remain but remain wholly unchanged and unaffected by such changes.

Electrons, positrons, protons, neutrons, all matter and antimatter can travel as and through a wave formation; remember form equals function. The discovery or creation of the equation describing antimatter and therefore anti-energy was made by the British physicist Paul Dirac in the early 1900s by using the looking glass of Einstein's most famous equation, $E=mc^2$, to help describe the quantum mechanical effects of electrons. If an equation has a positive charge for energy and mass, the equation still holds true for the symmetrical opposite, regarded as negative energy. Just as 2 x 2 equals 4, likewise -2 x -2 equals -4. This means anti-energy can exist alongside antimatter. This was Paul Dirac's famous insight, in which his equation combines special relativity and quantum mechanics and unveils quantum electrodynamics and anti-particles. Electrons, as described in quantum mechanics, exist and disappear for a Planck-scale instant, which is only half of a split between an electron and its other half, the anti-electron or positron. This antimatter particle instantly combines with its electron and then both cease to exist in their material form in space and time. This is happening instantaneously all over the universe all the time. Electrons can exist in the material form of energy and in metaphysical ways that we will never fully understand. Electrons have no real bounds in space or time. This helps greatly to explain quantum temperaments as well as their emergence into an observer made of the observed.

The universe, laden with its entanglements, superposition, wave/particle behavior, and the effects of observation, was theorized by John Wheeler and Richard Feynman, who made the compelling argument that the universe could in fact be kaleidoscopic perspectives of a single, polar, and balanced electron existing in the many changing forms of an energy wave (note that all electrons are identical) moving back and forth through time and space at infinite speed. It is interesting to note that most of the electrons that exist today are believed to have been created at the beginning of the Big Bang and through subsequent high-energy particle collisions. Electrons are also predicted to be created at the event horizon of black holes, also known as singularities, both at relative and quantum scales.

All electrons have a hypercharge and a weak charge. This is called the unified electroweak model, which combines electromagnetism with the weak nuclear force. Even matter itself has its opposite, antimatter. The closest we have come to a theory of everything is quantum electrodynamics, or QED for short, with string, superstring, and M-theory now being the prime contenders for a theory of everything, or quantum gravity (QG). However, string theory and many others are essentially unprovable, because the "strings" are too small to be observed. Any theory gains credibility when direct observations can be made. All of these theories, including the small-scale electrodynamics framework, no matter how amazingly successful they are, are still a far cry from being totally understood.

Electrons have their positrons, the antimatter opposite of electrons. One might say "what do positrons have to do with the practical side of life?" Positrons are considered to be virtual particles. Physicists believe that the entire universe may be continually creating electron-positron pairs that instantly annihilate each other, thus immediately disappearing after they come into a material and energetic existence and then, almost paradoxically, instantly reappearing in a constant cycle of perpetuity. The net energy before and after this "creation" and "destruction" is zero. Note that when an electron collides with its positron anti-particle, a flash of gamma radiation is released or transformed. We can see this flash on a P.E.T. scanner. The creation, interference, and annihilation cycle of this matter and antimatter pair is believed to be the fabric of existence. The duration of the instant cycle of this pair falls under the threshold of observation and beyond common sense because there is no time "between" instants. Furthermore, since this pair instantaneously exists, interfering with and destroying its polar traits, they or it cannot be exclusively in either a form of existence or nonexistence. Like a spinning coin, it's neither and both. They both exist and non-exist for eternity; they are just changing forms, sort of like looking at something through a kaleidoscope. It is all the same thing, just with different dimensions or perspectives. This is a reflection of the universe as a whole. Throughout this cycle, the inseparable pair is, on our visible and detectable scale, perceived as an electromagnetic dipole or electron. The spin of the electron or of a galaxy creates mass and opposing reflections in a fractal scale of energy amplification and transformation, allowing the observer to then sense various aspects of one physical law, such as gravity, electricity/magnetism, the strong/weak nuclear forces, energy/matter, space/time, quantum/relativistic physics, science/religion, colors/black/white, senses, God/natural selection, and the observer and the observed.

Dual Actions in a Single Process

Symmetry is described as the harmonious or aesthetically pleasing proportionality and balance that reflects beauty, perfection, or patterned self-similarity. Symmetry, in addition to the common view of it as a static characteristic of a thing, is a dynamic process. Anything added or taken from anything symmetric remains untouched by these changes. The Platonic solids (see p. 214) are quite symmetrical in terms of reflection. These solids have duals, which are two complementary forms that are symmetrical under many aspects of their relationship. Just as a point and a line are duals of each other, which means that, in time, an instant is eternal, as are electricity and magnetism, certain Platonic solids are duals or compliments of others. They are two forms or views of the very same thing. Symmetry is the dynamic relationship between the changing and changeless behavior of form and function in concert. Any change in the speed, position, or direction of a sphere, for instance, leaves it essentially where it was before the change. Symmetry is a characteristic law that creates the dynamic process of form and function. Relationships aren't solely for comparison or interaction, but go to the very root of any definition. All definition is the relationship of what the defined interacts and relates to.

The Scale of Symmetry

Is the world a vast, interconnected system of relations, in which even the properties of a single elementary particle or the identity of a point in space requires and reflects the whole rest of the universe?

(Lee Smolin, quoted in Cole, 2001)

Symmetry is an effect of the universe, or flowering singularity, that causes a living creature to see duality and variety in all shapes and sizes. Symmetry is the *active* behavior of all things. Look at your body; it is symmetrical and is made to move. Symmetry is a fundamental concept in physics, mathematics, and nature. In math a correct equation has to be a mirror image of values on both sides of the equal sign. In nature, sacred geometry is the manifestation of form and function and it is intrinsically symmetrical, as everything is the same. Everything is symmetrical, as the universe is a reflection of itself and naturally its source.

The recognition of beauty is the reflection of oneself. When something changes within a system that is beautiful and symmetrical, the whole remains unaltered. It's the observer/observed connection. That is why the connection exists. This is purpose. It's not a goal to be expected or realized in the future or remembered in the past. Symmetry that is broken, known as asymmetry, and seen as a one-way motion such as time, or as ugliness or incompleteness, isn't really broken at all, but can be thought of as folded or braided in a way that we only see and interpret as aberrant, and that we tend to see as anything but beautiful. Reflective or bilateral symmetry, which most comes to mind when speaking of symmetry, has lines, creases, or seams. Many animals, including us, have this mirror-like symmetry while jellyfish, starfish, or atoms, for example, have radial symmetries. Our symmetrical reality, however, is fundamentally seamless. Like a mirror, it consists of a wall that is struck by a light. But a sphere has no lines and is symmetrical under rotation across all angles along a central axis. Symmetry can exist in both stillness and extreme movement. Efficiency takes advantage of symmetry. Our Sun, Earth, and some raindrops, without interference from excess wind or other raindrops, are close to spherical, as a sphere is super-symmetrical and is very energy efficient because of this remarkable effect of symmetry. Balance is equivalence, order, harmony and symmetry. Balance doesn't have to be thought of as a still scale with equal weights on either side, but can exist in the most active processes as long as the net energy is equalized. Note that net energy isn't in tallying up the score after the process, but is a factor that exists instantly and constantly during the process.

Change is symmetrical, and analogous to a kaleidoscope that, like all things, is fractal in nature. However beautiful symmetry may be, perfect symmetry is something undesired by many artists. Broken symmetry, or asymmetry, leaves room for growth and gives a sense of incompleteness, or the notion of something to be added to it (which is most likely the observer's perspective). Fractal or natural geometry embodies these asymmetric, chaotic and unfinished aspects of art as well as containing absolute symmetry and order. It gives creativity wiggle room to observe more than the perceived static and boredom that perfection sometimes seems to communicate. If one wants to be abstract, interpretive, or ambiguous, then asymmetry is the avenue many artists take in whatever medium of art they may be working in. This gives a feeling of randomness, freedom, and disorder, which allows the observer of the art to actively contribute to the art just by looking at it, making it quite open and interactive. When art is created in this way, the creation becomes a two-way street, with the artist and the viewer collaboratively creating the piece, making it different and new each time someone looks at it. Alternatively, some artists, for example, mathematicians or musicians, simply adore the order of symmetry. Symmetry is a particularly crucial aspect in music. Classical music as well as most other genres utilize symmetry in their tone, pitch, and recurring melodies. Asymmetry and symmetry together provide untold creative freedom and are two equally valid and beautiful views of the same elegant landscape of nature. Birth and death are also duals of each other, two apparent sides of the same coin, with symmetry describing many, if not all, of the dual perspectives of a unitary truth.

Euclidean (Smooth) Geometry

Nature is an infinite sphere of which the center is
everywhere, and the circumference nowhere.

(Blaise Pascal, *Penseés*, quoted in Collison & Collison, 1660/1980)

The Sphere

Spheres are symmetrical, infinite, and unified. Have you ever wondered why solar systems, atoms, and so on rotate and orbit, and why they are in the shape of a sphere? It is from the curvature of the sphere that all geometric shapes (sacred geometry), biological and otherwise, originate. A sphere is perfect under rotational symmetry. The surface of a sphere is always an equal distance from its center. A raindrop is more or less a sphere which, due to this property of surface tension, gives rise to the beauty of a rainbow. A sphere can be described as having one side and infinite sides, not the 360 degrees or idealistic divisions we use. The horizon of a sphere is infinite. Its 360 sides can all be divided further infinitely many times, but the number 360 is easy to remember and math lets us get a handle on it. Note that ϖ (the constant ratio of a sphere's diameter to its circumference) is not a whole number but a fractal number with infinite decimal places.

If a sphere were cut into plane sections (think of an egg in an egg slicer), all of the slices would be larger and smaller circles. A sphere has the smallest surface area relative to its volume, and the largest volume relative to its surface area. The sphere is the only shape that does not have a reference point on its surface. A fixed and constant motion in all three dimensions will create a sphere seen in celestial objects such as the Moon, Earth, and Sun. The universe can be thought of as a sphere but without either a center or circumference. The sphere is perfectly balanced, super-symmetrical, and can be viewed without a defining perimeter as the universe and the mother of everything inside it. The universe is made of energy, and since energy tends to propagate in waveforms without complete obstruction from matter or other sources of energy, unimpeded energy will radiate spherically in every direction. The inside of a sphere is fully defined and thus completely dependent on and profoundly interwoven with the characteristics of its outside, like a hole, or like us and our environment. There is no separate outside and inside, but only both together and as one.

All stars and planets are roughly spheres that revolve and rotate 360 degrees around each other. A sphere is a three-dimensional circle with a circumference of 360 degrees. Two points in two-dimensional space with one or both rotating around each other form a circle. If there are three dimensions, you will get a sphere. The universe is a boundless, infinite sphere with its center being any and all equal points around it. A sphere cannot exist without both a center and a perimeter, so therefore a sphere has no real center and edge exclusively, which means anything considered a center and anything considered connected to that center, middle, or source point is really all the same thing. It is not a matter of coincidence that circles, or spheres in three dimensions, are a basic fundamental shape prevalent in nature both on the telescopic and microscopic scales. From the nucleus of an atom to droplets of falling water to the Earth and Sun, there are spheres everywhere, and in all manifestations of this basic shape. We are born of spherical stars; we are created from spherical atoms to create spherical eggs that subsequently grow into spherical zygotes and continue the process of dichotomy to create much of life.

The primary shape of the flower of life and of sacred geometry is the circle or, in three dimensions, a sphere. This sphere is where all of the platonic solids originate. A shape in the flower of life, after the *Vesica piscis* (two intersecting circles) and the Borromean rings (three intersecting circles), is the tube torus. The tube torus is a shape utilized in the study of black holes and their formation and is essentially a circle made of circles.

The essence of natural geometry is complete harmony and unity. Sacred geometry is an area of formational mathematics which states that certain sacred shapes are the blueprints for everything, such as matter, energy, space, and time in all their forms, that naturally bend to the awareness of a divine unifying framework, or the universe having an indescribable design and intelligence. This intelligence means there is no such thing as entropy, disorder, or random coincidence, as many intuitively believe. Nature gives us many blatant and subtle hints about this unifying geometry. Sacred geometry, fractals, the golden mean, and the Fibonacci sequence, all of which are described later in this chapter, all include each other in their descriptions, making them very much the same. They are interchangeable and, to a great extent, inseparable.

Shapes Made of Points and Lines

If fractal geometry is jagged-looking, then Euclidean geometry is its smooth and ideal opposite. Between these opposites is a common ground. Some Platonic solid shapes include beehives, seashells, viruses, pollen, diatoms, snowflakes, rocks, DNA, plants, animals, air, fire, and water and, unconventionally speaking, fractal geometric shapes, too. These are all examples of form/function using Platonic solids, named after Plato, who claimed that the basic elements were constructed from the regular solids. They are used in disciplines such as physics, mathematics, theology, philosophy, chemistry, biology, and art, to name a few. There are five Platonic solids, excluding the aforementioned sphere, whose names match the number of their faces. The Platonic solids are significant because the faces, angles, and edges are highly symmetrical and connect to each other with perfect and complementary precision. The straight lines that create the Platonic solids are considered to be male and born of the sphere or curved line, which is considered to be female. Some call the sphere the sixth Platonic solid. Remember that all Platonic solids originate from the sphere and all can be placed perfectly inside it. The five regular polyhedral or Platonic solids have an intriguing feature: when one adds the number of faces and points and then subtracts the edges, one will always get the number two. These solids are considered the prime numbers, table of elements, or building blocks of geometry. The sphere is the first prime, or number one (which many don't consider a prime number). A lack of any form whatsoever is where the sphere emerges, and from this sphere all other shapes originate.

The Five Regular Polyhedra

Euclidean geometry is based on points which are stretched and pulled into straight and smooth lines which then go on to form an enclosed and solid shape called a polyhedron, which means a solid form made with many faces. It is worth noting that all geometrical forms, however static and unmoving our minds make it to be, owe their existence to motion. For the first Platonic solid, let us start with the four-sided tetrahedron or pyramid, which represents fire and is "self-dual," which means the nodes or points match against themselves with the centers of each surface. The second is the cube, or six-sided hexahedron, which represents Earth. The third solid is the eight-sided octahedron, which is a dual of the cube, and vice versa. The octahedron represents air. The fourth Platonic solid is the twelve-faced pentagonal dodecahedron that represents the ether force or life force. The fifth solid is the icosahedron. This is a regular polygon with twenty equilateral triangle faces, and represents water. The dodecahedron and the icosahedron are duals of each other. There are only five regular polyhedra—six if you include the sphere.

Earlier in this chapter I talked about fractal geometry and how amazing it is, and after you have read this section you may see a disparity between fractals and Euclidean geometry, where the geometry of points and lines naturally agrees with itself but not with the rough and seemingly random geometry of fractals. It's like trying to mix Newtonian mechanics with quantum mechanics. The amazing thing is, it is completely possible and beautiful to combine and complement the two geometries. How? you might ask. It is easier than one might think. Euclidean geometry, along with hyperbolic and spherical geometry, is the framework for existence and fractals are scales of existence, so the Platonic solids and the sphere can be fractal, just like any shape born of these fundamental shapes. This is just one more valid aspect that shows there are no real paradoxes and that the universe is more unified and beautiful that most of us dare venture to realize.

The Golden Proportion

The golden mean or ratio, also called the divine proportion, is an infinite spiral which is roughly 1.6180339887, continuing on ad infinitum. This ratio is self-exact under any magnification or observation through scale, just like a fractal is. In other words, this iterated ratio is infinite, and any part is exactly like any other part as well as the whole itself. It is a universal truth and is fractal in nature, because any piece of this curve is an identical representation of the whole, where the only difference between the part and the whole is the scale of observation, which sees only a part in the context of the whole. It is interesting that neither the golden mean, the Fibonacci sequence, nor ϖ are whole numbers, therefore their decimal expansions trail off into infinity. Any form in reality will do for expressing these numbers, because they are fractal and thus infinite.

The Fibonacci Sequence

The Fibonacci sequence is an iteration of numbers between zero and infinity. The beginning sequence is: 0, 1, 1, 2, 3, 5, 8, 13, 21, 34, 55, 89, 144, 233, 377, 610, ad infinitum. This pattern of increasing numbers is seen in many settings in two consecutive Fibonacci numbers, such as the branching in trees and leaves, pine cones, the patterns of many kinds of fruit, ferns, seashells, flowers, curves of waves, spiral galaxies, water spinning down a drain, and many more. The sequence or process is self-conscious and aware of its own emergence, and this awareness provides feedback for it to emerge in the way it does. This self-organizing, logarithmic structure looks at the number preceding its present state and projects that number along with the addition of its present number in order to create the next number in the sequence. The spinning of a star tetrahedron creates pine cones. The spiral is actually an illusion, as the material and energy, being more than what meets the eye, are radiated from the center in all directions, but the spiral is the pattern that is created as a seashell is rotated in radial fashion, giving it its visual spiral pattern. Fractal, Euclidean, sacred geometry, the golden ratio, and the Fibonacci sequence are all the same thing. The number one is a scale of observation up from zero but also a scale down from infinity, all of which are totally equal. The process of proportion iterated through scale where any segment of the whole is a perfect replica of the whole is the merger of fractal geometry and supersymmetry.

Zero = Infinity

*The 'paradox' is only a conflict between reality
and your feeling of what reality 'ought to be.'*

(Richard Feynman, quoted in Gibbon, 1984)

Zero is often used as a symbol representing nothing, while infinity is a concept representing anything that cannot be fully defined, or that is regarded as having no end or boundary. A mix of zero and infinity create all the finite and calculable numbers arising from these two parents, which means that all numbers have their traits deeply linked to nothing and everything. Finding zero and infinity is easy. Each is contained in all numbers. Each is everywhere and nowhere. This makes them slippery—hard for the mind to grasp. Just look at some seemingly finite object in the room. It does not exist by itself, but is only described by relating it to yourself and other things. Reality is a combination of these polarities. Zero and infinity are two aspects of each other, like thunder and lightning. Any number multiplied by zero equals zero. Any number divided by zero will give any number. 1/0 gives infinity. Zero is just as hard or easy to grasp as infinity is. These statements may all seem pretty obvious and trivial; however, think about how they can relate to your daily life and they suddenly become greatly meaningful.

The midpoint of zero and infinity is one. Infinity is inclusive because it has the remarkable behavior of being everything, including paradoxes. Completely defining reality/infinity is intrinsically impossible with a finite language or system of symbols, because to define it would imply a limit upon that which is infinite. I find it interesting that large numbers start with a number, then have a trail of zeros going off toward the horizon. The same is true with small numbers, except that they start with a trail of zeros and end in a number. Numbers are used to determine a position of scale and magnitude between these apparently individual extremes.

Neither Big nor Small

To see a World in a Grain of Sand
And a Heaven in a Wild flower
Hold Infinity in the palm of your hand
And Eternity in an hour.

(William Blake, *Auguries of Innocenc*e,
quoted in Erdman, 1801-1803/1988)

Subtract any number from itself and you get zero, while a number subtracted by zero is left unchanged. Zero divided by zero is zero. Any number multiplied by zero is zero. One divided by infinity is zero, and one divided by zero is infinity. Zero is balance, just as infinity is. They are inseparable. They are both super-symmetrical. Together they dance with ample room for symmetry, asymmetry, simplicity, and compounded simplicity to sing. Zero and infinity are transparent mirrors for each to see each other and themselves at the same time. Zero is infinitely small just as infinity is infinitely big. Together they are nothing and at the same time everything. Most mathematical infinities arise from trying to divide by zero. Points in space, such as particles or black holes, are infinite, yet have zero dimensions, which causes much frustration among scientific observers. Point particles are of both zero and infinite dimension just as black holes are. Atoms are the infinite nodes of infinite waves. Finding zero and infinity is the same as finding the center of the infinite universe. Pick a spot and there it is. Pick a time and that's it. Due to this inclusive behavior of nature, it becomes unnecessary to engage in the act of picking a point at all. I believe this is a main hurdle that particle physicists have to grapple with in order to understand not just the point-like aspects of particles, but their entire background as well. Zero is at the center of all true equations portraying equality and balance. Waves vibrate about a point of equilibrium visualized as a point or line. Shorter wavelengths or frequencies mean that these waves possess more energy, so therefore the shortest wavelength—that is, the point or line having no wavelength at all—would not only be stillness but would actually have infinite energy as well. This is the elusive and unprovable quantum gravity. It is infinite nothingness. The universe is in the middle of these opposites.

The Silhouette of a Deeper Reality

Waves are the form created by the movement of zero (as the axis, orienting point, line, or equilibrium) and infinity (the wavelengths that endlessly extend from this point or line). Both are equivalent, just as the source is also everything emerging from the source. Deep and sustained inquiry into the relationship of zero and infinity ultimately reveals that their distinctions and similarities melt into each other.

Fractals are perfect forms dependent on the relationship between zero (the inner black portion of the fractal) and infinity (the colors radiating from the black inside), much like one's own eye with a black pupil and colored iris, or an invisible black hole and the visible galaxy around it. Any finite object is a true yet shadowy veneer of its deeper and infinite reality. A Menger sponge is a cubic representation of a fractal or a 3-D Cantor set, which paradoxically bears infinite surface area yet zero volume. The Cantor set, named after its conceiver, Georg Cantor (1845-1918), is a mathematical paradox where one takes a line, divides it into thirds, removes the middle third, and continues this with the remaining lines ad infinitum. The lines quickly become infinitesimal points, dust, or particles with no collective length. The Cantor set has infinitely many, infinitesimally small points and yet, paradoxically, their lengths combine to equal zero. A spiral converging to a point transformed into a Cartesian graph looks like the common representation of the electromagnetic spectrum, with large waves or squiggles decreasing into a flat line. A sphere has an infinite horizon. Net zero is when an immovable object meets an unstoppable force, creating a perfect balance that we see as a lack of movement, but with extreme potential or stored and unreleased energy. If you look closer and closer at your skin, you will see that there is no distinction between your inside and outside, similar to the fractal nature of zooming in to a tree line, connecting the land, water, air, or the fire of the Sun. When truth dissolves the barricade of illusion, the distinctions between the infinite and infinitesimal and the outside and inside become completely and utterly meaningless. Lava is to dust as water is to fog. Rock is to ash as ice is to a cloud. The air we see as separate is in our blood and breath. We effectively breathe in ourselves.

The perception of limit, or of an object being finite, is a matter of not seeing the scale of infinity. The limits of our perception don't allow, nor do they require us, to directly sense this truth from a sensory aspect. Sure, there are finite things, but they are within the scale of infinity that we don't generally incorporate into our perception of things. It's analogous to looking at a handful of sand and saying that there is a finite amount of sand in your hand. That's true, but you are excluding the beach from which you picked up the sand. There are beaches within beaches out there, and all we see is the handful of sand we disconnect from the whole and choose to see or analyze. Realizing the true nature of unity and infinity in nature and in oneself is real to the observer, and yet no more real than a dream to another who doesn't see it. It is hard to explain dreams, let alone the truth of reality, and have someone else understand them. This is the teacher's dilemma. The barriers are there and we put them up ourselves. It's hard to explain this in words, because our thoughts make it into something that thought has created, that is easier for the mind to take in, not what it actually is. Water and light combine to create plants and animals just as well as they do to create rainbows. It's difficult to see the process, but easy to see the results. The infinite universe is quite the context to live in, because by living in the universe we are logically more than simply a fragmented part of it, but are actually the whole universe. Viewing the universe as yourself allows both concepts to exist as a single, complete, and beautiful movement of reality.

In the Middle of Nothing and Everything

Zero is the balance point between the negative and the positive, effectively canceling out each of them. Two equal and opposing waves in direct conflict with each other cancel each other out completely in destructive interference. Waves of sound, when out of phase, can create silence, just as waves of light out of phase can create areas of darkness. The Maya discovered the concept of zero centuries ahead of the Asian and Arab cultures that brought it to the Europeans. The number zero is central to both mathematics and physics. Scientists remain on a quest to ascertain the temperature of absolute zero. Remember that when energy waves cease they become infinite, so absolute zero would mean infinite temperature, and thus the conditions theorized to exist inside a black hole. Absolute zero exists, but zero movement or stillness is also infinite motion and stillness. If the waves of electromagnetic energy (light and heat) reach zero, the energy increases to infinity—that is, the frequency/wavelength of the energy becomes infinite. In terms of simple math, $0+0$, $0-0$, $0/0$, and $0x0$ all equal zero. Using integers, negative zero and positive zero are exactly the same and are neutral between the positive and negative qualities. Zero may or may not be considered a number. It is not a prime number and is not considered an even number either, although in a sense it could be viewed as the most balanced and unchanging number. That's because zero is indivisible and all numbers are unaffected when divided by zero, if zero is accepted as a number instead of a place holder where there is no whole number. A scale with nothing on either side is in perfect balance. The Buddhist Nirvana is a sense of nothingness or emptiness and its corresponding infinite potential. The concept of zero is used by physicists to describe super-symmetry and singularities, such as black holes and the universe before the Big Bang. This is a good description of the universe as being one invisible and indivisible creation. Zero is variously used as a symbol for infinity, nothingness, and wholeness.

2=1+1

One plus one is two; so far so good. However, we tend to think of the number two as one solid number instead of as the numbers that create it. It isn't really the number two, but two ones. This may all seem achingly elementary and beside the point, but concrete concepts of finiteness, plurality and duality lay at the heart of all dogmatic logic, mathematics and hence the scientific method. Numbers are a describer or language of quantity, intensity, and magnitude. The prime numbers, the infinite number of building blocks for all other numbers that can only be divided by themselves or one, can be seen as wave formations, like atoms, that change, not unlike cymatics experiments which suddenly leap forward into a new formation when vibrating a medium such as sand or water as it passes a certain scale, energy level, or frequency. I believe the number one should be considered as a prime number and, indeed, the most important prime number, as it creates all other numbers into infinity. Like zero and infinity, the number one is often excluded and, with respect to the prime numbers, one is overlooked. The word "prime" means of first importance, so should it not stand to reason that the first prime be the first number there is—namely one? The prime numbers start with the number two because two has no common divisor except unity. Division always has the exception of unity, because one cannot be divided into another whole number. I propose the number one is the main oversight to solving the mystery of the primes.

Note that in our current view of numbers, one is a scale up from zero and a scale down from ten. All numbers are a scale of zero, one, and infinity, so the number one should be considered the first prime number. For mathematicians' purposes, calculating primes with the number one included may seem like a step leading to infinity and nowhere, which is exactly where mathematics leads them. Primes self-organize along the number line. Where the next one may pop up in the number line is unpredictable, because they are an emergent phenomenon. The main problem with mathematicians is that they view numbers as fixed. Pick a number and anyone will tell you it cannot be changed; in other words, it is dead. However, you can take that number and change it through interactions with other numbers. It's not the numbers that are important, but their relationships. Through interaction and relation, numbers become completely alive and transformative. Numbers are not the idyllic symbols in our head, but rather entities that are dynamic, emergent, and unpredictable. Think of how, in origami, one piece of paper, like the number one, can fold and flip into so many different facets and figures.

If one were to relate the waveform to the prime numbers, as the primes are related to atomic waveforms, then the primes, interfering with each other, would create all of the variety of numbers emerging from the number one. We see numbers as we see particles, individually and distinct from each other; however, they are completely interwoven into one another by means of infinite waves or fractions. Attempting to define numbers or atoms without relation to each other is ultimately pointless, rendering numbers and standing waves of energy (or atoms) distinct and yet also quite indistinguishable from each other. The difference between one and two, or any whole numbers, is, fractionally speaking, infinite. The ends containing this narrow and vast abyss between one and two are what create their relationship, such that we can then compare the relationship "between two things" to the relationship of each thing with itself. The "ends" of infinity are made of a single creation. Euclid proved that there are an infinite number of primes by taking any prime and adding the number one to it. Since primes cannot be divided into other primes, this means that there are infinitely many indivisible primes. These numbers exist as iterations of the number one, which is a fusion of zero and infinity. The problem with predicting or solving the layout of prime numbers on the number line is that they only exist when related. They pose no problem to themselves. They aren't counting and attempting to provide themselves with poof of their existence and place in relation to other numbers; we are. We are the ones with the problems. This relates not just to numbers, but to everything. Any number greater than one is still one, but to a human observer it is separate, with one in a particular spot and two or more being given different labels and separated from this single constituent. Any quantity greater than one is a magnification of one. Like a cell simultaneously dividing and multiplying we focus on the divisions of reality instead of the multiplications. All numbers are fractal, whole, infinite, and singular.

The Ether—The Formless Foundation of Reality

General relativity was believed to do away with the ancient idea of the medium through which all things travel. Interestingly enough, in both quantum physics and classical physics the notion of an ether, quantum vacuum energy, or energy of nothingness where waves and all things exist, is gaining popularity and credibility. Some say this is space-time itself and was first mentioned by a Dutch physicist by the name of Christiaan Huygens, a contemporary of Newton, born in 1629. Huygens disagreed with Newton and stated that light was a wave that traveled through what he called the "luminiferous ether."

Since we have been talking about the smallest of the small, I should ask a question that has to do with a certain dogma relating to space, and that is: is empty space really empty? Gas, liquid, solid, plasma, and so on are all states that are actually only different concentrations of atoms in a given space at a given time. These states are more or less the same. The most solid of states (technically there is no such thing, because states, just as life, are always moving), when looked under the microscope, is still basically empty. A vacuum void of gas particles and atoms is actually close to the opposite of our classical view of emptiness. Given the all-pervasive electromagnetic/gravitational and other energy fields, a true vacuum would seem completely idealized and imaginary however, the matter and energy we can observe and interact with could simply be pronounced manifestations of vacuum energy. We would then only be able to observe these pronouncements of reality and not the underlying ground from which the things we interact with (including ourselves) spring, much like noticing a thing in the air but not the air, or few rough grains of sand on smooth glass but not the glass. Furthermore, the vacuum energy or potential energy in one cubic centimeter is unimaginably vast. It has as much potential energy as the entirety of the universe so far able to be observed by our telescopes. It is suggested that empty space may be made up of Planck-scale black holes or singularities so tightly packed together, or one singularity superimposed throughout, that they create and destroy time and space simultaneously and instantly. This is why the blackness and emptiness of space seems so totally void of anything, because we can't sense it at all. It is everything at the same time, in the same space, throughout our universe. This stretches the imagination as well as rationality and sanity, but it does resonate with some scientists on the forefront of quantum and astrophysics, and it is entirely within the realm of possibility. Logic and reason usually tend toward the paradox of infinity and nothingness, yet many scientists dismiss them time and again. Scientists, the religious, and everyone in between all have their self-designed versions of reality that blur and hide the truth in one way or another.

A Drop Is the Ocean

How many drops of water can be removed from the ocean before it ceases to be an ocean? Is it in fact an ocean? One can remove far more than a drop and still have an ocean. What about a million or a trillion drops? What about a million-trillion? If one removes all the water from the ocean except for a single drop, is it still an ocean? The ocean is in every drop of water. The part is the whole, and vice versa. This example illustrates the composite nature of infinity and what we are in the universe. A slice of infinity is all of infinity, and fractals are exponential. Infinity divided by any number will always remain infinite, just as any number divided by zero is likewise unaffected. This is worth mulling over.

Allow me to explain how one can look at a finite object as infinite and unbounded. An object is seen as separate from another by the spaces between them. This is intuitive, whenever we see something we differentiate it from something else that we perceive to be "unconnected" to it. A cup is a finite and separate object from the table on which it rests. However, one could consider it from the point of view of looking at the morning fog on the "surface" of a lake. The fog is "part" of the lake, but it becomes fuzzy when one tries to say that it is the surface. Under the microscope, the hydrogen and oxygen atoms that make up the water molecules are intermingling with each other and with the molecules in the atmosphere. Similarly, with all objects at a quantum or Planck level of observation or beyond, atoms begin to become fuzzy and wavelike. When one also considers that the matter that all objects are made of is just different concentrations of energy, it becomes apparent that the energy fields in the cup, the table, and the atmosphere, namely electromagnetic and gravitational fields, the quantum vacuum, and virtual particles, are what the cup, the table, the atmosphere, and everything else that exists are actually made of. Matter is just more concentrated energy. Like the wind, we can't see all the energy or the tiny nitrogen and oxygen particles in the air all around us because they are too small or don't reflect enough light to be picked up by our eyes and registered by our brains. We can't see pure water either except for the distortions light makes as it passes through it. An object is to energy as a mountain is to dust. We can see the mountain and identify it, say "there it is," but dust is almost impossible to see unless sunlight is reflected off it within our line of sight. Objects can be looked at as finite, but they should be put into context, which is the infinite energy and process of the universe. We casually observe and, in effect, cloudily misconceive this skin of ourselves and nature, as we segregate objects and view them as separate—as anything other than the entirely and inclusively beautiful, and call these things the known in science, in faith, and in life itself.

Simple Is to Complex as Order Is to Disorder

It's not complicated it's just a lot of it.

(Richard Feynman, in *Take the World from a Different Point of View* interview, 1972)

Order is to disorder as simple is to complex. They are two aspects of the same thing. Chaos isn't just chaos but a fractal order. Chaos is a term used for the changes or disturbances in a dynamic and sensitive system, as in nature, that grow in magnitude where the system is more or less simple and contained in its parameters and variables but nevertheless exhibits wildly elaborate, unpredictable, and incomprehensible behavior. These chaotic systems that we consider separate from other events in nature are creations of simplification and categorization devised by and for the mind in our attempt to try to grasp and understand reality, because in nature and in the universe there are really no contained or separate systems, just those that are more related or less related to the observer and their observations. Chaos is order, because chaos isn't truly random, but is merely complex, sensitive, and dynamic. Chaos is naturally and primarily unpredictable, but so is simplicity multiplied by every movement fed back or affecting its motion.

Perceived chaotic systems possess endless variety, diversity, and freedom to become braided or interwoven into themselves, where order is seen as any pattern of a more comprehensible kind that is achingly obvious and straightforward. As described by Murray Gell-Mann (1994) in *The Quark and the Jaguar,* simplicity means "once folded," while complexity means "braided together." We see simplicity as a raindrop and complexity as a thunderstorm. Both are both. Laws or constants are to chance as order and simplicity are to disorder and complexity. Laws or truths are free to do what they will and mingle throughout or among themselves. They express themselves in the flow of creative universal consciousness. Entropy, or macroscopic events tending toward what we perceive as disorder, is said to make time asymmetrical. This leads one to believe that time does not flow in one direction. Simple systems give rise to complex behavior, and vice versa. What our minds generally perceive as disorder is just order on a different scale. Keep in mind the symmetries of fractal geometry. Nothing is random, no matter what we think. The universe is freedom and consequently we tend to view it as random or chaotic, mostly because of its complexity and unpredictability. Everything is governed by the consciousness of beauty, from the curl of a smoke cloud to one's thoughts and feelings to the flock of birds overhead that moves as one.

Heat seems chaotic in its entropic and thermodynamic radiation, where cold seems more orderly, constant, and aligned, as in the crystallization of common ice. Randomness seems uncertain and wild, although it's really just misconceived order, like the feeling of being inside an invisible cloud. Form and order emerge from the dance of symmetrical opposites. However, the opposites are used to define convenience, when the emphasis should be placed not on this illusory polarity but on the more complete reality of the unitary dance and the relationship between them. Opposites don't exist separately; rather there exists only the truth of unity that underlies the relationship between them. Our brains create these divisive oppositions. A shadow puppet can exist in so many different shapes and sizes when viewed against a backlit wall; however, in three dimensions, it is one single shape in motion. This is the same as our universe, where we see a limited dimension with such seemingly incomprehensible variety instead of seeing the singular comprehensive dimension from which all this variety emerges, the way the visible spectrum of white light contains all the colors that we can see, yet we still have difficulty in fully grasping the blurred shades that combine them, the unity among them. This is the relationship, dance, or process of the universe. It is creating, discovering, flowering, or awakening to itself like any artist does and, if we intentionally and carefully observe, we can see that everyone and everything *is*.

The Spectrum of Wave Form and Function— A Unified Polarization

From the perspective of physics, it is the interaction of the surface tension that pulls the water into a sphere, and the up and down movement of the plate creating 'push and pull' forces acting upon the mass of water, that is responsible for the process of formation. It is precisely at the moment of balance between the two polar forces, where the pushing force is already acting and the contracting surface tension can no longer hold the water together, that the form-building occurs. In the smallest drops, when the amount of water is below a critical limit, the surface tension prevails so that despite the impulses acting on the drop, it remains spherical and does not experience change in shape.

(Alexander Lauterwasser, *Water Sound Images: The Creative Music of the Universe*, 2007)

All things can be described as waves. Quantum waves, brainwaves, water, sound, the list goes on. But what is a wave, really? It's a mix of the obvious and the wonderful, to be sure. It involves the absence and presence of movement, frequency, and wavelength of a certain size, speed, and energy. For a wave, like perhaps no other phenomenon, presence and absence are the same thing, because one cannot exist without the other. They are inseparable. Both are inextricably interconnected, because they are the same thing observed from different points of view, in much the same way some people have a proclivity toward finding boredom while others can't seem to find it anywhere they look. A wave is naturally polarized as it oscillates in back and forth, ebb and flow, and in longitudinal/latitudinal motions. When the tip or extreme of a crest or pole is reached, the opposite force of the wave takes control and brings the energy back to create an opposing crest; this is a characteristic of all waves and vibration, and it explains many things in our cyclic and rhythmic life. There can be a destructive interference pattern (two waves of equal frequency but with opposing phases), which cancels out the wave completely if the crest matches a trough, and vice versa. And of course, there is *always* a vice versa! This destructive interference leaves a flat line or a node(s) in a standing wave with little to no vibration all in the midst of two perhaps very powerful waves. When two or more waves have coinciding frequencies, and phases or crests and troughs that match in size and periodicity, this creates constructive amplification patterns that double the magnitude of the wave pattern. Thus, amplitude is directly impacted by the superposition of two or more waves, which create a single magnified wave when in a supporting relationship with each other. Crests are the opposite of troughs, but in a higher perspective of reality it can be said that crests are equivalent to troughs, just as a valley exists only between the mountains which defines it. In short, crests and troughs are precisely the same when viewed from a non-dualistic perspective.

The Ripples Are the Water

If a water surface is set into motion by irregular impulses—for example through the shaking of a water glass—or if several waves are superimposed, perhaps through reflections of a wave at a shore wall, an unordered surging of different waves develops that leaves the viewer with an impression of unrest and chaos. But if a container is set to oscillate through a regular, consistent—like a sine wave of constant frequency—a wave movement will develop with a

definite and constant wavelength... In such a case
where the movement impulses do not disturb and
irritate each other, a stable structure can develop. The
observer gets the impression that the pattern is not
moving, rather that it 'stands' in equilibrium—and all
this in the midst of intense vibration and movement.

(Alexander Lauterwasser, *Water Sound Images:*
The Creative Music of the Universe, 2007)

The speed of light/presence of light is the same as the absence of light, also called darkness. On the quantum scale, waves rule. Since scale is fractal and self-similar, we can say that waves rule all scales. Quantum particles exist in a waveform or superposition of possibility, and as soon as this wave is observed it collapses, creating the individual particles of an observable reality. There are varied wavelengths and frequencies of electromagnetic energy. There are also gravitational and sound waves, plus many more types of waves. All waveforms that constitute reality are a dual appearance of singularity seen as symmetrical vibrations of crests and troughs. It is worthy to note that all of these waves more or less coexist without strongly affecting each other. We can see objects in varying degrees of brightness and color, feel heat by a fireplace, listen to the radio, get an X-ray scan, cook a hot dog in the microwave, and feel no discernable interference between any these waves. This is because they are all the same wave with varying degrees of length and frequency, which seems to matter little in terms of interference. Each domain has a specific frequency. They are interfering so harmoniously that there is no interference. Amazingly, there can be infinitely many waveforms existing in one specific location at the same time! The superposition of waves is elegantly beautiful in that it combines fractal geometry, superposition, entanglement, and infinity (just look at any cymatic image if you doubt this). If all things are made of waves, then this beauty of formation from oscillating energy is a perfectly natural behavior for waves to have. The frequencies of waves that create various atoms are analogous to the frequencies of the electromagnetic waves that present color.

The Stream That Ponders Itself

Everything can be explained with waves. A sine wave is a unique wave that occurs in physics, math, music, and elsewhere. Sine waves are unique because there is no interference of any kind when other sine waves of any number and of the same amplitude and periodicity are incorporated into each other. It is the only waveform that is able to remain as it was when other waves are joined to it. Sine waves are seen in light waves, waves of countless interacting water molecules, and sound waves. Translate a circle into a waveform and you get a sine wave. A sine wave in three dimensions creates a sphere. Oscillating stationary or standing waves have constant nodes at their axes, mean, or point of origin and a constant amplitude, and are a main means—if not the only means—for material creation.

PART 5

THE ELEGANCE BEHIND THE BEAUTY

*Surprisingly, everything in the universe moves
through the four-dimensional fabric of space and
time at exactly the same speed—the speed of light!
No matter what is moving, or how fast, change
in motion through spacetime remains absolutely
zero—no matter what.*

(K.C. Cole, *The Hole in the Universe: How Scientists Peered over
the Edge of Emptiness and Found Everything,* 2001)

Electromagnetism—Let There Be Light!

Light gives us our insights into the nature of reality. This makes sense because it is increasingly becoming apparent that everything is, in one way or another, a form of light. Almost all religious creation myths refer to light as primary and divine using the expression of en*light*enment when one has seen truth or God from the previously unknown darkness. In 1543, Nicolaus Copernicus published his observations on the movements of the blinding orb of light in our day sky, which proved that we revolve around the Sun and not the other way around. At the beginning of the 20th century, Albert Einstein gave birth to his relativity and quantum theories which rest on the absolute speed of light and the idea of the photon. Indeed, energy is equivalent to mass when mass is multiplied by the speed of light squared. The speed of light squared is the linchpin that unites matter with energy. How light moves revealed to early scientists the waves/particle behavior of matter. In 1666, Isaac Newton's splitting of light into its constituent colors with a prism allowed for a better understanding of what visible light is made of. James Clerk Maxwell (1831-1879) proved, in part by using the *field theory* invented by Michael Faraday, that electricity and magnetism were two forms of the same thing and that visible light was itself a thin slice of electromagnetic radiation. Our eyes are what give us most of the information about our surroundings. Looking up, we can bring far-away light up close through the magnifying lenses of telescopes which reveal things in the universe previously unimagined such as distant planets, stars and galaxies. Looking down, microscopes revealed the world of the micro cosmos shedding light, so to speak, upon the minutest of microbes, cells and atoms. All of these inquiries into the nature of light have improved our understanding of our world through new ways of looking at it. Simply put, light allows us to observe reality; it inspires the exploration of truth and beauty and it is at the center of life.

The visible section of light in the electromagnetic spectrum can be analogous to comparing the width of an atom to the height of the CN Tower, where white light is a superposition of all the colors of the rainbow. Red light has a wavelength of .00007 cm, violet is .00004 cm long, infrared is .00008 to .032 cm, which we feel as heat, and ultraviolet has a wavelength from .00003 to .000001 cm long. The spectrum of the electromagnetic field as we understand it now, from largest to smallest wavelength, is: radio waves, microwaves, infrared, visible, ultraviolet, X radiation, and gamma radiation. We would not exist if it were not for electromagnetism. The electromagnetic spectrum can be perceived to begin at the Planck- or quantum-scaled wavelength and reach wavelengths as large as the universe. It is worth emphasizing that the spectrum has no definite beginning or ending, because the magnitudes or wavelengths of electromagnetic energy extend into the infinite and infinitesimal, meaning that the finite scale we confine to this continuum as being the beginning and ending of the spectrum cease to have any foundation in reality. The larger and smaller wavelengths have no limit to how small and energetic, or how large and weak they can be. They are continuous, without origin or conclusion. Don't let the linear diagrams beginning with radio waves and ending with gamma rays fool you. Now, when I say "wavelength," try to imagine the varying wavelengths as the concentric shells of a jawbreaker, since electromagnetic waves radiate in every direction. Amazingly, each wavelength has its own frequency or speed of vibration, pressure, temperature, energy level, and place in space-time. This electromagnetic jawbreaker is infinite, but each shell has its place, form, and function. However, unlike a jawbreaker in the finite sense, electromagnetic energy is scattered across the universe in an infinitely more interconnected and dynamically energized sense, like the dance of the rainbow on the film of a soap bubble, tangled ubiquitously like a ball of yarn, awash in all dimensions throughout the universe. The frequency or wavelength is what gives the energy its form and appearance. Iron atoms vibrate at a certain frequency, and because of this we perceive them, when concentrated and many, as solid, hard, and red (when reacting with the energy frequency of oxygen); meanwhile, with electromagnetic energy, colors such as blue and red are simply varying frequencies of energy that our mind interprets as blue or red accordingly.

The Sea of a Single Wave

Scottish physicist James Clerk Maxwell (1831-1879) is credited with developing mathematical equations to show that electricity and magnetism are not separate phenomena, but a singular phenomenon with dual aspects. The carrier of this energy is the photon wave/particle in an electromagnetic field, which is absolutely everywhere. In field theory, an idea created by British physicist Michael Faraday (1791-1867), a photon doesn't travel like a bullet from one place to another, but is considered a wiggle or disturbance of the electromagnetic field traveling as a wave of energy, the way the jiggle of a Slinky sends energy throughout its length. In this sense, photons are not really particles or waves but a twitch in an energetic field the size of the universe. This means that photons of light, as classically perceived quantized chunks of radiation from the Sun, do not travel from the Sun, through space, to reach Earth eight minutes later, but the jiggle from the Sun travels through the electromagnetic field or ubiquitous Slinky, and we see this as light and feel this as heat on Earth. Within quantum field theory, the amazingly successful theory explaining the interactions of the electromagnetic field with electrons and their anti-particle positrons is called quantum electrodynamics. Whether subject and object, energy and matter, particles in space-time and waves in fields, or magnetism and electricity, all appear distinct and split from each other, but they are really the same. Electromagnetism is a feedback/emergent scenario in which the magnetic field creates an electric current and an electric current creates a magnetic field. Calling electromagnetism either electricity or magnetism is not unlike calling water either hydrogen or oxygen when it is both. Magnetism and electricity amplify each other because they are feeding on themselves like the ouroboros (tail-swallowing snake). They are never separate, just different forms or aspects, the way fog is a low-lying cloud and rain is just condensed, heavy, and falling clouds. This aspect of the singular force is accountable for many things in our daily lives. The forces involved with atoms, of which we are made, can be traced to electromagnetism, as every proton and electron in an atom has an electric charge. Everything we perceive with our senses, every vista, touch, smell, sound, taste, hug, kiss, emotion, laugh, thought, is attributable to electromagnetism. Electricity has opposing negative and positive orientations, as does Earth's planetary magnetism with its north and south orientations.

More Than Meets the Eye

Light is timeless, motionless, constant, absolute and at rest, like the universe. Energy is equivalent to mass when the velocity of mass is the speed of light squared. Electromagnetism travels at 299,792,458 kilometers per second in a vacuum (more or less, because although particles can be taken out of a specific space, energy and gravity waves are impossible to negate in any space). One light year is exactly 9,460,730,472,580.8 kilometers. It is a traditional measure of distance, not time, as the word "year" would have one infer, although space and time are the same; light travels this distance in one year. The starlight we see may have taken thousands of years to reach us, and galaxies far away, seen with the Hubble Space Telescope, may be billions of light years away. Think of just under ten trillion kilometers that light travels per year multiplied by billions of light years. A rudimentary way of estimating how long visible light has taken to reach our eyes is, if an object is one light year away, the light we see from it would have left on its journey to us one year ago. The Hubble Space Telescope can see objects roughly ten billion light years away, or ten billion years back into space-time. Light, as with everything else, behaves as both a wave and a particle. It stands to reason that the fastest thing in our space-time existence is perceived to be light. This does not coincide with the entanglement observation in quantum physics where time does not exist; light with its finite speed is based on time. It is all instantaneous. The brain, a finite observational tool, perceives things in a finite range that forms the basis for our construction of reality. Speed without observation is infinite, thus instantaneous. This is why photons have no relationship with time, because light doesn't really exist in a finite reality alone. Light and all matter as specific particles and as infinite probability waves are at home (except for the observations of humans, and, I presume, of many other life forms) in both aspects of the finite and infinite world, which is why they behave as both finite particles and infinite waveforms.

We see the whole of visible light as white. The page you are looking at is white because it reflects the entire visible spectrum from a source of light such as a lamp into your eyes while the words absorb the full visible spectrum making them slightly hotter than the rest of the page. This is why on a hot day you know to wear white clothing instead of black to stay cool. The frequency of waves hitting our eyes that we can detect and react to is roughly 600 trillion waves, crest to trough, per second. Sound is to your favorite song as light is to your favorite painting. However obvious these truths may be, they are worth mentioning because they show how beautiful and awe-inspiring something so simple and common can be. White light is a very narrow collection of wavelengths that, when split up, we see as color. Colors, which we see so distinctly, are just different aspects, intensities, or scales of the same thing. All colors are vibrations, as are smells, tastes, and so on. They are playful distributors and forms of energy, as they are all made up of energy, which we then react to through one or more of our senses. If there were no interaction, we wouldn't sense anything. Note that we don't actually look at any object; we only look at the number and intensity of the photons that enter the small reverse flashlights we call eyes. Imagine a time when something was touching you, and because you and it didn't move for a time you lost the sense of it's touching you at all. If all things were uniform and constant, we would not be able to sense anything. It is truly a great thing that we have a capacity for distinguishing contrast.

Light Is Hot and Loud

What happens when photons enter our eyes? They pass through the lens into the pupil and reach the back of the eye, or retina, where they jiggle millions of rods and cones, and this jiggling is then translated into an electrochemical signal that creates a little lightning storm in the brain, which is then interpreted by the brain as an image that, one hopes, we can make sense of. Reality, when translated into an image in the mind's eye, can be likened to lightning and thunder. We absorb figments of reality through many psychological refining and distilling methods to gain a comprehensible perception. We are thus only experiencing the thunder without the lightning because of the process which brings reality to us as conscious observers. When reality is observed in this way, our way of viewing reality essentially becomes our emergent and often dualistic and conflictive feelings, viewpoints, and emotions. We observe reality through the filters of our thought process, which split the now into the past and future and categorize life into subjects and objects. As a consequence, our accumulated knowledge, self, or ego allows access only to a thunderous remnant, an echoed silhouette of reality. The lightning of complete reality, including the observer, exists only in the present moment, and can only be clearly seen and left pristine when the mind is peaceful, silent, open, and at rest.

Together, light and heat stream down on us from the Sun continually. There is one day: Sunday, all day, everyday. Just by seeing that the Sun shines on our spinning Earth and allows life on it to flourish should be enough to instill a deep sense of awe. We see the beauty in our everyday lives as less than miraculous simply because we see it as old, familiar or bourgeois.

An increase in pressure increases heat and thus light. Pressure, temperature, and electromagnetism are essentially different names describing the same phenomenon. Even light and dark are the same thing only with variable intensities. Many people think light and dark are completely different, but they are fundamentally the same. Light red and dark red are just the same as light grey and dark grey, because the only thing that differentiates light from dark is the intensity. A dark color is simply less intense in brightness than a lighter color. Light is both wave and particle just as water droplets are water waves. A single photon interacts with itself. One raindrop is a rainstorm in and of itself. There is no fundamental distinction between a raindrop and a rainstorm, because one emerges from the other and thus they are basically equivalent, just as a bee is the hive, a bird is the flock, a grain of sand is the beach, and you are the universe.

Gamma, X, and radio waves, microwaves, heat, color, and so on are merely either slower or faster, or less or more energetic distributions of electromagnetic energy. Higher frequencies give rise to the particles used in nuclear reactions and in stars, cooking them into different forms of particular energies. Pressure and heat mash simple atoms together to form other more exotic atoms, like sunlight being made into plants, animals, coal and petroleum, which in turn are made by man into solvents, rubbers, and plastics that can be endlessly transformed. Energy is versatile. Pressure and heat turn steel into a liquid, just as the absence of pressure and heat turns lava into stone. Sand is just small stones. Mountains are just hardened lava from the Earth's core, and in time these will be broken down and eroded into rocks and sand. Diamonds are the same as everything I just mentioned, but more pure in their carbon content. That's all. Indeed, all life forms are made of carbon and its cycle of movement throughout the biosphere is crucial to all of Earth's inhabitants. Plants, animals and single-celled organisms retain carbon in their bodies from the atmosphere and food they eat and release it during respiration, their decomposition and combustion such as burning wood or fossil fuels which then dissolves into the water. With the recent advent of the fossil fuel age, we have greatly disturbed this carbon cycle. All the carbon that is taken in and released in all life on Earth came from the stars. It's why the Sun shines and why you feel good when you are bathed by it. We refract or break the light of observation into categories, classifications, names, and the like when we are made to radiate and reflect it.

Red Is a Certain Shade of White

We see the color red and we can easily agree that it is indeed red and we should call it by its commonly agreed-upon handle. The color red is, very simply, the longest wavelength in the visible range of the electromagnetic spectrum, with a wavelength roughly .00007 centimeters long, wide, or deep. Any wavelength longer than the wavelengths of the color red is categorized as infrared and cannot be seen by the naked eye. Hug someone, rub your hands together or sit next to a fire until you feel infrared radiation as heat. We see heat as a distortion or shimmering of visible light, such as a mirage in the desert. That is the part of the electromagnetic spectrum that is closest to red and just outside our visual range called infrared. The activity of every cell in ones' body culminates as body heat which is about ninety-nine degrees Fahrenheit. Heat is just as red as any other color, but we see these colors differently instead of feeling them. Red is different from blue only because its waves are more ripple-like or tsunami-like. Red has a tendency to evoke strong emotional reactions and is one of the most evocative colors in the visible spectrum. It is associated with heat, energy, blood, anger, passion, love, and fire. Blood is red due to the oxidized iron content in hemoglobin. Red is also the first color or energy wavelength in the spectrum to be absorbed by seawater. The old saying about "seeing red" relates to anger because it is an emotion that gets our blood flowing. In Chinese mythology, the color red represents fire. It can also represent anarchism and communism. Red gets our attention when extra awareness may be needed and is often used for warning signs, the most common being stop signs and stoplights. The color red advertises the ripeness of some fruits, and the red petals of flowers draw the attention of pollinators so that they will drink their nectar, fertilizing the plants in the process. It also advertises the highly poisonous characteristics of some creatures in order to warn away predators. Plants and animals use a specific frequency of electromagnetic energy to reflect back to an observer in order to defend or conceal themselves in the process. Red is attractive to birds because they see light most similarly to humans, while insects see things in a more blue/ultraviolet range. In astronomy, objects moving away from an observer exhibit a Doppler or red shift because the light is stretched; making the wavelengths longer, less frequent and red in appearance. The Hopi have three symbols for important coming events for the Earth. The first two are the swastika and the Sun, and the last is represented by the color red, which is considered in the Native American medicine wheel to be an energy giver.

A decrease or increase in light is not only that. Like all opposites, the truth is in the shades between these mental concepts, because complete dark and complete light don't really exist by themselves; nothing does. The threshold of reality is between opposites, which is the pivot of the fruition of understanding. It is the eternal moment in which contraction meets expansion and where all other opposites are connected.

Stars—The Self-Organization of Gas and Dust

In addition to gas and dust, which are the ingredients of stars, galaxies can contain billions and even trillions of stars. Our Milky Way galaxy alone contains over 400 billion of these bright celestial wonders. Galaxies, stars, and everything on the surface of the Earth are all held together by gravity. Stars would not form, our planet would not spin, and we would not be able to move if it weren't for the attractive properties of gravity, or curved space-time. New stars are "born" from "dead" stars. It is movement which is the foundation of creation. Stars are born of condensing gas and dust and unpredictable violence. Stars are born from the subtle and not so subtle force of gravity.

The forces at work here, and everywhere, are so precise that if there were off by an unfathomably miniscule fraction the universe would cease to be in balance and would fall from its precarious flux of equilibrium and into certain oblivion.

Everything we have on Earth including the Earth itself came into existence from the processes of the generation of stars. The air we breathe and the water we drink are the "waste" from the explosive radiation and redistribution of star stuff. There is a time in a star's life called the "main sequence," which is about halfway through its lifecycle, and this is where we are today in terms of our star. The force of gravity pushes against gravitational collapse, creating equilibrium. A star's commonly perceived form begins, lives, and ends as a singularity. It is a choreographed, determined, and yet open and unpredictable emergent experience. There is a certain relation to homeostasis in this aspect of the equilibrium maintained by stars. Once a new star is born and lives out its life cycle, if it is a large star, it will explode as a supernova. This is an example of the self-emerging character of the universe and all of the processes in it. In this way stars can actually change their own environment, exactly the way emergent species can change their environment, as we are doing with such disastrous results. Energy evolves into stars through sophisticated self-regulating and emergent processes.

$E=mc^2$ Transformers

Atoms such as carbon, oxygen, hydrogen, nitrogen, and all the other elements that are essential for life as we know it are created or mashed together by the process of nuclear reactions that we see as stars. Some stars end in explosions called supernovas which create all of the heavier elements such as gold and uranium. Our Sun takes hydrogen atoms, the simplest and lightest of elements, with only one electron and one proton and, with heat and pressure, combines them in what is called nuclear fusion or stellar nucleosynthesis, creating helium atoms. As helium is created, the extra energy is given off as photons. These helium atoms later combine to form carbon, oxygen, calcium, iron, and the other atoms that are the building blocks of all life. Ultimately they go on to merge into other elements and continue all the way to carbon, the chemical basis of life and, finally, iron, the last element to be created by nucleosynthesis. The nucleus of the iron atom is relatively stable and is useless to a star's fusion process, as the fusion of the iron nuclei would require more energy input than the star would receive, so the star continues fusing other atomic nuclei into iron as its natural ceiling or limit to this process. All other heavier elements beyond iron require much more energy to fuse their nuclei and are thus created not by the constraints of temperature and pressure in nucleosynthesis but by unimaginably high-energy supernova explosions caused by the abrupt gravitational collapse of a large star, the largest and most energetic explosions in the universe. Only supernovas can create elements heavier than iron, for example, nickel, silver, gold, lead, zinc, and argon. They can also create heavy and radioactive elements and lightly sprinkle them onto planets like Earth, elements such as uranium and even trace amounts of plutonium, the main components of atomic bombs. These elements have great energy density and are highly radioactive. Atomic bombs are essentially very tiny stars.

Supernovas, Neutron Stars, and Gamma Ray Bursts

A supernova is the explosion that occurs when a star is in its final stage of life and has reached a sort of critical mass in which the star's gravity collapses into itself. At that point, it either turns into a singularity and creates a black hole or creates yet another one of the largest explosions since the Big Bang. Supernovas are agents of cataclysmic change, for better or for worse. The Milky Way galaxy is overdue for a supernova, which occurs about once every century per galaxy.

By way of gravitational collapse, a star may also change itself into an unimaginably dense and compact star known as a neutron star, effectively creating a mass of neutrons by fusing together the constituents of atoms: electrons and protons. These neutrons can fly clear through our planet. With no electric charge, that are essentially invisible, as they do not react to electromagnetism or light. When any large star dies, its heavier materials and strongest energy is radiated into space, and thus when later generations of stars are formed, some of that material and energy coalesces into rocky planets. If one of those rocky planets, such as Earth, then happens to lie in the habitable zone (not too hot or cold), it may generate a stable enough environment to sustain organic life, and indeed allow plants and animals such as us to flourish.

Gravity

In what is called the first great unification of physics, Sir Isaac Newton created a theory of gravitation that united the attraction of things on Earth, toward the Earth to the movements of moons and planets. As obvious as it is to us today, this is still a huge leap of insight into nature. Gravity is the attraction of everything. It creates every size and form that planets, stars and galaxies exhibit. Gravity exists in and with a star through its entire life from dust to star to dust again, and in a wider sense allows everything in the universe to exist. It is why we have an Earth and why there are stars and why everything on Earth doesn't go floating off into space. It is responsible for our orbit around the Sun and every other orbit in the universe, including those of electrons and all other sub-atomic particles.

Gravity isn't really considered a force but an effect of space-time curvature. The theory best explaining this phenomenon is the Theory of General Relativity, which states that gravity is the warping of space-time caused by anything with mass, and since mass and energy are, in essence, the same, energy and gravitational fields naturally interfere. Einstein, in his General Theory of Relativity, states that space and time are altered by mass. Gravitational fields obey the inverse square law. In other words, if one doubles the distance from a source of gravity, the energy is spread over four times the area, hence the intensity is reduced to one-fourth. This law is the same for electromagnetic fields. Gravity, like most aspects of physics to the average person, is instinctively thought of as being something "out there," or as a nebulous phenomenon affecting planets and objects from afar. However, like infinity, quarks, or God, gravity is us, front and center. It is everywhere. It is a constant yet changing geometry of space-time. Although it is considered to be a force, it can also be viewed as simply the geometric curvature of space-time. To embrace physics is to confront the ideas of paradox and conclusion. Quantum gravity creates infinities, which mathematicians and physicists don't really care for. They are seen as incalculable and hence incorrect. However, infinities make perfect sense when combining the quantum-scale universe with the large-scale inverse square law of gravity, where the smaller the distance the greater the increase in effect or energy. Zero distance between anything is infinite gravity or quantum gravity. When there is no space between tiny objects with mass at the quantum scale they are literally one and have infinite gravity. Gravity is seen as the weakest force until it is observed at the quantum scale, where it becomes the most powerful force in strength and influence. The intensity by scale gradation is important to the emergence of all other physical phenomenon, including the biological emergence seen in self-organization and natural selection, as well as in the emergence of stars, planets, and galaxies. I feel that God isn't the guy who made the laws in his chambers and set the universe off to follow them, as we may tend to think. These physical truths exist as their own generator and operator without any authority, allowing the balancing tendencies of nature to simply do what they do. These laws are created by the election of each interaction at each stage of emergence, much like any truly self-governing, populous. The law or truth operates on its own. God is this law or truth, seen in all of creation, down to the most minute of aspects in all harmonic things.

Black Holes—The Eye Is the Storm

Matter tells space how to curve, and space tells matter how to move.

(John Wheeler, quoted in Cole, 2001)

Gravitation can, in addition to creating planets and moons, creating and collapsing stars, igniting Supernovas and subsequent neutron stars and forming galaxies, also create black holes. The most bizarre and destructive and quite probably the most creative things in the universe are black holes. The propensity of a star to collapse under its own gravity is delicately countered during its active lifetime by the energy that comes from fusing hydrogen in its core. Once this balance has passed its prime, or main sequence, the process of gravitational collapse will take place. Black holes contain the most immense gravity in the universe and there are millions of them throughout the Milky Way, with a super-massive black hole right at the center of this, and all galaxies. Black holes, shooting out opposing jets of large amounts of matter and energy are believed to give rise to the galaxies in which they reside. This is a perfect example of how nothing is equivalent to everything. Black holes are also called singularities, because the mass and energy is compressed into such a minute space that space and time cease to exist. Think of a speck of dust. Then try to think of something a trillion-trillion-trillion times smaller, and you still aren't even close, because size, distance and movement don't exist wherever space and time don't. Gravitational collapse compresses a very high density of mass and energy into an infinitely small point that eludes even space-time itself. This intense force gobbles up matter and energy when it gets near the point of no return, the boundary past which nothing, including light, can resist the attraction force, which is called the event horizon. Black holes don't have to be large; they can also be microscopic. Furthermore, all black holes emit radiation known as Hawking radiation, named after its discoverer, Stephen Hawking. Black holes normally grow larger by attracting more and more matter and energy, or sometimes by joining with other black holes. Black holes attract each other, just as matter and energy do, to create stars, planets, human beings, and everything that exists. The only way we know black holes exist is by observing their relationship with and effects on the material around them. It is impossible to directly observe black holes because of their complete, 100 percent absorption of everything, including electromagnetism or visible light. Astrophysicists discovered a super-massive black hole at the center of our galaxy, and later found that all galaxies share this phenomenon. Super-massive black holes can be millions to billions of times the mass of our Sun, and the one in the center of our Milky Way is about four million times the mass of the Sun.

The largest black hole discovered to date is larger than eighteen billion solar masses. That is pretty massive for a singularity, or a point of zero size. Black holes are often viewed as existing in deep space and at gargantuan sizes; however black holes could just as easily be infinitesimal, popping in and out of existence inside us and all around us like anti-particles do. Tiny, fleeting black holes, as well as large, longer lasting super-massive black holes could be what the entire universe is made of: nothing or infinite and infinitesimal space-time curvature. This could perhaps aid in explaining the paradoxical view of everything being equivalent to nothing.

According to General Relativity, space-time curvature is responsible for gravity and thus acceleration. If the force of gravity or acceleration is constant and uniform such as in a spinning black hole, it would be at complete rest no matter how fast it is going. I would think that the spin of the black hole, like that of an atom, would have centrifugal force thus possessing the tendency to accelerate its contents away from its centre along the entire, infinitely curved path of its spin. This tendency however, is more or less balanced by the centripetal force of acceleration which has the tendency to accelerate things toward its centre along a continuously curved path.

Black holes are places of infinite gravity, density, space-time curvature, and have zero dimensions, volume and thus zero size. It is interesting that the inverse square equation for the force of gravity/ acceleration is also the same as the law for electromagnetism. Black holes are just parts of the universe we can't see because they don't reflect any light to our eyes the way objects do, but that's the point; black holes are not objects. We don't actually see objects; we only see the light that bounces off them; if no light bounces back, we see only blackness. We can assume that physicist John Wheeler coined the term "black hole" because black absorbs light and a hole denotes emptiness and the unknown. In similar fashion, Dark energy and dark matter are additional names for the unseen and unknown. What we see is something that happens uniquely between the light and our eyes. Keep in mind that the observable universe of regular matter and energy is only four percent of the entire universe, and that is only if one were to look at the entire observable universe all at once. Observing the known four percent of the universe is not possible from the vantage point of individual consciousness. This means that there is only an infinitesimally smaller percentage of that four percent that we can actually assimilate due to our localized slice of experience. Observing life as it is around us and not millions of light years away does not take away from the beauty of this singularity. But if we fail to notice the awesome beauty right in front of our faces, it might as well be millions of light years away, which is coincidently where many see God and Heaven as being located, far away. It is an interesting parallel that ninety-six percent of the universe is unseen and unknown, while ninety-six percent of the world's population believes in some form of faith-based religion, or in some form of higher being. Black holes can also be perceived as a variety of star, because stars are energy and mass transformers in some way or another. So whether we are talking about black holes or the matter and energy they contain or conceal, the known is just as beautiful as the unknown because they are two blurred shades composing the exquisitely united spectrum of reality.

Black holes are commonly viewed as inherently impossible to observe directly. The pupil of an eye is black to an outside observer but not to the person to whom the pupil belongs. That is where the light enters to be transformed by the brain into a conscious electrochemical experience. Black holes appear black, but what if we were to put ourselves in the eyes of the black hole? Would we see everything? We have never seen a black hole, but they exist. We see how black holes relate to empirical observations, which is how we describe them and everything else, in terms of relation. It's the same as describing the hole of a donut. We start by giving the dimensions of its boundary and end up describing the donut instead of the hole. To describe this cosmic donut hole is to describe the donut. Are black holes areas of nothingness? Describing nothing always has the sneaky tendency to end up describing everything. This is interesting because, paradoxically, nothing is everything. Interestingly, in the Bible, the world was manifest as *creato ex nihilo* or "created from nothing." This correlates to the Buddhist view of emptiness and its infinite potential as well as the scientific view that all reality is an emergence from the Big Bang, coming from nothing and the quantum vacuum energy or unbounded potential energy of nothingness. In short, everything came from nothing because they are the same thing. The seed is the forest and it all came from nothing. If the eye of a hurricane is peaceful in the midst of all the motion, what would the eye of a galaxy be like?

Are black holes nonexistence, the absence of presence, the space-time nothing natural philosophers, the religious, and scientists have been seeking for so long? Nonexistence is the absence of existence or the existence of absence and, paradoxically, nothing, and nothingness can never exist by itself; it only exists in unification with everything. The simple fact that reality exists is pretty amazing. If nothing is a concept, then it exists just as readily as concepts like love, fear, money, and hatred do. Black holes are described by their relationship with the existing material around them. We can say that a black hole sucks things in and that is the end of it, or we can say that the size of a black hole is either so many solar masses large or that it is microscopic, but either way we are describing the size of something using anywhere from two to four dimensions of our space-time fabric of reality with which, apparently, the black hole has no relation. We say it is a void of matter so wide and so tall. It is an absence of something. This is a lot like describing nothing. Nothing, like the black hole, can exist in relation to something else which also exists. This is classically seen as a paradox, but if we take the view of infinity as equivalent to nothing, they beautifully complement each other, and the paradox balances itself out, as we have previously seen.

Matter is to space as energy is to time. Einstein pointed out that matter is energy, so matter is what we can see and energy is what moves it, because mass is always moving. Existence is truly a miracle and it is awe-inspiring. Like the chicken and the egg, infinity and nothingness, the answer probably won't suffice to the logically thinking person, but it can make some sense. Isn't it crazy that anything exists at all, let alone in the way in which it does?

A question that arises in this context is: *What is the universe?* The universe is everything, existing as an infinite creation of conscious and harmonic intention. We see this intention as space, time, matter, and energy. The universe is amazingly beautiful, and it is impossible to fully comprehend within the confines of thought. We live in and as the Sun, just as well as we live in and as the center of the universe, whether we can fathom this or not.

The Singularity of Time and Place

If it were always present; indeed, it would not be time but eternity.

(St. Augustine of Hippo, *Confessions,* Quoted in
The Fathers of the Vol. 5, 398/1953)

Time is commonly viewed in three parts: past, present, and future. This trinity is intuitive yet a fundamentally flawed mental construct because it splits time into three parts and divides it from space as well. Space-time is the basis of our experience. Everything that exists does so within a certain space at a certain time. Every organism, event, thing, smile, tear, emotion, or memory has its time and place. No space is separate from another. Where is the "other" space? At what point does the future become the past? When does the present become the past? At what point is one point of space divided from another? What is this moment we call *now* and is it at all separated and cut off from the past and future? The entirety of space-time is singular and continuous; space can't be divided into bits and neither can time. That is why it's called the space-time *continuum*. We see physical changes in space and call this time. Think of the movement of a guitar string. At rest we see the line, but with movement we perceive it as wavy blur of ups and downs. It is the movement of objects that gives us our sense of past and future playing out on the background stage of space and time. Space is not an unmoving background or stage where things and events play out in it. Things and their motions are not, in any way, separate from space. Particles and energies don't push space out of their positions, their existence does not displace space but rather they are manifestations *of* space.

The fundamental laws of physics with respect to time work equally well both forward and backward, but we view time as an asymmetry, separate from space and only moving forward. This, I believe, is due to thought, and our thinking in this way causes a separation of the present moment, or the separation of time into moments. This is the illusion or misconception of time, and it is brought about by the limits of thought.

The Stitch in Spacetime

According to quantum theory, the shortest span of time, called Planck time, is 0.000000000000000000000000000000000000000000 001 of a second. That is forty-two zeros with a one after it, for those who don't wish to count them. So-called Planck time, 10^{-43} seconds, is connected to Planck space, which is about 10^{-33} cm across (Clugston, 2004). This is a moment in time and a location in space that is theorized as the smallest possible scale of space and time. Mathematicians and theoretical physicists are getting close to the full truth and meaning of infinity by adding more zeros and decimal places, and eventually when they get to infinity there will be no need for these measurements and place holders at all. Concepts of space and time are derived from our finite view of the world, through which we make artificial distinctions, the fictitious beginnings and endings of things and happenings. Limitation is an illusory yet useful concept, whereas infinity is a truly tangible abstraction most cannot or will not fully realize.

What is this moment of now? What is an instant? What separates one moment from "another?" Why is "here" perceived as separate from "there?" There is only one moment and there is only one place, but the mind divides it into manageable, relative bits. An instant or moment is traditionally thought of as relative, a concept of separation from the eternal moment; however, if space-time is an illusion, what does infinity or eternity really mean? Well, infinity and eternity mean space and time, but not in the way we normally look at them. Our ideas of infinity and eternity represent the real unlimited, unbounded wholeness of existence without separate spaces and without separate times, because where are the gaps between these moments and spaces? A specific moment in a specific space is a concept which separates, thus creating our narrow and incomplete worldviews of entropy, chaos, cause, effect, time, individuality, and other separate and conflictive illusions. The space-time illusion is the same as a card trick, or the trick of pretending to pull one's nose or finger off and reattaching it, making a naive observer believe it is true. But the space-time illusion is a *real* act or trick, with real cards, fingers, noses, and actions; it is misdirected, and not the whole story. We have made space and time into our own card trick that we play on ourselves with our sleight of mind. The illusion is merely a misunderstood and somewhat hidden reality. Stage magic and deception are all about misdirection and being led to believe. The here and the now are everywhere and all the time, as well as nowhere. Try to wrap your head around that!

No Time But the Present

The moment of now is the Big Bang, or creation, over and over again in a continuous flow. To be in this now is to experience the greatest vitality. It is all of creation in one absolute and everlasting moment. The one perfect moment beyond our perception of space and time is eternal. Past, present, and future exist as one as with the "here" and "there." The reality beyond space and time is the here, now. This here, now exists within the complete inclusion or negation of classical space and time. It is all in the here and now. This is the forefront of creation. This probably isn't a very satisfactory description of our space-time experience with reality, but within the confines of the finite symbols of a single language, and our limited ability to grasp the fullness of this concept, it comes close. For the most part, this reality isn't perceived, because of our limited senses, our reliance on separating cause and effect, including our notions of thought and action, and other divisive contrasts. When we perceive, we are aware and observing, which separates us from the greater reality. To be aware we must paradoxically be unaware, knowingly yet wholly unintentionally; this is the experience of awe and beauty that stops the mind in its tracks. Thought exaggerates instinct, ego, fear, pleasure, pain, and everything that branches out of these. We have changed with over-thought and in effect, oversight of beauty. We have, under the guise of fear and ego, been painting ourselves into this corner for some time now. Synchronicity (two or more things in tune at the same time) is even an illusion or fragmented awareness. Simultaneity is a word that is also appropriate with unity, action/reaction, space/time, and consciousness (although, as with all language, still portraying the same sense of duality).

Cause and effect, action and reaction, are a single process split by thought into dual concepts so that the conditioned hemispheres of the brain can comprehend them. Flow is the harmonic connection between the observer and observed. Experiencing flow begins with the unthinking acceptance of ones' existence as the natural, moving, and creative way of things. Intention and acts of bliss and compassion are innate. For example, if one is accepting and in flow and sees that someone else is hurt, they will naturally and spontaneously try to relieve their suffering. However, if one is indifferent, or in denial of flow, there is a freezing of this flowing river where the actions of this intention, or the entire lack thereof, shut compassion, inspiration, and natural reaction out of ones' consciousness and life. Denial is the resistance to truth and beauty, while acceptance opens the door, allowing the energy of nature to flow through the individual self. Indifference is when one is embedded in the illusion of a time and place other than the present moment; one appears cold, distant, removed, and withdrawn. When one is in the present moment, there is an acceptance, compassion, engagement, immersion, rapture, care, receptivity, peace, and flow. Living in the present moment is reality in all of its peaceful totality. The mind splits this balanced and singular totality into fragments, creating unbalanced and conflictive fear: denial and escape on one side, and violence, anger, and aggression on the other. I have no romantic illusions as to how harsh nature can be in causing suffering and struggle, or about the efficacy of survival responses. Nature doesn't have to be without suffering to exhibit profound beauty. The issue I intend to address is The persistent, generalized and unnecessary psychosomatic, (rather than purely necessary) fight or flight response that so many humans get caught up in, which affects humanity as whole. When the dualistic mentality of fight or flight is left engaged because of illusory psychological conflicts—when they are not necessary for basic survival—peace and flow become hard to maintain. We create conflicts around such things as goals unattained or progress and happiness unfulfilled and our brains then take these dysfunctional thoughts and ideas and turn them into a way of viewing the world that requires the fight or flight response to remain constantly in our conscious and subconscious minds. The denial of reality and the subsequent loss of the flow of experience creates the world we see today.

The present moment cannot be completely grasped by finite, rational, and calculable languages, arts, concepts, symbols, or mathematics. We need a new approach in which the observer can see the "now" with the mental lenses of science and religion totally combined or negated to reach an understanding of Einstein's worrisome problem of now. Einstein said that space-time was relative to each observer, although the observer and the observed are the same, because it is when there are separate observers or egos that things become relative. Einstein also said that space and time are illusions, which means that relativity theory, quantum theory, and everything that is qualitatively and quantitatively relatable to our space-time is a biased, selective, and incomplete view of reality. Relativity says that reality is divided by the perceptions of observers and quantum theory says that reality is divided into distinct and separate grains, packets or quanta. These two theories of our world are true yet terribly incomplete. When one is aware of the totality of relationship in life there is, in a sense, no longer relationship, that is, there is no longer just a relation or connection between one and another or two or more categorized things, but a deep unification of duality and relation into an utterly singular reality. When one ponders and seeks, one finds or reunites with beauty that is not in the past or in the future but ever-present. All that peace requires is the clear and serious intention to discover and recognize oneself as the unity and beauty in everything that is. Time is our theory or "way of looking," like a theater audience. The illusion of reality is our view of time created by our psychology, which is then projected upon our observations of physical things. This is where our thoughts cause problems, not in the root of thought itself, but in how our perspective of time being split three ways skews our thoughts.

A black hole or singularity theoretically collapses the notion of space and time. All personal experience consists of things and events in space and time. Since our existence is based on this space-time illusion or a misled partial reality, it is obviously important to reexamine it. The smallest theorized measure of space is the Planck scale, which is far smaller than anything that can be seen with any tool. In theory, a moment in time and a point in space are infinitely small, so small that they cease to have an observable existence. This is called a singularity or black hole. Once observations begin to fall behind theory, physics can slip into metaphysics quite easily.

There is only one present moment in one dimension, and since one equals infinity, then there are infinite moments in infinite dimensions. The present moment can be seen as either a prison or as ultimate freedom in all its degrees. The prison—or reality filtered by our ego/mind—is self-created. Our mental reality is a scaled down, incomplete, and limited world in relation to the completeness of reality. In reality, we aren't caught or stuck in the middle of opposites, small and large, past and future, but rather swimming and flying through them freely. Power in scale certainly holds true when related to infinity. Deeper than mechanical, chemical, and atomic reactions there is an infinitely sized scale of energy that is the essence of all creation. This is the immeasurable nature of love.

Instants are indistinguishable from eternity. Instants are a fractal perception of what we think space and time is, and try as we might we end up with an immeasurable and unobservable theory. We can measure to a certain degree of accuracy with exceedingly small and large numbers, with more and more zeroes, but this is our illusion. It is relative and very dynamic and we only accept clocks and rulers due to society's collective agreement and need, which in turn is the sole reason we believe in and value it, rather like money. All measurement is created by that which measures. Standard and metric are two standards of measurement. Even the paradigmatic kilogram that all other kilograms are compared against is mysteriously losing weight, mass, or energy in its very secure container. Nobody knows why this is, but I tend toward the notion that any container will never completely contain what it attempts to because matter and energy are always busy interacting with other energy fields, decaying radioactively, losing and adding electrons, heating and cooling, and are never as static, unchanging, and contained as we tend to think they are. Time is even managed by Daylight Savings Time, first proposed in Paris as a joke by Benjamin Franklin, and atomic clocks in different parts of the world have incongruences, with pulsars now being a new and improved constant for measurement. Finally, there are many calendars throughout the world that measure the same concept of time differently.

Gravity is an important factor in space-time, because anything within the fabric of space-time has a gravitational effect, even in the seemingly empty vacuum of space. We don't really know which caused the other, since they are really the same, and the question of cause is flawed to begin with. When we combine antimatter, dark matter, and energy into the mix, space, time, and gravity create a cycle with no beginning and no ending, and everything ends up being the same. In our minds, time separates cause and effect, past and future. Time is a component of a measuring system used to separate events, in order to relate events and the intervals between them, in order to quantify the motions of objects. Time is relative, as seen by an observer, and since time is really space-time, space is also relative to an observer. This means it depends on the observer and how fast or in what direction, if at all, things, including observers, travel in space and time. Any speed or rate of change involves motion. Motion is a general idea of change, or a matter of something being either non-static or at rest. It is the relative movement of the position of a reference point or observation that is also moving relatively or changing its position. Change can be called variation, revolution, or transition. Change is to make a shift from one state or form into another, creating a difference, contrast, and variety. We see the motion of an object only if it is related to itself in a different space which was previous to where it would be now. Motion, change, and all the differences we see are thought of as different from before, but aren't. It's just the illusion of our memories that creates the past, and the projections of our thought that create expectations and predictions in the future, always leaving out the reality of the ephemeral and eternally changing yet changeless now.

Cause and effect are separated only by our psychological interpretation of change. Newton's third law of motion states that for every action there is an equal and opposite reaction. The observer of space-time separates cause and effect and action and reaction. This leads to entropy or chaos theory and is simply a distinction or separation made between macro- and micro-scales of perception. How do you split action from reaction with any definite precision or conclusion? We do this in our crafty minds, which create but a silhouette of the complete reality. They are both intimately joined together, like the infinity of fractions connecting any two whole numbers, superimposed and entangled, so when the veneer of space and time are looked at closely and broadly enough, cause and effect, as well as space and time, are indistinguishable. Change or life is a flow or cycle with no apparent or constant frame of reference except the ego, because life is eternal and infinite. Supernovas or exploding stars transform life. They emit cosmic waves that compress space-time like a sound wave. Since you can look back into space light years away, you can also look back into the past according to the law of transference. Space alters time. For example, a spaceship in space has a small difference in time than on Earth, according to relativity theory. Thus time affects space also, much like electricity and magnetism. This makes perfect sense, since they are the same thing. And since matter and energy are the same thing, anything in space, including matter and energy, is the same as time, just as gravity, electromagnetism, and strong and weak nuclear forces are different aspects of the same thing (super force theory).

The word "aspect" means a varying view, dimension, relation, or scale of observation, which is essentially limited by our focused, conditioned, and ego-filtered senses and consciousness. Therefore, when we say "aspect of the same thing," we are really saying it is all the same thing, just with variation. It is the wholeness of reality viewed as separate and hence distorted fragments. All views of an exclusively separate reality are distortions and thus reach only partial limits of truth.

We are trained to see contrast or anything deviating from "normalcy." We can thank natural selection for this simultaneous gift and obstacle. We might experience excessive noise or harsh light as annoying or painful, but there is nothing fundamentally bad about a constant high frequency of pressure waves or heat waves any more than the certain range in the visible spectrum that gives us the color blue is fundamentally blue. We see blue, we judge "bad," but they are not really bad or blue. Neither bad or blue cares what we think of them, but we care. They exist only in our self-defined view, only insofar as we want to see them. They are concepts that can be manipulated and interpreted by us, but their basic definitions aren't of badness or blueness by themselves. Electromagnetic frequencies need us to complete the equation of the observer and observed and bring blueness or badness into reality; this goes for more than just the color blue, things that might be bad, or electromagnetism in general.

General relativity, quantum theories, and physics equations all allow for time travel into the past and the future symmetrically. This is probably because no matter where you are, you are in the past, present, and future at the same time and spot. The past is a memory and the future is an expectation. Both are imagined thoughts realized in the moment of now. There is only now, which includes the past and future. The present moment can be said to be an emergence of the combination of these two opposites, or these opposites can be said to be an emergence of this one truth.

In a sense, if you want to see something in the past all you have to do is look at something. The objects you see are already in the past, because it takes a fraction of a second for the photons to reach your retina, and then for your brain to interpret this information, so from this perspective everything is in the past. The time it takes those photons to reach your eye from the object is immeasurably tiny, but there is nevertheless a fractional time lag from what is being seen to your seeing it. On a grander scale, modern telescopes such as the Hubble Space Telescope can see back into space billions of light years in spatial distance, or eons into the past, because the light takes about one year per light year to reach us. Photons themselves have no relationship with time, as they travel at the speed of light, and light has no reaction to time. Reality or change is the change in our perception or dimension; it is not a change in time or space.

The most accurate or regular measure of movement in time that man has discovered is the atom or, more recently, pulsars. Humans have made these natural phenomena as well as the relationship of Earth with the Sun into clocks that essentially measure our cognitive illusions, but nature has processes that are simply reliably consistent. Scientists who create and use these atomic clocks use the signals that electrons emit when they change energy levels, which is quite regular and frequent, a perfect mix for high accuracy. The same is true with pulsars that spin like electrons but differ in the measurement of how often the pulsar jets (rapidly spinning neutron stars emitting radiation in beams) pulse or point toward Earth. Think of a lighthouse in outer space, but greatly sped up. The world's most accurate atomic clock measures the vibrations of a single atom of mercury. However accurate this atomic clock may be, Earth's rotation is slowing, and a "leap second" must be added every few years. Space-time is the "ether" or framework in which we live and experience all things. We are simultaneously experiencing past, present, and future in the eternal now.

The Quantum Realm Is Our Own
Anyone who is not shocked by quantum theory has not understood it.

(Niels Bohr, quoted in Gibbon, 1984)

The old adage "truth is stranger than fiction" is certainly accurate with respect to quantum physics. Einstein never embraced quantum physics, mainly because it is based on the opposite of his certain, orderly, and yet relative view of reality. Relativity theory, his baby, and quantum physics, his grandchild and nemesis, are two views of the same thing, just at different scales to the observer. Einstein spent the last years of his life trying to find the unity between these views of the large and the small and missed every time. Quantum effects are like a frozen yet vigorously oscillating lightning bolt, or a tree starting at its roots, amplifying with a self-organizing and emergent effect along the scale until we see a single experience of lightning or a tree. Quantum effects as seen from our scale appear random; however, when amplified, they create processes of considerable order. Quantum physics is the flowering emergence of the vibrating and conscious universe.

Quantum theory asserts that anything and everything that can possibly happen in the universe does, and does so simultaneously. Why and how is it that a theory that has no rational correlation to everyday life creates technologies such as lasers and computers? Quantum theory exemplifies the inclusiveness of the moment of now, and how we so often overlook it. All subatomic particles, and every other thing and process for that matter, interact with gravity, electromagnetism, weak and strong nuclear forces, and dark energy and matter. Everything that exists does so within these forces that we narrowly perceive as condensed energy or matter and their motions.

Waves, just as everything in the universe, have a beat or rhythm. These are rhythms of the on-off harmony. Mathematics is called the universal language. Geometry is physically manifested mathematics and, used as a describing tool, geometry elegantly and beautifully emerges and transforms into all of the shapes and sizes of life. Spiritual disciplines such as Hinduism, Islam, Buddhism, Christianity, Judaism, and so on, and the sciences: mathematics, biology, chemistry, quantum/relativity, classical Newtonian physics and all the rest, all in their own way describe the infinite and unified beauty of nature. The cosmological constant that was later included to Einstein's Theory of General Relativity provided an add-in and fudge factor to describe and permit a nonexpanding universe. The force opposing the potential runaway expansion of the universe without this cosmological constant, now believed to be dark energy/matter but unknown when Einstein released his original General Theory of Relativity, is precisely tuned to 1 in 120 powers of 10. Einstein was disappointed when his cosmological constant was apparently repudiated, when it was discovered that the universe is expanding and was not static and nonexpanding as his cosmological constant portrayed. However, the discovery of dark matter and dark energy could turn out to be a balancing factor describing neither a static nor rapidly expanding universe, but rather an expanding universe accelerating at a constant and very precise rate. What are the odds of the expansion of the universe being as precise and constant as it is? It is not luck, random, or accident. It is completely perfect and absolutely intentional. The fascinating thing is that the intention is not separate from the intender and what transpires. Nature is its own intention with humanity as a part of it; we just don't see it.

Wave/Particle Duality and the Double Slit Experiment

Electrons have a dual wave/particle behavior, as studied with our limited observational tools. Isaac Newton said light was a particle, then Christiaan Huygens said it was a wave, and next Thomas Young agreed that it was indeed a wave. This went on and on until Einstein joined the ongoing argument with his statement that it was a particle. Einstein had a continuous debate with other scientists, particularly his good friend, the Danish physicist Niels Bohr, who said light behaved like a wave. Many others during the early 20th century believed it behaved like a wave. The debate ceased when it was later confirmed that light behaved as both a definite particle of particular experience and as an oscillating wave of indefinite possibility, interference patterns and all. This is yet another strong confirmation of singularity. Similarly, separation, duality, and ego are all illusions by means of disconnection from their inherent opposites.

Wave/particle duality is the inseparability of the wave and particle aspects of light, the quantum wave function and atomic particles. It shouldn't really be called wave particle duality but, rather, wave particle unity. The set-up of this double slit experiment is very simple to understand, but the deductions are utterly jaw-dropping, to say the least. Richard Feynman, a well-known physicist who is thought by many to be second only to Einstein, was fond of saying that all the characteristics of quantum mechanics could be understood from the particle/wave and observer/observed paradoxes which arise from the double slit experiment (Gibbon, 1984). It starts with a flat piece of material with two vertical slits cut into it to allow matter to travel through to the other side. First, particles are sent through the two slits, naturally creating a two-lined pattern on the opposite side. Next a beam of light, consisting of many photons, travels through and creates, on the other side of this material, an interference pattern on a background like waves of water. This indicates the wave nature of light. Interference patterns happen when waves interfere with each other or one wave interferes with itself. Next, a single line of photons (particles) is sent through, one after another, also creating an interference pattern on the wall behind of varying intensity, which is seen as light and dark stripes. How on Earth can a single photon interfere with itself? This is because a single photon does not exist by itself. A photon has no mass and no charge and as a result is effectively its own antiparticle, which relates to the theory that because energy can only be transformed, rather than created or destroyed, the energy of the universe is zero. Photons have no center or boundary, although we think they do because they appear small, which reflects the universe: without center and without boundary. Photons are excitations of the electromagnetic field which is the size of the universe, so the universe is really just one infinite and infinitesimal photon, because photons have no relation to time, and thus space, and all facets of physics are attributable to photons. All the of matter and energy in the universe is the result of the actions of photons, as collisions of photons create matter/anti-matter and collisions of matter/anti-matter create photons, which are all the light and all the heat in the universe. Even our bodies emit photons as heat which we have accumulated from the plant-based food we eat that gather their photons from the Sun. The wave character of light enables photons to independently travel through both slits separately, together, all at once, and not at all. All possibilities are happening at the same time. This is just the tip of the iceberg. As soon as we add an observation or measurement device pointed at the two slits, this interference wave pattern of the single stream of photon ceases and becomes a two-lined pattern of "regular" particles. Now that it has been observed and measured, the light behaves like a particle and is noted to always be absorbed by the screen behind as discrete individual particles, and not as interfering waves. The very act of observing collapses the possibilities of the wave function. This is called the quantum wave function, in which the very act of observation or measurement, perceived as a duality, collapses the wave of probability as soon as it is observed. Observation or measurement collapses infinity and creates the finite observation. We create what we observe just by interacting with it. Energy without observation is potential energy, unrealized, and in waveform. It is important to realize that when one particle or wave node "recognizes" or interacts with another, they effectively observe or acknowledge each other. It is not only the human brain that observes. Every object and indeed the entire universe is superimposed in every moment in our perception of space-time, but our narrow observations only tell us the story we tell ourselves. The gap we create by observing the observed as separate destroys its potential and makes it actual. Seeing the observed as the observer combines the potential with the actual. It is the real dream. This is the Copenhagen Interpretation of quantum mechanics minus the anthropocentrism.

The quantum wave function or electron probability wave is non-localized and spread throughout the universe until it is observed, which is when the probability of the observed being throughout the universe drops to zero and the probability of the object being observed in a certain space, at a certain time, rises to almost 100 percent, or near-certainty. This probability wave function is not specific to photons, but has been scientifically seen in atoms and even some large chemical molecules, clumps of atoms that are electrically neutral and from which all things inorganic or organic such as cells, organs, and organisms emerge. The only main distinction between organic and inorganic is that the chemical composition of life favors sunlight, hydrogen and oxygen linked together in a liquid form, and carbon, the only element that can naturally form chains and rings without any coaxing. Perhaps the entire universe is one big probability wave function that collapses when observed or interacted with, which allows for the emergence of many different kinds of elements such as carbon, radiating stars, chemical compositions such as water, calcium, lipids, hemoglobin, and hormones, macromolecules such as nerve cells, skin cells, stem cells, DNA, cytoplasm, vacuoles, mitochondria, single-celled sperm, eggs, spores, viruses, and bacteria, which can then lead to specific and complementary organs and organisms of many similar and wildly varying species whose home is this single biological film on Earth's crust.

When we conduct the double slit experiment again and block one slit, it only increases the brightness and darkness of the interference patterns on the screen behind the slit. This is explained by the greater intensity of the wave function going through the slit and causing the interference pattern. Any modification of the apparatus, such as adding measurement tools, cameras, or the like, where the purpose is to observe and record a definite measurement of which slit the photon goes through, destroys the interference wave pattern, and the light becomes a regular acting stream of individual photon particles with no bright or dark spots and possessing only a single line of light intensity. Now when the electrons go through the slits, this creates two slit patterns on the backboard, not interference patterns, as anyone with elementary physical knowledge would conclude. This illustrates the particle nature of electrons. Two objects can demonstrate both wave and particle properties, but not at the same time. When a photon is observed, it exists as a single photon. When unobserved it acts as a wave, in a characteristic back and forth motion with every possible variation from the tip of the crest to the bottom of the trough, and of course every position in between. This double slit experiment can be performed with photons, electrons, atoms, and even some molecules, all of which the human body and everything else is made of. Gravity, electromagnetism, nuclear forces, matter, energy, space, and time can all be propagated by the form of wave motion. Entanglement is the superposition of singularity. Our consciousness divides this singularity from infinite waves of possibility into the finite particles we perceive. Particles are perceived as particular and finite, but this is only our view of waves interfering in an infinite manner that produces constant nodes. The particles exist in a wavelike continuum. Every particle is contained yet infinitely interactive with itself and every other particle.

Things Are Made of Atoms and They Are Not Things

*What impresses our senses as matter is really a great
concentration of energy into a comparatively small space.*

(Albert Einstein and Leopold Infeld, quoted in Cole, 2001)

There is a theory in physics called Superforce Theory, which states that all of the forces of the universe at the time of creation were one, due to infinite and uniform nothing and everything, from gravity to electromagnetism (both having a range of infinity), to the strong and weak nuclear forces (although infinite in range, having only an appreciably finite range of human observation). All aspects of the universe are theorized, at the beginning of the universe, to have been a singular and indivisible force. This holds true today. Everything is energy and all it does is transform.

Scientists are currently aware of over 200 subatomic particles based on observation, although there is really an infinite variety, and most of the general public only knows of three: protons, neutrons, and electrons. It's funny how the word "atom" means "indivisible," and yet we have divided it further in both the standard model and in the periodic table of elements. The real atom, in the sense of its meaning, is actually the universe in its entirety and not just quantized bits or particles of matter.

Matter is energy, so particles are their force carrier meaning one must not only look at the thing but also at the behavior of the thing and their interactions with other things to get a wider understanding of what is being observed. Four percent of the universe is proposed to be the percentage that we can physically observe and interact with. This includes stars, planets, asteroids, meteors, comets, and so on, and yet the predominant three point six percent of that four percent is interstellar gas. Atoms, or the matter our bodies are made of, such as hydrogen, carbon, and so on, are the same atoms that make up rocks, trees, stars, plants, and animals, but they all have different forms, aspects, or relationships. Atoms are tiny agreements of vibration in relative equilibrium that are more or less reactive or stable. Water is a molecule made of two hydrogen atoms and one oxygen atom. Steam, fog, gas, mist, rain, ice, liquid, or crystallized solid are many forms of this molecule. Water molecules are hexagonally symmetrical due to their tri-atom configurations, which gives ice and snow its shape, as well as its surface tension, and all of the other miraculous characteristics of two hydrogen atoms connected to a single oxygen atom. Beautifully enough, snow, frost, or ice can only form when there is a central particle of dust called a nucleator as a place to begin growing, and until there is one, water will remain super-cooled, below freezing temperature yet unfrozen. Temperature or ambient energy transforms water into all these other forms. It crystallizes snow in the same way that it does diamonds. Temperature and pressure, as two different forms of the same thing, change energy, matter, form, and function just as electric currents change magnetic fields.

Concerning the balance of nature, scientists believe that for every hypothetical billion-and-one particles there must in turn be a hidden billion virtual or anti-particles; otherwise we would not exist in a material world. The anti-particle of an electron is a positron, and when these particles collide it creates a pair of gamma radiation bursts traveling in opposite directions. Alternatively and amazingly, two gamma ray pairs that collide create electrons and positrons. This is the transformation of energy into matter and matter into energy.

These creations and annihilations are not pointless, as some may have supposed, because without these interactions there would be no sublime beauty and diversity of matter or energy. The pointless creation and annihilation point of view of some can be related to how some view life and death, because people feel there is no purpose to being born or created, given that, ultimately, one eventually dies or is annihilated.

What amazes me is how the vibrations of creation's intention can collect in concert such that we see them as the physical laws that create clouds, stars, light, plants, animals, and humans, enabling us to ponder these things and ourselves. If we were to try to follow an atom as it traveled through our body from the time it entered to the time it left, where would we start? Where would we end? These are arbitrary points of origin and fate, because there are only finite beginnings and endings in the larger context of that which is infinite and ever-present.

It is common knowledge that atoms are small bits of matter made up of subatomic particles, such as a nucleus with electrons spinning around it in shell-like orbits like a microcosmic solar system. This is the classical view and not entirely accurate. The overall size of an atom is a thousand million million, or ten to the fifteenth power bigger than its nucleus. Ninety-nine percent of the mass of an atom is in its nucleus, which is made of varying interactions and flavors of quarks, just like the Sun and the solar system. Atoms are mostly empty space with a small amount of highly condensed energy at their centers. Even some of the densest materials such as steel and rock are, up close, just empty space. Molecules (many atoms stuck together) also vibrate. Everything vibrates and everything is a wave function in one way or another. Atoms are enthusiastic musicians, but they are not just the performers but the performance as well. They are themselves the instrument as well as the music and the performance. Their harmonic interactions create each other's sound, form or shape, and function. The instruments of nature in all their forms are also the corresponding masterpieces they produce.

There is one law of nature. It appears as different laws because, like a fractal, it is iterated throughout observable scales of reality, and thus shows us differing strengths and appearances. Blue and red are essentially the same except for their frequency or intensity; to a wider extent this is also the case with all of the forces and matter in nature. The laws of the universe change with the size or amount of matter or the intensity of energy. One law changes or grows as the complexity, scale, or amount does. The laws of nature vary in scale, which is why a complete theory of quantum gravity is still, after so many years and so many brilliant minds tackling it, as yet unfound. Evolution and biological life are considered more complex and special than other forms of matter, yet we are all made of the same matter or energy. Energy combines harmoniously into matter to create floating spheres, just as it unites to create a tree with roots, leaves and branches, a giraffe with a spine, eyes, mouth, legs, and ears or a human with our similar implements. The single law of nature refracts and reflects throughout the scales of the universe, which is why things become heavier with increasing mass and why water evaporates and falls in such a perfect and exact way that it allows life to exist as it does. The Sun powers this water or hydrologic cycle on Earth. The Sun's energy gently lifts water from the oceans, lakes, and perspiration and respiration from all plants and animals up into the atmosphere. This vapor simultaneously condenses into fog and clouds which then falls as rain, snow, sleet and hail. This precipitation is stored in glaciers and settles into rivers, aquifers, lakes and the oceans only to be lifted up again. I believe we have lost sight of this beauty, and the repercussions are a disrupted hydrologic cycle evident in our everyday lives, just as the beauty is.

The universe is made of energy in all its many forms, so the only difference, if we can use that word, is in its transformation, intensity, and distribution. Think of the universe as being like chunky peanut butter where the chunks and smooth "butter" are both quite easily distinguishable even though both are made of peanuts. We are but a chunk in a chunky peanut butter universe. Everything is energy. It is the ability to move. The prime mover is creation, which is everything. This creates form, function, color, the senses, our feelings and judgments surrounding these words, and everything else. One thing is everything. If one truly understands one thing, one has the opportunity to comprehend the whole. The universe is a package deal. We can superficially divide it up all we want, but all that does is give us a new perspective from which to learn the same thing. Some people understand beauty through thinking, singing, painting, or playing with mathematics. The sense of unity, usually seen as partial in some way, is the big lesson most students seem to miss.

Dark Energy and Dark Matter

Scientists have discovered an unexplained energy and matter that make up most of our universe. Galaxies are moving farther and farther apart as the universe itself expands. This creates more space and time at an accelerating rate. It has been speculated that the remaining ninety-six percent of the universe is composed of so-called dark energy and dark matter. Dark matter is a type of matter that is theorized to account for about twenty-two percent of all the phenomena in the universe. The remaining seventy-four percent is believed to be dark energy. This unseen matter and energy is called dark, like a black hole, because it hasn't been completely confirmed by observation yet, but astrophysicists are convinced it exists because of how observable phenomena are affected by these unseen forces. See how faith and observation mix in science as well as in religion? Since dark matter is still matter, it reacts with gravity, which is the main reason we know it exists. Dark matter is supposed to explain gravitational lensing or mass bending light and the rotational speed of galaxies. Dark energy permeates all of space-time and is supposed to be what is accelerating the expansion of the universe.

The Heisenberg Uncertainty Principle

The Heisenberg Uncertainty Principle is a successful explanation of our world proposed by Werner Heisenberg's quantum wave equation, which states that the paired or complementary values of variable physical quantities such as position and speed, or the momentum of a subatomic particle or larger event cannot be simultaneously known with great precision. In other words, the more precisely one variable is known, the less the other is. The principle also posits that a particle or waveform cannot be completely still or in a static state possessing zero movement, because then the position and momentum would be precisely defined; this would also be the theorized temperature of absolute zero. The uncertainty principle is not an illustration of nature in an entirely objective sense, but also pertains to the limited and unpredictable observations of the observer itself. This means that the uncertainty principle describes not only the sensitivity of a single event or experiment in relation to everything in the entire universe, but also how an observer's conscious limitation, by being localized in an organism in space-time, naturally perceives observed events. To exactly know or observe one quantum state with perfect precision, one would have to perceive the entire universe relating to it as a large-scale quantum state in eternal flux. Using our brains and thoughts to observe the infinite details of any event is simply not possible; however, an event can be experienced without the activity of our behavioral organ upstairs. This is why scientists will forever roughly, however correctly, guess, using probabilities.

Whatever a particle or waveform does is, of course, absolutely certain and determined as it happens. The unpredictability and incompleteness of an event is perceived when attempting to accurately measure the time and place of an experiment, which is always dependent on the scale at which the observer observes something. An experiment or event may only appear to be relatively small in size or place as well as existing in a closed and localized system, but of course it is in fact "located" in the completely open and non-localized system of the universe, just seen at a relative scale by an individual observer. Any event, along with the observer, always exists in the present moment within the singular space of the universe; however, the observer's perceptions are usually transformed into thoughts by the observer's brain, and then the event ceases to remain as it is and is then diminished and constrained, reflected upon and predicted by the thoughts that then become figment observations and not truly complete observations. There are abundant practical and entertaining reasons for the mind to twist reality into something more manageable, but a complete understanding of reality is then out of reach as a result of the organism's preoccupation with basic survival.

Uncertainty is simply the limits of our individual measurements and observations. It should really be called our "spotlight exclusion" theory. If it's a part of observation, then it's a part of the observer and his or her observations. Momentum is the same as position, just as spin is the same as mass. Position, like momentum, needs an observer to measure it, thus creating a nearly definite and observable fixed locale and/or speed. Observing reality and thus contributing in its creation is a fundamental aspect of the most generally accepted and experimentally applicable interpretation of quantum mechanics: the Copenhagen interpretation (for more in depth information on the Copenhagen Interpretation, see p.159 in *In Search of Schrodinger's Cat: Quantum Physics and Reality* by John Gibbon).

An observer or observation, not restricted to the human species but all interactions in the universe (and therefore the universe as a whole) must logically influence the creation of any and all observers and observations simply by existing, observing, interacting or collapsing the wave behaviors in things such as atoms and molecules such DNA which are the basic constituents of all material and biological forms. The behaviors of quantum mechanics, gravity, chemistry, weather, evolution and all other categories made by our mental attempts to describe the universe are really combined as a single reality, all of which involve feedback loops of repeated interactions of nature with herself which brings about the emergence of many unique observers. The process of emerging and changing observers occurs in order for life to exist as an extremely diversified and self-balancing aspect intended to expand and complement the whole in every movement within our earthly and cosmic womb. If the self-balancing, unified and adaptive implications of quantum mechanics, gravity, weather and evolution and all other categorizations of reality were not true and perfect in their behavior, it would be primarily impossible for anything to exist let alone the existence of organisms with all their varying abilities to adapt and be aware of their selves and surroundings.

Entanglement

There is an effect in quantum physics called entanglement that provides a way of looking at a singularity or the universe as a whole. In an experiment, a pair of electrons is separated by space and time. A stimulus is delivered to one of the electrons and, amazingly, it is also felt simultaneously by the other electron. The distance record so far for a scientifically observed test of this entangled unification effect is eleven kilometers. At the scale of an electron, relatively speaking, eleven kilometers is a gargantuan distance. This effect reveals that electrons, the building blocks of humans, rocks, and everything else, are connected in ways we haven't been previously aware of. Things are so connected that they are really one, in that quantum physics states that the non-locality of particles is really a field, a smear, or a superposition of energy waves across the universe, which is at the heart of entanglement. Particles are not entangled as such and do not exchange information. Rather, particles may be more than pairs: they may actually be the same particle or wave function, and this would coincide very much with the complete unity of the universe. The universe, like consciousness, is not a finite and distinct thing, as we all naturally tend to think, but rather a unified and infinite process. Space is ubiquitous, in that space can't actually be divided in any real way. Only our heads split space into digestible bits.

Superposition

Does entanglement mean that there are two separate electrons in their own space-time that affect each other, or could it be that they are the same electron which is in a wave-like superposition? Superposition is another facet of quantum physics which posits that electrons can be in "super" or multiple positions, not localized in one point in space and time. Superposition, entanglement, and interference are terms that can be used interchangeably. Superposition is the different parts or frequencies of a wave traveling toward an observer from different paths or angles. When an electron, or anything which can be observed, is observed, the waves of possible motions and positions collapse or condense into a single measurable and definite position or motion. However, anything unobserved remains in a superimposed, undetermined, and entangled wave state. When some thing/event is observed, its probability wave or quantum wave function collapses to a nearly 100 percent observable certainty concerning its measurable position or momentum relative to the observer. In the act of observing the infinite paths nature can take, we effectively diminish the infinite behavior of nature into a more manageable and finite world for us as observers to somewhat understand and live in. For example, white light is a superposition or waveform of all the colors of the rainbow. In keeping with observation as central to quantum physics, an observer can only see a rainbow, the blurry yet visible colors or diffracted frequencies of white, visible electromagnetic field jiggles, due to the location of the observer in relation to the Sun and the water in the air. This is why there is no definite location for a rainbow, because it is light which is seen across the ever-changing sky, and it is also why nothing can be described to be in a definite location or have a determined motion to more than one observer at a time, because everything is relative to each observer. Another similar example of the effects of observation is the superposition of the colors of the rainbow in white light when refracted on an oil slick in which we can see the colors that have reached our eyes, but the vision we see is completely unique to our consciousness only, and will look different to another's eyes and consciousness respectively. This is because the photons you "see" enter your pupils and travel along your optic nerves to create an image and individual reality that is uniquely and relatively yours. Each observer sees the world through their own filter.

The Theory of Everything—
A Door Between Two Pillars

String theory, or superstring theory, is a proposed theory of everything, describing matter and energy as profoundly small strings of energy that can exist in a closed string loop or in a string with open ends. It might also be called shoestring theory, because of the endless twists and turns that a single loop or string can create with knots and braids and layers. These strings theoretically vibrate at various frequencies that give rise to all matter and energy. I believe this is very close to what actually happens. This energy need not be only in string form, but can be infinitely transformable. Superstring theory was created in an attempt to describe quantum physics and gravity. In essence, at the smallest Planck scale or quantum scale levels, there are tiny vibrating stringlike structures that make up our universe. They can exist in loops or membranes ("branes" for short), and string theory is a compelling candidate for the GUT (Grand Unified Theory). I think these string forms are no more than a conceptual and visual aid, and thus an unnecessary form that can be done without. The theory could be simply seen as vibration theory without all the strings, but then, what energy or material form would vibrate? Since matter alters space-time and space-time alters matter, perhaps what vibrates is the symmetric geometry of space-time itself? This wave energy of space-time is to the quantum aspects of atoms as electromagnetic waves are to color. One may ask, "How did these vibrations or frequencies come to be?" In my opinion, they always were; they have always existed. There was no initial condition or beginning in "time," such that before it no vibrations or frequencies existed and after it there were frequencies or vibrations.

The "holy grail" of physics and even general science is to combine quantum physics (the very small) with relativity theory (the very big) to come up with a so-called Theory of Everything. A theory of quantum gravity is needed to combine and explain these two aspects. As it stands, each includes a dualistic perspective of reality by, in one way or another, separating the observer from that which is observed and thus each is nearly complete in itself and needs to be combined or integrated to be fully complete. Until then, neither is false or wrong, just incomplete. These two very successful theories have provided the science that has allowed us to manipulate nature to create such things as cell phones, computers, lasers, GPS satellites, and so much more, and yet all of this rests on theories that, while very close to a full view of reality, remain incomplete due to their foundation of dualism.

With respect, Albert Einstein, Stephen Hawking, and scientists could not, cannot, and will not find a theory of everything (quantum gravity), or a grand unified theory (quantum field theory that includes the electroweak force and quantum chromodynamics) because they were, are, and will be looking at the problem from a view that is polarized and subsequently unsolvable. We are unified and live in the Garden of Eden, but we apparently choose not to accept the wholeness of the spiritual and the material, Heaven and Earth, the divine and the human. We see this unification as manifested through a veil of half truths. The universe is made of movement, processes and change, not static things and restrictions. It is too dynamic to pin down with a GUT or even an equation. All simplicity iterates the creation of an emerging unpredictability, as seen in quantum physics, the concept of emergence, and chaos theory. Every theory in mathematical language will always be finite in its description of the infinite.

Throughout his entire life, but especially in his last thirty years, Albert Einstein, a heavily right-brained discoverer and unifier, was intensely occupied with finding a unified field theory that would combine his theory of gravity with the periodic table of elementary particles and forces known as the standard model. There is a difference between the grand unified theory of the unification of matter and the force of gravity and a theory of everything, that is, a theory of quantum gravity, but for the intents and purposes of this book, these terms are used more or less synonymously.

General relativity and quantum physics are the twin triumphs of 20th century theoretical science. Today the Holy Grail is to unify these twins into what is mistakenly named the theory of everything—mistakenly, because it's not completely everything. In a technical sense this theory of everything would only be a more encompassing theory combining the current understandings of gravity along with the interaction between gluons and quarks, or strong nuclear force, and the force combining quantum electrodynamics with the weak nuclear force that is responsible for things such as radioactive decay, or the electroweak force. String theory is a school of thought that is an attempt to be a door between these pillars. The thing with string theory is that it hinges on the form of a string and the fact that there are so many versions of the theory and there is no way of directly proving or disproving them, as the strings are too small to be observed. This is a big problem for scientists. Regardless, the general idea of unity, especially when linked with super-symmetry and superstring theory, remains strongly favored by the theoretical physics community.

Everything can be fundamentally interchangeable due to the nature of the unity of all things. Keep in mind that everything is energy and all it does is change form. Entanglement, quantum wave function, the Heisenberg uncertainty principle, special and general theories of relativity and matter, the very essence of space and time, are all aspects of the same singular process.

In attempting to combine quantum physics and relativity, physicists have come up with infinities as their result. Mathematicians and physicists don't like it when equations create infinities. Infinities aren't conformable, calculable, or clearly useful for anything. They just are. These mathematicians and physicists see infinity as a meaningless dead end. But they found it. That's it. Infinity is discussed throughout this book and is a central truth of reality, but we look past it every time as a nonsensical concept or miscalculation. All solutions to any equation that describes reality are believed to be finite because we believe reality itself to be finite. Thought sees infinity as untrue, because thought cannot comprehend or rationalize it. It's not false if one doesn't understand it, and it doesn't go away if one ignores it, except in terms of a specific individual's feelings, thoughts, or presuppositions.

For years now, we have been finding smaller and smaller aspects of reality within atoms and subatomic particles, down to their constituent quarks and waveforms. Why is it that we can believe in an infinitely large universe but not an equally infinitesimally smaller one? Mathematics is called the universal language, but our mathematical vocabulary and eloquence in understanding the cosmic textbook is too limited and too human. If the universe is infinite, creating equations such as quantum gravity and fractals, for example, to equal infinity is not an abstract quirk, flawed phenomenon, or disposable aberration realized only in playing with numbers and tailoring equations, but a commonly found theme and perfect representation of life and existence. It's the same thing, just at appreciably different scales and to perceptibly different observers.

A true theory of everything innocently and unintentionally defies a prim and proper explanation, because a description can never exactly match what it describes. In order to explain something, it must be compared to something else, or somehow separated from itself. In describing everything, you can only compare it to itself, or to nothing. It is all energy, mass, space-time, and the processes by which it emerges and changes. A description of infinite singularity is described as itself with nothing separate from it. Current quantum gravity hypotheses predict that the universe underwent not a "Big Bang," as most would think, but a "Big Bounce." This is a universe with no beginning and no end that is growing from a singularity to a point of collapse and back again, repeating infinitely not unlike a dynamo, a catalyst, or a heartbeat.

Quantum entanglement theorizes that everything was a singularity before the "Big Bang." All the particles were one, and then were split as the universe expanded, allegedly and, contrary to Einstein's idea of light, faster than the speed of light. This single point of origin is why all aspects of reality are intrinsically interwoven with the entirety of existence. Thus, as the universe expanded, everything—material or energy, which is the same thing according to $E=mc^2$—is equivalent and still entangled with everything else, and the universe is still primarily a singularity. Mathematicians and physicists attempt to explain nuclear forces, gravity, electromagnetism, and all other energies including dark energy, and all matter dark or otherwise, as being divided or separated from the initial singularity, which at the time of the Big Bang was a "super-force" of all energy/matter and space/time combined in strength and infinite concentration. This explanation by division is paradoxical, as duality—a paradox being two opposing views that are irrational when joined—usually is. So far we have theories such as the super-force made of all the known forces, super-symmetry, super-position, and super-gravity…clever names, I know. All these theories try to explain the singularity, which is only seen as different because of the kaleidoscopic facets or viewpoints of the singular consciousness.

The infinite probability wave of creation becomes finite and particular through our perceptions which have been honed and ossified by the basic impetus to survive. Whether micro or macro, an individual's measured, comparative perception is a matter of size, and size is completely relative to the way something is observed by the observer. With the revelation of the unity between subject and object, human concepts such as macroscopic entropy, randomness, and disorder disintegrate, because they rest on closed systems and naive interpretations of narrow observations. Complete reality is singularity, which is unity. The orders of magnitude of fractal observation give scientists and other observers these perceptions of separation and distinction. Look at the colors red and blue, for example. However beautiful they may be, they appear to us to be very different, separate, and distinct, but this is only because we perceive certain scales of electromagnetic radiation in ways that suit us best, not as they are in the unbiased entirety of creation.

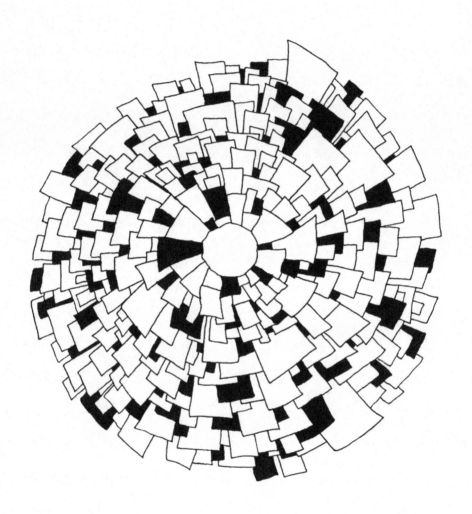

PART 6

A LAND BEYOND COMPARE

Nature uses only the longest threads to weave her patterns, so each small piece of her fabric reveals the organization of the entire tapestry.

(Richard Feynman, quoted in Gleick, 1964/1993)

The Teacher's Dilemma—A Willing Student Is the Teacher

What is it to teach and what is the motivation to be a teacher? Obviously if there is no teacher there is no student. Teaching is a process through which a mentor sheds light on some subject or phenomenon to themselves or someone else—the student. The most passionate teachers are often the ones who have been affected by that knowledge so deeply that they wish to pass it on. The "revealer" or teacher in turn wants to help the student by imparting that wisdom or knowledge. To teach is to reveal or present truth. They are only the humblest of arrows and, like any road sign they can be heeded or ignored. Philosophy, to some, is the love of truth which includes searching, questioning, and sharing what one feels is true. I believe that the natural compulsion to teach comes originally from the thirst for answers or the feeling of discontent of the teacher which has been quenched or tended to, and thus the teacher cares to pass the beauty on. Any teacher naturally desires to spread truth and beauty where there is illusion and conflict. Teachers are compelled to show others the ways that they themselves bridged the gap between questions and answers once perceived as two halves of a problem. Most teachers were probably not fully developed or completely aware of truth and beauty at the outset of their lives; they grew and learned and acquired insight, which they then desired to show to others. Remember that to heal means to make whole. Isn't it astounding that organisms can heal themselves when injured!? What if a teacher or philosopher couldn't relay his or her insights to others? What if Jesus, Buddha, Mohammed or any other well-known teacher could not give their message to others? Jesus, for example, was a person as well as the spirit of God's love in his teachings. If you really see teachings for what they are then you become the spirit of those teachings. When one encounters beauty, one wants to bring it to the attention of others. This desire is spontaneous and completely intentional whenever one can see suffering, fragmentation, or an emptiness in others, whom they recognize as themselves, since no person is at all separate from the rest of humanity, and one simply wishes to stop the unnecessary suffering in the only way they know how. It is as natural as sharing a good recipe because you yourself found it tasty, filling and satisfying. The deep hunger pain and suffering of humanity, and of all life, belongs to us all. It seems as if humanity is deeply dissatisfied no matter what. Teachers are healers; some treat symptoms and some treat the source to varying degrees. Any effective teacher will explain to the student that there is no difference between the two, that in reality the student is the teacher and the teacher is the student. If one is lacking in care, attention, openness, or sincerity, and concern about the gravity of the problem of ignorance and suffering, then the other lacks these things also.

Lost in Translation and Interpretation

In 1495, William of Occam postulated his famous Razor, namely that a theory making the fewest postulates tends to be the correct one. And yet, the most fundamental of truths seem to be the hardest to explain and understand. The words used to describe an experience will never do it justice. In many circumstances even appropriate and carefully chosen words can be poor vehicles for conveying understanding. Generally speaking, no matter how much we believe we understand something, and no matter how passionate we are in our feelings about it, it is difficult to convey the concepts with any sense of accuracy and lucid interpretation. This is the trouble with explaining counterintuitive and less than self-evident truths which challenge the taken-for-granted views of reality. When we tell a story in detail or describe something funny that happened to us and it doesn't have the anticipated impact, we often respond by saying "I guess you had to be there." In other words, it is often hard to convey the vibe of the moment. Words may mean something close to their loaded emotional triggers, but words will always be a separate and inert amalgamation of letters that are interpreted by observers in their own ways. We are an emotional, self-conscious species that puts emotional weight on events and memories. Everything that is objective is also subjective. The words we connect to or understand join us to the words, so much so that the observer becomes the observed and each observer ends up having their own unique interpretation. In other words, things and events will always mean something a little different to each person. It's like eating a pineapple and trying to explain it to someone who has never eaten one. You can try explaining its texture and its citrus taste and its unique sweetness until you are blue in the face. The other person will not understand unless they have eaten what you have eaten. We have to eat and experience the same thing in order to understand.

Sometimes we view happiness as a destination and the reaching of a goal, achievement, or potential; we believe that by doing certain things we will become complete. Other times we view the path—the "journey"—to happiness as more important than happiness itself, although in my opinion, with this approach, happiness is always out of reach. Ultimately, the path is not separate from the happiness, although we don't see it this way. This is why we strive for betterment, progression and improvement rather than simply observing peace and perfection. We are caught in one big vicious circle, and the only way out, it seems to most, is to ask someone for the answers or follow someone who claims to have them. Yet it is not about escaping the circle, but about seeing it differently. Eternity can be a curse or a blessing. It is the same cycle; it just doesn't always seem like it to our limited perception.

If you had a problem with your sight, how would wearing someone else's prescription glasses help you? We want to be happy and to know things for ourselves; however, when we outsource this responsibility to guides or teachers of all sorts, we can get lost along the way. Ultimately, you are the teacher and the student, the guide and the guided, and you are the lock and the key to seeing the miracle. If you are a willing student who is ready to be open and to learn, then you are your own teacher, and a teacher is only as good as the student.

Jesus came to teach and to reveal what reality is and what every one of us is. His name translates to "I am free," just as the name Buddha translates to "I am awake." We are all one and the same and both Jesus and Buddha saw that.

The tree of life is a seed; it is also a forest. It is one reality with endless roads toward realizing the awe of it. The ego is a stepping-stone that we only use to ascend to the next stone. It is about seeing value in yourself, which isn't a bad thing; this is the positive side of ego. It begins with the individual self, but grows or emerges to include everything. Seeing the importance, value, and beauty in all things is what ego is supposed to guide us toward. However, sometimes we think we have reached a conclusion and sit on it for a while, rather than trying to continually move forward. Trees bear fruit only to spread their seeds. This I think is the nature of teaching, revealing, or unfolding. He who plants the seed of life has that seed take root, and then those seeds grow their own tree which then comes to bear fruit, and so on. Amid the motionless dance of the forest and the silent song of the waves, it is a beautiful thing to chop wood and haul water. Understanding requires the acknowledgement of the natural flow towards change and growth. If no value is seen, then there is no interest. One cannot learn if something is not relevant to them, or if they are inattentive. The lesson will go in one ear and out the other. We are selectively blind and deaf, filtering out information that we unconsciously deem nonessential, and turning the filters off requires a careful attention and sense of awe so that we can see beyond them. The teacher is the middleman between the knowledge and understanding of the truth and the students' illusions about it. There is a teacher in all of us that clarifies things. This love of clarity can give one a taste of more truth or less truth, depending on the value one has for clarity and truth. And yet it represents a dilemma of sorts, because how can one teach the value of clarity and truth to someone stuck on valuing superficiality, suffering and division? Moreover, how does a teacher teach a student who is himself his own teacher? To resurrect is to wake up the dead. How does a teacher or guide communicate the idea that thoughts are a problem as well as a solution without using thought? There are multitudes of people who are constantly teaching illusions to themselves as well as to others, and they have thus created superiority, inferiority, and overall conflictive views of life; this is why the world needs everyone to be their own teacher and student dedicated to understanding the reality in front and behind our left and right eyes and brain hemispheres. Only you can truly teach yourself, including how to care and how to listen without being subject to any superior/leader, punishment, reward, routine, or mechanical method dictating how that is to be done. An effective teacher must present reality in such a way that the student can clearly see and understand. An effective student must have doubts balanced with effective questions and complete openness to all shades of truth and illusion. Teaching oneself love is deceptively simple and even automatic. The fullness of one's care and attention is required for understanding beauty. As with all observations, we miss the crucial ingredient that doesn't get mixed in, namely ourselves, our immersion in the world and the process.

The desire to teach anything is seen throughout the human race as well as the entire animal kingdom at large; the compulsion to teach arises naturally. Teaching allows one to exist and perceive a wider understanding of the relationship between oneself and their surroundings. The truth of reality is as naked as we are underneath our clothes but we add layers of concealment to truth from the innocent ideas we have made reality into. The intention of teaching is to reestablish the awareness of the raw union between everything and oneself. To summarize this section, the teacher is the student; if one is lacking, so too is the other.

The Reflection of Life as Death
In death, I am born.

Hopi proverb

Beyond the sight of day and night, life has trouble existing without the ability to distinguish itself through contrast, distinction and relation. We could not drink, eat, procreate, or ponder our own existence. The behavior of the creative vibrations that propagate as waves are the reason we are alive. We tend to believe that this life started at birth, which I call the "birthday fallacy," and ends at death, or what I call the "death fallacy." These are fallacies because life does not begin or end; it just acquires different forms.

Death is always on the edge of one's thoughts, but we never really discuss it, or we try to familiarize ourselves with or desensitize ourselves to this idea in order to feel more comfortable about it. Death is such a taboo subject that it's always avoided until it is thrust into one's life, only to be avoided again just as quickly as it is dealt with. Remaining relatively alive and pain-free is an important motivation in our lives. Death is constantly in our conscious and subconscious minds, so far away and yet so close.

There is great debate around the beginning and ending of consciousness or the beginning and ending of life. When does life begin? Abortion versus right-to-life is a heated controversy, where some say life begins at conception, whereas others say it begins when the senses are reactive, or when there is conscious movement and brain activity, or as soon as the umbilical cord is cut. When does life end? some specifically believe that death is "brain death," when brain function has ceased. This is the current legal definition of death. Many agree that the irreversible cessation of electrical brain activity constitutes death. Some believe that when the function of the neocortex, the part of the brain responsible for consciousness, ceases, this is the point where death occurs. But this is controversial. Others posit that "clinical death," where the heart stops beating, is the point where death occurs. The point I'm trying to make is that there is no one set of criteria for defining the beginning or ending of life, where one can say conclusively that someone has become alive or that someone has died. Biologically speaking, death is a process, no matter how suddenly it happens. There is no one way to pinpoint birth or death, because it doesn't really exist as a moment or instant, but is rather a continuous flow in the ongoing stream of life.

All goes onward and outward...and nothing collapses,
And to die is different from what any supposed, and luckier.
Has any one supposed it lucky to be born?
I hasten to inform him or her it is just as lucky to die, and I know it.

(Walt Whitman, *Leaves of Grass: Song of Myself,* 1855/2007)

Whatever we may think or believe about the cessation of bodily processes, it is perhaps the letting go of the possessions or attachments of consciousness that everyone would agree constitutes true death. Consciousness is life, or the awareness of oneself as limitless. We fear the unknown because it is uncertain. Seeing what little humanity can comprehend through knowledge is like standing on a beach and dipping our familiar toes into the vast ocean before we take the dive into the unknown commonly abhorred and referred to as death. The reason we perceive uncertainty is because it is unlimited, and we are governed by the authority of our limited thoughts and consciousness, which are always seeking to understand that which cannot be fully understood or comprehended. As the flow of what we believe to be the known, our thoughts create the past and future which are repeated throughout our lives and will always create the sense of time, conflict, and the feeling of separation. However, thought with insight and awe is an animal transformed. Thoughts are now freely governed by an experience beyond the personal realm of consciousness. This is pure consciousness. With straightforward and uncomplicated insight into the change and movement of creation and not just our personal psyche's time, change, and movement, there is an awareness of peace as a single living universe. It is chopping wood and hauling water in a whole new light. This insight does not come from the merely therapeutic escape of wishes, chants, mantras, recitation, meditation, and heightened periods of stimulating thought or any imagined comforts that will indulge us and our loved ones now or later. These all occupy and focus the mind, but mainly serve to cloud true perception. These pleasurable techniques are similar to a relaxing getaway vacation. Moreover, making insight a distant goal to struggle toward will only prolong one's suffering. Rather, a fully integrated, simple and clear view of life as it is is all that is needed. This only requires one to place great value in seeing this and demands no strain or effort. This may be easier said than done, however, as our view of ourselves and the world are an illusion based on separation, which is a powerful trick of the cunning, overactive human mind. We provide our own stumbling blocks against this perception. The awareness of what is complete and what is not merges and reinstates the illusion, the trick, back into the fullness of the reality where the illusion originated, not isolated and caught in a filter or a piece of reality as in the mind or the thoughts. The illusion of duality arises only in isolation. Only in the perceived and believed disconnection between the perceiver and the wholeness of that which is real does conflict arise. Insight and wisdom comprise the reunion of oneself with the wholeness of nature. To be in nature means to be born with it continuously. The awareness of oneself as nature is our constant birth, Genesis, baptism and Big Bang in all things.

Living and Dying Simultaneously
Everything dies; nothing perishes.
(Ovid, *Metamorphoses*, 8 AD)

However pitiful, sorrowful, beneficial or pleasurable they may be, the ideas of loss and ownership are clearly flawed. "Destruction" is an absolutely essential process woven into the design of creation. Nature in *all* her death and decay is deceptively beautiful and obviously creative. Death is similar to that of a star "dying" in a supernova explosion, releasing its energy for other life forms to utilize.

We see solid forms and objects as still, but they are in fact teeming with motion. Electrons are spinning around their nuclei at hundreds of kilometers per second, but our eyes don't need to see this, so they don't, nor are they capable of it. We can all agree that our fingernails grow without stretching our imaginations, but we don't actually see them grow. This is the process of life that we see as death. Death isn't an abrupt event at the end of one's life, but is factored into and included in the life and processes leading up to it and after it.

Death is the opposite of birth; it is not the opposite of life. Death is birth and birth is death. There are unimaginable amounts of death in nature; this is why nature means to be born because death is a birth with all that happens in nature. This life includes both aspects of itself. Life is the canopy under which everything transpires. You were alive before birth, you are alive now, and you will be alive after death. You are bigger than your personal identity and the form is always changing. Death is a release of the ego and life's necessary possessions of consciousness. The brain is merely a container of these navigational aids. This is not who we are any more than a GPS receiver is the essence of a vehicle. When living without that sense of "me," there can be room for the instant catch and release of the moment. Our body has a collective consensus to live. It's in our atoms, DNA, cells, and organs. They live their lives for the benefit of the organism for as long as they can (as they do in all plants and creatures). However much we think we "own" our bodies, that's just our ego telling us that. And that is how it should be; however there is more to it. We borrow this agreement for a cycle of time called one's life. Once this agreement expires, nature speeds up her process of transformation to create other agreements. Learning the language of creation enables us to see nature along with ourselves as the message. This message is nothing less than the truth behind the words: truth, infinity, nothing, unity, love, and beauty.

Quantum physics shouts to anyone who will listen that a state does not exist. A state indicates something static and unchanging at a particular fixed point in space and time. This does not exist in observed reality. The truth is that the act of death simply transfers energy from one eternally moving moment to the next. An act of death is occurring every second of your life as each of your 100 trillion cells ages, dies, and regenerates new cells, repeatedly, invisibly, and silently. It is this process of birth and death together that creates the heartbeat of life, like Pacific salmon carcasses carried into the forest floor or the forest that drops its trees and the tree that drops its leaves only to reabsorb them through its roots and its symbiotic fungi as the decay of salmon, leaves and branches become soil. One can compare the visible change of life into death to the simple burning of a piece of paper. The process of fire combusts the paper and transforms it, creating light, heat, and ashes. Any process, whether it is death, fire, or anything else, is simply the redistribution of atoms and their bonds. There is some matter that is left over as ash and smoke dissipate into the atmosphere, but that matter isn't in the form of paper anymore. This is the natural cycle of change from composition to decomposition and back again, which is just a repeated movement of the same thing. Some of the matter is changed into energy. This is $E=mc^2$ in full bloom. This is what stars, ourselves, and all other things do. Einstein's famous equation states that energy is equal to mass when the mass is traveling at the speed of light multiplied by itself. The process of material and energetic metamorphosis is a continuous and universal process. Life is the infinite cycle of change. This is happening simultaneously across the cosmos and in your own cells. Space and time (as they are commonly thought of) are only our misinterpreted constructs, through which we convince ourselves that cause and effect are separate, or that past and future are separate also. These opposites only exist with the observer in the middle of them, joining them together. The past and future only exist when relative to the present, just as "there" is related to "here" or the observed is related to the observer. This illusion of duality and separation, I believe, must be acknowledged in order to live a peaceful and balanced life in harmony with nature, as nature. Humanity as a whole has not done this. Separation is the root cause of all of humanity's—and now Earth's—conflicts. Questions have answers and answers have questions. The left side of the brain has its right side, up has down, hot has cold, space has time, positive has negative, heroes have nemeses, life has death, good has bad, male has female, big has small, pain has pleasure, past has future, light has dark. The list goes on: spend or save, supply and demand, sink or swim, begin and end, love and hate, alpha and omega. They are complementary, balanced, reciprocal, and no opposite can exist without its twin, so they are forever one, as a mirror image must have its double. Where would north be without south? If you find a globe, point a finger somewhere in the northern hemisphere and move it further and further north and see that it becomes south. They are both just points of reference. We all have two parents just as they had and their parents' parents' parents' parents had. We exist due to a long line of pairs of men and women we call parents in all their changing adaptations to their surrounding environments. This is why children of the same parents look like a mix of their parents, why people develop more melanin in their skin in sunnier and hotter ecosystems, and the reason for all human diversity. We all have in our DNA a double helix pattern rotating around itself in a lovely embrace, like two dancers who both follow and lead at the same time to create an eloquent display of perfect attraction and repulsion.

Birth and death are analogous to a rainstorm. Clouds gradually and silently gather and increase in size until a limit is reached. They then collapse under their own weight to fall as rain, creating floods, wind, lightning, and thunder. It's a very dramatic and energetic event, all from a slow, quiet, and easily overlooked process. It is worth pointing out, however obvious, that after the storm the weather returns to the same slow and quiet process that preceded the thunderstorm that we tend to focus on. It's also impossible to say which started first, because the question is faulty in its predicate of something beginning (or ending) in an infinite process. Like the chicken and egg paradox below, the "you" the "me," the rainstorm, the ocean, and the cloud are all one process in different stages of its cycle. One mustn't get attached to the cloud form regardless of the beauty and love one has for it. Forms change. That is all they do. See the cloud as the rain and the person as the tree and all the other infinite intricacies of nature's scale and form.

The Chicken and the Egg

Do you want to know the answer to the chicken and egg paradox? You may not accept the answer, but it's *both*. It's the same life cycle but at a different stage of form. They cannot exist without each other because they are the same thing, just in different form. We have made the chicken and the egg forms distinctly separate in our minds just like everything else. This is an illustration of the illusion of duality and how utterly self-convinced we are that duality exists and is the rule. Believe it or not, the chicken and the egg are one. "But what came first?" you may still persist in asking. Perhaps this is not the answer you want to believe because it goes against common sense, but it is the very question of "what came first" that is flawed. We are so caught up in the form of things that when they change, as in death or in the emergence of a chicken from an egg, we can't really comprehend the truth of how and why they transform. Our reason and logic hit a conceptual brick wall. A chicken comes from an egg and an egg comes from a chicken. We narrow reality into isolated things and events. There is no "first" or "last" or individual species in the continuum that is the process of the universe. Life, death, infinity—all cycles have no real beginning and no real end per se, so the answer is both. They exist together and cannot exist without each other. Natural selection is a process, and simply points to forms always changing and never really being in a static state of permanence.

A dandelion is a beautiful and obvious display of life and death. For imagination's sake we can start this journey arbitrarily as a seed from its parent flower. This is blown in the wind until it lands on the ground, settles, and begins to grow. It grows into a beautiful flower and continues its cycle of change. It loses its color and its petals become seeds that are, like its parent's seeds, blown in the wind to settle and begin this process all over again. There is no death or birth; only the process of change called life. There is no static egg or static chicken, but a constant movement of change and form. Energy and matter are the same thing; it's just that they go back and forth and all we see is what we consent to see.

To live is to die or release each moment over and over again continually and only once, depending on how one looks at it, allowing the moment to enter and exit seamlessly. The fabric of life, woven from the single Möbius thread of birth and death, is seamless. It is the energy, matter and the space-time ether moving along with nature that makes life the loom made of its own fabric. This is why death is so hard to deal with, because we are so possessive of what can never be possessed and that is life. Life is always moving, and we stubbornly perceive ourselves, through accumulated knowledge, psyche, or ego, as largely unchanging, as having a definite beginning and ending in birth and death. It's worth emphasizing that the very mechanisms responsible for deluding us that we are unchanging—our ego, our perception of "self" with a specific personality and separate individuality—are the very things we perceive to be unchanged themselves. When we speak of death we say words like "gone," "lost," "passed away," "departed," "gone to a better place," "beyond," "with God now," which are all based on distance and separation, beginning and end. In death, as in life, there is no separation. We find comfort in the past and fear death in the future for the simple reason that we don't want to lose what is known. Before, during, and after the cradle and the grave we cannot possess, have, hold, or own anything, including our belongings, love, beliefs, memory, arms, legs, brains, and egos, all of it. We own nothing, including ourselves, and everything we think we can hold onto is a conflictive delusion separate from love, and will never lead to true and sustained happiness. Death is the opposite of birth not of life, and since opposites are the same, one can say that death is birth. The hoarder mentality we have for life's things and experiences is the frantic attempt of a thirsty man running to drink all the raindrops in a Sun shower when all he need do is open wide to the awe and beauty of it as it passes. As illustrated beautifully by the poet William Blake:

> *He who binds to himself a joy*
> *Doth the winged life destroy;*
> *But he who kisses the joy as it flies*
> *Lives in eternity's sunrise*

(*Several Questions Answerd*, quoted in Erdman, 1792/1988)

The Seam in Between

Reality is not in conceptual or idealized opposites, but in the singular relationship between them. It is the balance of dualities that conserves the harmony of their unity, like a top spinning in one spot due to the equal force balanced in all directions. Without contrast, there is nothing. Remember what nothing is equivalent to? Balance and imbalance, matter and antimatter, they are all relative, and together they are one. There is no north unless it is related to the south, no evil until related to good, no death until related to life, no *Genesis* without *Revelation*. There is no experience without reflection. I think the part people have trouble with, understandably, is the illusion of its polar duality. Reality emerges when opposites merge. Our common sense, or normal thought process, creates the illusion of duality. It has convinced us all. The beautiful truth is complete and eternal unity. The combination of past and future is the present or "being" of a human being. This moment called "present" is only present for the moment. The dual illusions of past and future meet halfway to become the present moment. It is the reflection of itself.

People's observations of duality aren't wrong, but they are what they seem to be in themselves. It is plainly a lesser or fragmented scale of "picture quality," much like a very crude and pixilated photograph of reality. It is seen as fuzzy and distorted instead of clear. It is our unbalanced proportion of dimensional perspective between the observer and the observed.

Our polar reality is convincing and ever-present. We, in large part, choose to live our lives the way we do with this dualism in mind. Viewing the reaches of life as a whole miracle is heaven. Viewing the universe and also yourself as detached and not miraculous is a certain sort of hell. Reality is heaven or hell depending on how little or how much one intends to see of it. If one chooses to see two halves instead of a whole, then conflict will always be their companion, but if one opens to the freedom of totality, then conflict dissolves and the clarity of truth and beauty comes sharply into focus. It all depends on the range and balance between the degree to which one more or less chooses, shuts out, and segregates, or accepts, connects, and lets in.

The death or transformation of our present form awaits us all—tomorrow, a few years from now, or whenever it may be. We all have our own personal doomsday, as most tend to think of it. Many people have an indifferent or "who cares?" attitude towards life and death. The shame is that one can't care about the beauty of life and death if one isn't aware of it. It is a common paradox and paradigm, in that we all know we are going to die, yet we act as if we aren't, and at the same time we still fear this great unknown more than anything else. The illusion and power of fear, and more precisely the fear of the unknown or losing grasp of the known, has gotten us into trouble in the past and into the trouble we are in now. Strange as it may seem, love is stymied by thought, memory, and fear, which are all conflictive and separate. It is clenching the past and projecting it into the future, all of which is based on divisive observation. Every effect of conflict is essentially the root from which it springs.

When Fear's Necessity turns Surplus

Fear is an emotion arising from a defense mechanism that is activated by real or imagined danger and subsequently real or imagined pain. It triggers the flight (avoidance) or fight (conflict) response. Instinct is an automatic biological tendency, indistinguishable from a habit, and is an action of nature and nurture for the survival of the organism. Fear is a perfect example of a natural and beneficial habit run amok. Animals have this fear, but it's carried on through their biology and genetics to benefit the species, not through ego and conflict founded on social or political ideas and mental conditioning based on individual experience, learned and compounded generation after generation. This I believe is the main problem facing humanity and Earth. Fear is a defensive mechanism. It creates and drops atomic bombs. It helps us imagine the worst and see the flaws in everything. It is necessary for our survival. If we imagined the best and felt no fear, we would not last long. However, this once balanced and effectively beneficial natural instinct has become exaggerated through our psychology and ego, and as long as the much coveted, misunderstood, and limited aspects of thought and ego remain skewed toward the important, there will always be conflict in this world until it self-destructs, which is its inherent natural tendency. Nature tries what works and when it doesn't work, it is either phased out or grows out of control and collapses. Animal instinct, mixed with our relatively newfound power of thought, clash with and also unknowingly feed off each other. This may give us some comfort, but overall it has created a world of problems for thousands of years and these turbulent times of transition serve as an appetizer for the imminent main dish. This perfect storm has given us more than enough warnings. The effect of this constant negative awareness is subsequent discontent, which long ago was beneficial for our species to reach its goals of basic survival. Of course, we have goals today, yet we have made these into more than they should be by way of disproportionate ego and fear. This illusion has given rise to discontents such as sadness, fear, and anger to name a few. These are all different forms of the same suffering, just as surely as rain, fog, snow, and ice are all water.

Psychologically inflated fear, founded on hope, the past, and the future, fosters conflict. Fear exists because it helps the organism remain alive. Without any fear we would not last a week, but when fear is left unchecked and unacknowledged, like an unweeded garden, the mind begins to cultivate fear from the seed of automatic instinct, such as the automatic response when startled, into a psychosomatic disorder, cutting the observer off from reality. Fear propagates from attention deficit, denial, hope, escape, and also from too much attention, aggression, and opposition against it. This disorder of hyperactive fear leads to chronic uneasiness, unhappiness, panic/anxiety attacks, and phobias. We as a species are essentially phobic, as our psyches grab hold of automatic and beneficial physical responses to a dangerous situation and transform them into debilitating phobias and superstitions. Phobias are a mental disorder or excess of fear which makes the subject irrational and instills unwarranted feelings of danger, extreme dislike, and even hatred around an event or circumstance. Our perception transforms a peaceful moment into a dangerous one because the fight or flight response kicks in and gets things moving. Our minds ceaselessly create stress, a force to dominate and conquer, and so we ceaselessly tend to withdraw or confront because of our constantly active perceptions of many types of hopes and fears. Our minds fabricate their own dangers because our egos crave something to achieve, dominate, and conquer. Creating undue perceptions of danger and things to be overcome, creating conflict when there is none, is a prevailing addiction of mankind. When the ego is understood and the mind is quiet the midpoint between these reactionary extremes is peace, which is an unbiased clarity of reality. We live unbalanced lives of dueling opposites instead of living between these extremes; when we are unbalanced there is always a conflict of two or more forces, but when we are balanced there is only one, unified force. Fear is psychosomatic and thus constantly governs and clouds our thoughts, feelings, and bodily behaviors. We allow the dictates of fear to control us almost outright. If fear—or any other thought pattern meant to be used only in appropriate conditions—is unnaturally constant enough and intense enough it can become manifested as a physical illness, as well as numerous mental disorders and even mild psychosis, all resulting in a general loss of connection between the observer and reality. We are our awareness, among other things, and we have become a fearful species. Fear is born out of separation, out of conflict against reality and the flight or fight responses to escape reality. Sensing an imminent risk of pain and/or death is obviously quite useful; however, it is not a complete view of reality. Notice how the fear response instills an acute focus on the situation at hand and excludes everything else. Fear works extremely well in all organisms that use it, but there is a tradeoff; it excludes a clear perception of reality during the time it is utilized. Our mentality creates, uses, and sustains fear longer than necessary. When one is fully present with fear, a keen sensitivity to reality emerges: one becomes what one observes. Fear only arises as a protective motivation in an organism and is thus not a salient feature of the totality of reality. Therefore, when reality is observed with fear, hope, anger, despair, expectation or any other distressing mental state being understood, included, and not reacted upon, the subjective reactions lift and dissolve. The dissolution of illusion is a result of its complete comprehension and incorporation into the larger context and beauty of reality. This can be called the flow experience, and it doesn't have to occur through the acceptance of fear alone. In realizing fear, the observer and the observed (in this case fear) become one, and fear stops due to the dissipation of thought and overall separation. In the totality of acceptance of all that is observed, the observer and the observed are one, and this is called peace. Ignorance may be a superficial and fleeting slice of happiness, but the acceptance of total awareness is the whole satisfying and meaningful cake. In this awareness there is only here and now and it is filled with love, which is simply another word for everything. Like the contrasting and distinguishable colors of yellow and blue mixing to become green, you and that which you observe (fear in this case) are no longer distinguishable. Yellow and blue cease to exist when their combination transforms them into the color green. Separation and thus conflict are what create fear and unhappiness. If one is aware of their connection to everything then there is a sense of deep and everlasting happiness or purpose, where nothing is lacking and nothing is excessive. This awareness is the perfection of reality and the purpose of life.

The Truth and Silence of Illusion

What is truth? This question implies another question: What is not true? Truth as separate from untruth is the very essence of the simple yet intricately repeated and limited view of reality that creates all of the misguided questions that mankind asks. Everything is true when taken in consideration of the varying angles and intensities of scale from which it comes. A lie or an illusion can be true in the sense that liars might not know they are lying. Similarly, if someone believes in something that is untrue, that person's belief is sufficient in itself to make the thing true and real due to their very automatic belief in it. All illusion and deceit are true to a degree; they are just not the whole truth. Understanding the idea of something being untrue or false is like a cake with a piece taken from it. Someone removes a slice from the complete cake and then declares, "This piece of cake is not true." But anything that can be considered untrue is essentially true, just a smaller and smaller piece of the whole truth. Hate is just as true as love and is simply a very small and scaled-down piece of the beauty and love of reality. Anger and sadness are two forms of the same lesser truth—or a piece, to follow my analogy—of the complete truth of compassion and joy. Anger and sadness are simply a lesser truth or dissociation from the complete truth of love, and as such they constitute a certain void, or loss, of love and its totality. A piece of reality is always a piece when separated from the whole; however, when the piece is not dissociated from the whole, it is also the whole.

We are like spectators at a magic show. We allow ourselves to be voluntarily misguided by the performers and the performance, except that we ourselves are the players, our actions, and nature, in order to revel in the ignorance and lesser bliss of its entertainment value. We enjoy the mystery because we are not being shown the whole process. It is a self-engaged act of deceit, which is why the world is living in a highly conflictive and self-defeating paradigm of blissful ignorance. This is how we live our lives in reality; watching and living in this distracting and conflictive illusion. Is all this game-playing necessary? Surely it has value in a perverse way, in that it can teach us a lesson about its artificially concocted and fragmented nature, all of which make it unnecessary. Reality is a Magic Eye image in motion; however, the process of seeing it is reversed. In the normal approach of looking at the pictures in a Magic Eye book, one looks at the images of combined random uniformity and engages in a method of seeing the beauty behind the surface of the otherwise ungraspable colors and patterns. However, the way that we seem to go about viewing reality is quite to the contrary, due to our thoughts and conditioning. That is, we tend to largely overlook the reality of the order, beauty, and unity of the universe that is of and behind the surface of things, because it all seems random and utterly incomprehensible to us. We see instead the final image as a world and a universe of many separate, conflictive forms, functions, and objects, all unrelated in our minds. We constantly and automatically engage in this technique to see contrast and opposition, as well as to validate our own narrow view. It's as if we are looking through a kaleidoscope and convincing ourselves that the single truth is actually the many truths that we see. We utilize this method to divide and separate our perception and our world in the quest to fulfill the basic needs on Maslow's pyramid. We must unlearn our concrete and habitual ways of seeing in order to look beyond the surface, because however pleasurable it may be short term, it always results in pain and loss later on due to the hollow and counterfeit happiness generally striven for by people today. Biological adaptation, Darwin's survival of the fittest, demands that we see the world in this contrasting way; however, it can also help us see the truth behind it. Nature gave us eyes to look and, perhaps now, to see. Remember, adaptation isn't about progress. It simply serves to strike a balance or fit between the observer and the local environment, allowing both healthy survival and harmonious unity. We are adapting from an unsustainable and conflictive approach to one that is sustainable and in balance with our inner selves and consequently also with nature. Einstein stated that space is time, energy is mass, past is present as well as future, and that all of these are relative to each observer, and all of it is an illusion. Anyone's individual view of reality is merely a sliver of the creation cake, because we can only partially perceive it, but because we live in an infinite universe, one can see the whole in the part and the part in the whole. However, illusion and conflict can and does arise by our chosen belief in everything our senses and thoughts tell us and the conviction that what we think we know is all there is to reality.

Smoke, Mirrors, and Shadows

Everything is real, but we are simply distracted, and thus we miss the totality of our true beauty within this amazing universe. Our egocentric mental veils or filters, despite their known benefits, also serve—or dis-serve, I would submit—to hide and distort reality. They are our double-edged swords.

Magic tricks, for example, dupe only the willing and the knowingly blind. We, the many, are fooling ourselves because we like to be fooled. The perceptions and convictions of these illusions create an imbalanced reality between the subject and object that unnaturally splits them in two. Close your eyes and imagine a colorful sunset with the sound of crashing waves upon the sandy beach of a beautiful island paradise. This image is as real as any other. It exists in your mind, and if you imagine it well enough, you can almost taste the salt spray and feel the wind flowing between the palm trees. There is no denying that hunger, pain, pleasure, taste, sight, ego, and fear are real feelings, but they are all restricted to the observer, created by adaptation as an advantage for survival, in the observer's body and mind. These feelings, as with the image of the island, are what I call a real illusion. We get caught up in all of these images and feelings when there is so much more to life than this. There are more nutritious foods than candy, but perhaps they're not quite as tasty if one has a sweet tooth. One becomes caught and held captive by the illusion of taste, for example, if one only tastes, thereby forsaking real nourishment. We become lost in the imbalanced focus of our senses. Evolution gave us our sense of flavor as positive and negative distinctions of taste. The chemicals in the food we eat reach our taste buds because they look and smell good, the pleasure centers of our brains react favorably, and thus we crave more. Food that has "gone bad" looks, smells, and tastes the way it does to send us a message not to eat it because it will make us sick. If we still don't get the message, our stomachs will vomit it up for us. Sweet isn't really sweet by itself, but this illusion gives our body the motivation and energy it needs. The object needs its other half—the subject, observer, or experiencer—for taste or any other sensation to exist. There is no observer without reality; however, reality still exists despite ones' lack of awareness to it. Perception is a substantial and intimate glimpse of reality, but reality is not only one's mental perception. We generally trust what our gates to reality (or senses) tell us, and so we easily become lost in them and their interpretations. The color red isn't exclusively red, but it attracts our attention for many reasons, as seen in so many examples in nature, art, clever advertising, and so on. Fear, pain, color or any other perception needs an observer to make it so. This is at the heart of all quantum and relativistic physics, as well as true spiritual teachings. The observer is the observed, and without one aspect, the other cannot be; this means that the non-observer, or the lazy and uncaring observer, is also a part of the non-observed or ignored and conflictive view of reality. There is difference only when the observer creates an in-between world. As you walk through a valley, notice the mountains which create it. Observing separation, conflict, and suffering only occurs because of the perception of focus and isolation and thus the loss of the context of wholeness. Earth's balance is an even ground so when we bulldoze nature to elevate and expand humanity we simultaneously dig a hole for all other species to die in. When there is a clear understanding and balance of one's self, needs, desires and senses there emerges peace and wholeness in ones' consciousness. With the peace of the observer, there emerges a beautiful interaction and awareness in which the observer meets the observed in such a way that nature becomes the true and whole experience of itself. All interactions throughout all scales of awareness and interaction create the true, ultimate reality. The illusion is in our views of limitation and separation and the subsequent imbalance of these interactions. Our world is in the context of an infinite universe, not in our personal corner of repetitive little goals, habits, and discrete sensations. The reality we present to ourselves is a lesser and partial view of what complete truth really is. It is because we don't see the fullness and beauty of reality that we are generally unhappy.

Duality

There is a story I heard on a trip to the Mexican Yucatan Peninsula concerning two trees which always grow together and that I believe illustrates the underlying unity in the midst of apparently obvious separation. During the 1970s and 80s the hotel boom on the Peninsula was in full swing, resulting in many trees being felled to make room for roads and development. Many of the laborers, for reasons unknown at the time, had to be hospitalized due to the development of severe painful rashes on their skin. The local Maya told them about the trees they were cutting down. As the legend goes, long ago there were two Mayan brothers who died, and when they returned from the underworld, one emerged as a poisonous *Chechen* tree and the other as the *Chaca* tree whose sap contained the antidote to the poison. These trees always grow together in pairs and all the workers had to do to heal their ailments was to simply rub some of the sap from the *Chaca* tree on the rash that was causing the pain and irritation. I believe that this parable uniquely summarizes the unity in nature, which actually exists in profusion in the countless symbiotic relationships between plants, animals, insects, microorganisms—and man—and among the diverse forces of nature. Unity is a law that is never broken; it is just sometimes ignored and forgotten.

Sir Isaac Newton stated that "For every action there is an equal and opposite reaction." Action is reaction because they are deeply interconnected by the infinite chain of indistinguishable actions and reactions. Action and reaction are just two names for the same process that we choose to divide arbitrarily, much like the numbers one and two or any whole number connected by infinite and arbitrary fractions. Waves have a crest and a trough, ebb and flow. Like the birth and death of a bacterium, a grasshopper, or a human being, all are a reaction to an infinite chain of actions, and this infinitely chained event will continue after individual life and death because, like space and time, life and death are traditionally limiting concepts that are much more than what we narrowly think of them. As with the concepts of space, time, energy, and matter, we must rethink the way we have always thought about life and death. We must give a serious second look at life because the first look was hasty and divisive. Infinity is a continuum. Smoke and shadow obscure the truth and also serve to divide this truth into a false dualism.

Two Halves of a Whole

Without contrast there is nothing. However, these polar oppositions form an inseparable and singular relationship. All conceptualized opposites are joined into a unity because they are totally and thoroughly defined and dependent on each other. Choosing to believe that the observer and the observed are separate makes it so, as we discovered in the *OBSERVING AS AN INDIVIDUAL* part (p. 7) and *The Quantum Realm Is Our Own* section (p. 258), and thus we cannot observe anything without becoming it and affecting it. It is because we are conditioned to view entities and existences as separate that we see life this way and divide it. Suspend the act of thought-filled, logic-driven observation and you will see reality as it beautifully and completely is. This can be difficult and take time, or it can actually be easy and instantaneous. This action of awareness dissolves all separation, division, conflict, and opposition, creating in its place freedom, beauty, love, and unity, which is truth.

Whether it is a person, plant, animal, or object—or anything we slap a label on—we grasp little of the infinite depth of what is represented by our shallow symbols, images, categories, and mistaken translations. Names and images do not equal true understanding, although we tend to think they suffice. If we know the name or appearance of something we don't really know the thing itself, we just know the name or image. We know the handle we attach to it so that it's easier to identify or imagine in our heads. We divide ourselves from creation. Life and love are restricted by our imagery, memory, symbolism, and abstraction. All of these tools of resistance live only in our practical thoughts; they are meaningless within the context of the vast, unlimited reality that exists without all of the imagined borders and chains we put on it. These are the many finite symbols we use to conceptualize our infinite world, a task for which they are utterly inadequate.

Science and art are the same. Explaining or expressing the inexplicable and inexpressible through equations, theories, paint, letters, or philosophies is an eternally transient comprehension that we hope sheds a sliver of light on the truth. One has to be entirely open for this. How can reality present itself clearly when we are strangers to the nature of it and ourselves? The symbols we cling to, instead of letting go of them and understanding how we act in respect to ignoring reality and ourselves, serve as arrows. However many and however correct in their representation, it comes down to the individual to see these symbols for what they are: a tool, a compass that shows everything at its axis.

People choose to be unhappy, whether from a mix of active and conscious awareness or unconscious and habitual unawareness. One can run and hide from the truth and, indeed, from oneself for an entire lifetime. We go to church, read our books, throw around ideas, theories, tips, tricks, traditions, commandments and stories, all in the attempt to feel genuine joy and peace, and so far it has generally been for naught. Through our discussions, debates, and arguments we usually only partially understand one another's viewpoints due, in large part, to the limits of communication, and thus it is mainly viewed as entertaining or pointless, like the magic show. And yet only one thing has been misinterpreted, and that is everything. We think and talk and, more often than not, we leave the practice and the action out of the momentum of the revolution and beauty of reality. This is perpetual half-assery and there are, generally speaking, no real groundbreaking shifts to come out of all these discussions or methods of devotion and self-help. How do we bridge the gap between thought and action? The only answer is through love, as a motivation that must be nurtured and sustained. Love or beauty is action all on its own—the alpha and the omega. This is freedom, freedom from knowledge, fear, and everything else we humans have blown out of proportion to escape and distract ourselves from the flow of creation, which most of us see as bad and full of pain, sorrow, and death. What we habitually and uncontrollably desire is pleasure, fun, escape, comfort, and ease. Many people are stuck in the habit of working hard and playing hard with nothing really in between these excessive extremes. This is our bodies speaking to our minds and vice versa based on our own survival mechanisms and habits accumulated from thousands of years of evolution, in order to survive in times of worsening scarcity and mounting discomfort. Survival is our singular biological imperative. In the animal kingdom, of which we are members, survival is all about the struggle for food, water, shelter, and the ability of species to propagate. In our modern world, at least in developed countries, humans don't really have to struggle too much for these basic necessities, at least not compared to in the ancient past. Our society has only transformed these basic struggles into physical and psychological wars of greed and ignorance, competitive and aggressive job markets and economies, the striving for status and prestige, all focused on the middle echelons of Maslow's hierarchy. Without self-actualization, conflict always remains, even if the forms and circumstances vary. I am optimistic that we may have domesticated ourselves to such an extent that this process may possibly lead us back to the normal struggle and appreciation of the life that nature creates, however it may happen. This explains our big brain, our technical knowhow, fear, hope, and curiosity, all self-serving to the survival of an individual organism. If the individual organism survives, it collectively helps the entire species and the balance of life in general. We are an overly successful species when it comes to survival. We have focused on what is important to maintain life and have, like all species, self-beneficial instinctual patterns and behaviors. We navigate these unconscious, instinctual, involuntary compulsions through the dominance of the mind with its thoughts and ideas. These thoughts and ideas have elevated and separated this organ from the rest of the body through a conscious and active sense of its own importance. The brain's mental processes are essentially an individual's ego, which many think lives on after the body dies. Our strong sense of ego has made an individual soul type of entity out of itself. Certainly a strong sense of individuality is advantageous for survival; however, it comes at a profound cost to one's ability to experience truth and peace. Furthermore, in ancient times our focusing, choosing, and deciding thoughts needed to be quick and self-serving; otherwise survival would have been even more difficult in a harsh prehistoric world with little wiggle room for mistakes. This is where prejudices, stereotypes, the strong sense of ego arising from our overactive brains, and our conquering mentality come from. Escape, denial, ignorance by choice/selection, aggression, violence, fear, and the illusion of time are all survival mechanisms built on the basic perception of the individual as separate from others and one's surroundings. The stresses, dangers, and subsequent actions of living in a wild world require that our organic computers (our brains) assert their individual characters in order to initiate and maintain these defense mechanisms and self-preserving behaviors

Certainly, we can only see things through our own eyes, and thus each of us has our private, relative views of what is good and bad, our values, beliefs, objects, and people we relate to and care about. Each person's perception of reality is unique, but at the same time it is also essentially quite the same to those of others. We can't afford to be careless with this powerful influence we have upon ourselves and Earth.

What happens when one can't afford something? The prudent individual doesn't buy the item, but the extravagant one borrows and buys it anyway with the intention of paying for it later, and hence becomes instantly in debt. We have certainly not been prudent. The idea of later eventually progresses into the present, and that time is now. Now is the time we start paying for the heavy loans we have taken from nature. So far we have lived in a global model where everybody wins except nature. Now is the culmination of illusions, where nature and its resources face exhaustion and humanity must pay up.

If we cannot recognize our stupid habits and attitudes, which is the first step to understanding, accepting, and moving to transform them, and then multiply this ignorance by the number of people on Earth, we are unwittingly steering ourselves, and all life on the planet, toward a place far from where we expected to go, assuming we even had an inkling of a specific expectation. This, of course, is both good and bad from certain perspectives. We separate the ideal from the actual, and everyday life from the imagined fantasy goal, and we separate the true from false, good from evil, and the material from the spiritual. All of this separation is illusion. We are and have been lying to ourselves. We are fish in the ocean that see only the things in water and we then imagine these observable things as the whole world. The universe is an undivided oceanic continuum to which we really don't pay the necessary attention. The illusion of duality rules our view of nature and of ourselves, which creates conflict and leads to our unsustainable and dangerously failing stewardship of our now dying world. The veil is lifting, and the destructive nature of our ways is presenting itself.

Uniting the Divide—The Universal Process of Joining and Splitting

Many have spoken about oneness and unity, but to actually see it for oneself is an entirely different story. This is to be expected with faulty communication that always seems to present an air of uncertainty, or a lack of complete understanding between the speaker and the listener, who only seem different from each other, though they really are not. People may speak about the same thing, but almost always from different aspects or perspectives, even if they are only slightly different, because of the way each individual perceives those things—with their individually procured attachments of meaning, experience, and knowledge.

Imagine a sphere. Now put two arrows inside it at opposite ends with each pointing in the opposite direction in line with the perimeter. When we spin the sphere in the direction of both arrows, the arrows go in the same direction, like a dog or snake chasing its tail, the regenerative symbol called an ouroboros. Thus, two opposing arrows in a cycle or circle travel in the same direction. It is all a false dichotomy. Only in our minds do we contend that life needs something more, because we feel as if we are missing something, whether it is in terms of our goals, expectations, hopes, ambitions, or happiness. It is really only our unbalanced instinct augmented by thought. We are simply on our own frequency. Like a radio, we are tuned in to our own individual signal, and we need to tune in to the signal of the universal station, instead of tuning it out. We are out of sync. This is why we are always looking for more in life, but generally only in places that we know, the realm of the familiar and safe. This vain search can be likened to looking for something you lost, but searching only on the surface of things where you can see, or in places that you are familiar with and where you thought the mission object would be, never in the dark and risky places that might challenge your entrenched and cherished views. This is our approach to understanding the unknown by means of the known. The finite known has its place, but in the end it only serves as an arrow toward the infinite unknown. This is the linchpin of discovering the true beauty that the majority of people lose sight of, much as looking directly at a star causes it to appear to lose its luster. We create religions and theologies of many kinds, based on sheer fear and hope in some shadowy plane of existence beyond this amazing and unlimited universe. And yet, even with the concept of some "afterlife," we separate our limited perceived reality, and ourselves, from a divine and usually anthropomorphic symbol of an even "more" unlimited truth and beauty, as if the one we have isn't enough. Or we seek and isolate the special and amazing things and experiences within the continual yet unseen amazement of every thing and all experience. Or we go on digging deeper into the atom, splitting it apart into smaller and smaller pieces, or looking deeper and deeper into space trying to find answers to the question of where exactly we fit in the middle of all this. It's all the same damn beautiful thing. Imagine a world where everyone sees the beauty in life because it's reflected and recognized in themselves. The world has been painted ugly by almost seven billion painters and their predecessors, and who will see the beauty of it? Who will accept it and love it instead of hating and creating conflict with it? If we become an opposite force, we are caught again where we conflict with the conflicted and become it as we aid in its growth. We will feed on each other in an endless cycle, with two opposing arrows chasing each other, and if one is lacking so the other is also. We are all responsible, yet we outsource that responsibility and predictably blame "them" for our problems. With opposites, if one is missing, so too is the other, and if one exists so does the other. We create our conflicted reality by and through the neural web connecting our thoughts, perceptions, experiences, and memories; this web strengthens these connections by repetition in the vain effort to help us live better in the world of what we know or sense. Opposites are inextricably linked, so we view the false dichotomy as a relationship between two or more opposing forces instead of seeing the infinite unity that this incorrectly perceived limit arises from.

Singularity excludes nothing, including nothing. In the beginning there was light; this is something science and religion can agree on. Big Bang or creation or whatever label you choose, it is the same thing; these labels are simply versions, perspectives, viewpoints, localized and hence fractal perceptions of the singularity. The Big Bang or creation wasn't just in the past; it is the past and the future which are right now. Terminology abounds, but ultimately this narrow view of reality is the misinterpretation of our space-time, exclusively material reality borne out of our limited and fearful awareness of things. It is probable if not certain that there have been infinite creations before this one and that there are infinite singularities that await us in the future. It is still *one* infinite creation, just with points of reference arbitrarily designated by us, where we assume that singularities "end" and "begin." A singularity is described as a point that is smaller than an atom, an electron, or a Planck-sized object. It is both smaller and larger than anything beyond space in time. This singularity has no traditional concept of space-time, which expands to create universes and contracts to create the singularity. It is the dance of the seed and the forest.

Stars and planets are formed from gravity and magnetism and all other forces attracting gases and particles. Many of these stars will eventually collapse under the force of their own increasing gravity, or explode and redistribute these particles to form new stars and planets. This cycle is infinite. The universe is timeless beyond eternity and spaceless beyond infinity. The universe sprang from a singularity and in reality still is one. It is unlimited growth, life, death, love, hate, possibility, thoughts, feelings, ideas, pain, and pleasure, all existing as opposites in a single indivisible moment, which is right now as you read these words. The universe is everything happening everywhere all at once forever. Forever isn't a long time, as most think. It is actually right now. Likewise, when we think of infinitely small or infinitely large we think in common terms of size. Something infinitely small isn't really small and something infinitely large isn't really enormous either. This can be hard to fathom. Our illusion of the senses governed by our self-imposed laws of separation, on-off or contrasting sensations, cause and effect, past, future, and so on create this faulty point of view. The illusion is simply a perspective of belief in what we see as opposite or separate in order to escape fear and ignore the pain and sorrows of life. Thus we remember the past and plan for the future in order to always remain ignorant, too busy planning or too busy remembering. You see, an illusion is that which eludes us, an erroneous perception clouding, hiding, concealing, and disguising our clarity, much like a magic act or a veil.

The Singularity—The Observer Is the Observed

The singer is the song and the one song that exists is sung by God, so God, the song, the notes, the spaces between them, the you, the me, and the universe are all the same thing, echoed perfectly in Walt Whitman's poem *Song of Myself* in *Leaves of Grass* (1855/2007):

I celebrate myself,
And what I assume you shall assume,
For every atom belonging to me as good belongs to you.
and
I and this mystery here we stand.
Clear and sweet is my soul…and clear and sweet is all that is not my soul.
Lack one lacks both…and the unseen is proved by the seen.

Relativity states that what I experience is different than what someone else experiences, based on our varying and personal observations. Quantum physics also states that all possibilities in reality are superimposed in a waveform, and as soon as we observe them the wave collapses into an observable experience. Touch a snowflake and it melts. Both of these scientific views are still focused on observation through an observer. True reality is the complete immersion of the observer so that the observed and the observer become one. This is where all science that is based on measurements and observations will fail time and time again to find its holy grail of a unified theory, because there will always be separation between what seeks the theory, the theory to be found, and the act of finding it. With the study or observation of things, also known as science, there will always be separation between the observable and the observed and the known and the unknown. Stephen Hawking, Einstein, and many others, including spiritualists, have devoted their lives, time, and energy to trying to find a "theory of everything," and it was always out of their reach because of the separation of the observer and the observed. We play hide and seek with ourselves.

Relativity shows how things relate to the observer and quantum theory shows how both uncertainty, and how we relate to the observed indelibly affects that relationship. Both are correct in their domains, just like red is defined by its proprietary wavelength—its scale of size or intensity. The combination joins the object and subject in a fundamental way. Everything from measurement to physical laws to religious beliefs are all about how the observed relates to oneself and what he or she observes. The non-observer, the habitual or unconscious observer, is the fragmented, concealed, and conflicted non-observed. Anything finite is still only partially observed, while anything infinite can never be fully observed, unless one sees infinity as oneself; then the world opens up.

We live inside and outside of a combination tool called mind and body. This will change in death when our physical tool is no longer needed and the energy that we consumed from nature as food, water, and air will move along the flow of life to create bugs, fungi, plants, and animals, which in turn will pollinate and reproduce along the motions of life over and over again, because it is all cyclic and this is the infinite conscious energy of creation/nature/God being manifest in perceptually different forms and functions in all the variations of life. This is reincarnation without the self or ego being needlessly reincarnated and preserved as some separate, selfish entity, so it could be better described as a naturally perfect and beautiful transformation of degree and scale, not kind, just as birth is. Your life or purpose isn't even truly yours alone. How odd it sounds to say "my life" when nobody really owns anything! All you can really do is share your love and life with all of the other shareholders, analogously the way a company benefits its shareholders with their investments.

Imagine everything as a mirror. Your purpose shouldn't be so narrow and specific and selfish as to reflect only what is good for you alone, or only what you want to acquire and have for yourself, to the exclusion of others, because that is all based on separation and ego. You are the nucleus and circumference in a boundless sphere, just as everything from a source is the source. You are the infinite circumference which is also the infinite center. One cannot force this revolution upon others, because force simply compounds and continues the problem. All one can do is present a level of awareness that starts a seed, and the growth of doubt of the known and a spur of love of the wonder of reality. After that, what the observer is presented with and what they do with it is up to them. Based on their memories, experiences, and thoughts, they will accept or reject it. This is something one can only partially explain, but ultimately it must fully be felt by each individual. Love your enemy because you *are* your enemy. You are your own worst enemy. We are really one big family of galaxies, stars, planets, moons, friends, enemies, tools, garbage, stones, fire, water, wood, lightning, thunder, rain, snow, clouds, and atomic bombs: All of it. Some things in life are like distant relatives, some things are closer, some things intimate and some estranged, but that doesn't negate the fact that life is one family, however familiar or unfamiliar.

A spark is only a spark when separated from the flame from which it was thrown. A spark within the flame *is* the flame. A droplet of water is only a droplet of water when viewed in isolation from a body of water. A droplet within the ocean *is* the ocean. Alone, a droplet of water may not seem like much, but millions of droplets of water can absorb and reflect light, unify and harmonize that light to create a rainbow. In this way hydrogen and oxygen unite with electricity and magnetism to create the awe and inspiration of one of the many beautiful sights in nature. This rainbow can be seen in everything, even in the most unlikely of places, like an oil slick, or a puddle topped with spilled gasoline in the streets of a slum. If you choose to see it, everything, however "ugly," can be viewed in the same way as a rainbow. This is the beauty in life. It's the same as seeing the grooves on a vinyl record and regarding the sound that comes from them as boring or even irritating when they are made by scratching a fingernail across them instead of being ridden by a needle running smoothly and harmoniously with them, then suddenly realizing and hearing the music hidden in the valleys. The notes become fuller, the blues are bluer, and the sweets are sweeter. The creator has an image and it is in all things, seen and unseen. We are sleeping in heaven, but we are dreaming a nightmare, and all we have to do is wake up and open our eyes. It is analogous to a lottery, except we all have the winning numbers, and the jackpot belongs equally to everyone and everything. Our problem is that we don't see the miracle that we already have, and we are letting the gift go unnoticed instead of claiming and appreciating it. We thoughtlessly ignore the potential of beauty and love while embracing our own little "real" or self-perceived world.

The creator and heaven are right here, right now; all we have to do is see it and realize that it is everything and live in this awareness in our everyday lives. Instead we seem to choose to see our lives as boring drudgery, as painful and sorrowful, even as some sort of moral test or waiting period of hardship, even suffering, before we eventually die and can finally receive the reward of "eternal happiness" with God or in the spirit world of eternity. This all just seems a bit silly to me. We love our lives so much as to fear death greatly, and yet we view our lives as tribulation and ordeal. Our lives are common, and it's up to the individual to choose to see this normality as boring, empty, and ugly or as full of life and beauty. Only complete acceptance, surrender, and freedom can evoke serious change for our Earth, and it inevitably will, because in conflict and imbalance lie the seeds of collapse and dissolution. The utterly complete awareness of conflict and fear for what they actually are effectively dissolves them, transforming them the way the water in a vast sea of ice might transform into droplets in the atmosphere to create a cloud. It is seeing the solution to a puzzle with absolute clarity. With new sight the puzzle is no longer a puzzle.

The puzzle of reality is always seen to be in innumerable pieces only in our brains, because in reality it has always been, and always will be, one piece.

For some reason, most tend to think of Jesus, Buddha, Mohammed, the Creator, creation, and ourselves as separate and distant from each other. This is heaven, right here and now, not just eternally in the clouds after death. We are the split piece of wood, the color, heat, humanity, stone, nature, and everything. We all have it in our greater selves. This is why we sometimes refer to God as a higher being or power. Knowing God or creation is our higher being, our higher power. Satan, fear, and hate are what create the illusion of separation, and hence our sleight of mind reality is why we are a fallen humanity destroying everything in our path. We only see a sliver or, in essence, a singularly individual, localized, ego-view of the truth and beauty of life. In a traditional, sociological, and interpersonal sense, we are of course separate from each other; we have separate bodies, separate minds. Many people really feel this way and they are utterly convinced that things are separate, and thus they act and speak from their convictions and beliefs. From the water we drink, to the air we breathe, the food we eat, to the people, plants, and animals we share this world with, it does all seem so separate, doesn't it? It is intuitively obvious without thought. This is the commonsense and highly practical and pragmatic view of the world, which enables us to navigate our lives through it. This concept is painfully elementary and considered dogma without ever being given a second glance. A lot of us need to take another look at many things. Conventional Reality 101 says that everything is clearly, obviously, and distinctly separate. But consider that common sense is an evolutionary prejudice that an organism has developed in order to live long enough to the age where it can effectively produce, and in some cases raise, offspring. Common sense is not the whole reality. Even within our bodies we have separate organs, systems, molecules, atoms, elementary particles, quarks, electromagnetism, gravity, and quantum wave functions all doing their own thing and in relation to each other. You can name everything in existence and come up with a non-labored and very convincing argument that they are indeed separate. It's just plain old objective, empirical truth, right? It is my view that this paradigm or social and cultural dogma is hopelessly limited and scaled down to basic practicality, and that it is completely incompatible with the infinite and unknowable and utterly beautiful truth of actual reality. Opposites are not at all separate from each other. This limited truth exists only in the context of the infinite; it merely has its place in a small corner within the whole grand scheme of the universe.

All experience is this relationship of feeling opposites vibrate together in harmony, and this feeling is then recreated by our consciousness. Action and reaction are illusions of separation interpreted as such by our senses. Action *is* reaction.

The word "paradox" means anything commonly perceived to be contradictory that, regardless of these views, may still be completely true. Some may see ample contradictions in the vision presented in this book; however, they are simply paradoxes that may oppose and challenge one's conceptual foundation of dualism, separation, and opposing mental extremes. These paradoxes do not actually conflict with worldviews based on dualism, although they may seem to at first, but rather they serve to humbly expand them to the whole context of truth. Reality is seen through the illusion of separation which causes conflict. The universe is one all-inclusive song that is a harmonic and flowering vibration. Listen to your breath and feel your heartbeat. You breathe in and out, but it is the same breath one cycle after another. Feel your heart. Your heart contracts and expands as your breath rejuvenates each beat with oxygen. Our breath is the same repeated heartbeat over and over again. Blink. Your eyes close, then open repeatedly. The rising and setting of the Sun and the waxing and waning of the moon are cycles or processes just like the universe, with which, of course, they are in tune. The universe rises and subsides. It has an infinite beginning and an infinite end that are one and the same. A fractal universe has a beginning and an end only as an artificial reference point of experience for the sake of our meager orientation or perception, and is really and simply infinite.

Serenade of the Whole

Love

Love is perfectly equivalent to life, heaven, God, energy, matter, time, space, nothing, everything, you, me, nature, the universe, beauty and truth. These words are empty symbols, triggers, or arrows that only serve to lead to the meaning behind them. Love is connection, and forgiveness is acceptance; thus if we simply accept connection, then everything falls into balance. Love as we think of it is not really love in the fullest sense, because the love we commonly feel is given and taken according to human, social circumstances and conditions. In a sense, you can buy and sell this superficial love at a market, not only with money but also with the many other conditional, circumstantial forms that selfishness creates to feed itself. The love we think we feel is not love if we are afraid of losing it, because it then becomes fear, not love. Likewise, if you are greedy with love it then transforms into a selfish and conflictive possession, not love. Complete love is unwavering and truly unconditional without the desire to give or take, and without the notion of punishment or reward. Even when we view love and compassion as good, we have the negative and opposite side of the coin in the corner of our minds, just as surely as any opposite has its companion. However, when one becomes both opposites, not separating, escaping, denying, or avoiding, but accepting those opposites as coexisting, all is then seen as one and one is seen as all, because conflict, fear, hate, and all the other symptoms of separation dissolve, because the roots and branches of duality cannot exist on their own. A sad or angry person who is open and present is no longer sad or angry, and the same goes for a person with fear or hope. This openness and simultaneous awe cancel out illusion and conflict, leaving only what is. When one becomes the observed there is no judgment, thought, or observation by a separate observer. There is just what is. You become the beauty of it and in this there is the flow of love and true freedom, different words for the same thing. There are truths and lesser truths, the known and unknown, past and future, and they all exist together. With observation, the observer may transcend the fragmented view of the universe, and thus see that the smaller can be in the larger and the larger can be in the smaller. Any part is representative of the whole. Separation is always a lower degree of intentional observation in the scale of unity.

Displacement

Love your enemies.
(Jesus Christ, Matthew 5:44, *The King James Bible*)

Cold isn't really the presence of cold, although I can imagine many arguments to the contrary, because one can clearly feel cold. Rather, it can be understood as the absence of heat. From this perspective, concepts like hate and Hell have no substance in reality except for when there is a perceived void or absence of the reality of love and heaven. Illusions only exist when there is an absence of reality. The opposite of reward isn't punishment, but simply the absence of reward. Where there is hate, it is a displacement, void, or separation from love. In the process of displacement the negative energy is only negative when separate from its opposite positive energy; however, when the energies are balanced and united there is no negative or positive but a perfect harmony of motion. We attach many symbols to reality in our effort to put some sort of handle or comprehension on that which cannot be fully grasped by the mind.

Being in real love and falling from it into anything else is very similar to how we view the transformation from genius into insanity. Profound and absolute love involves nothing else. Superficial love, however, can easily become tainted and transformed into many diverse forms of that which is not love. Love can become twisted into fear by thoughts of trying to keep it which come from thoughts of the possibility of losing it. The desire for more love becomes greed and the motivation to defend it and fight for it transforms love into aggression and violence. This is how subtly partial love can become twisted and lost. One may not notice the moment when love crosses seamlessly into hate, anger and so forth because one is not aware of love when this occurs. Love is conventionally viewed as irrational, which is probably why we can't make sense of real love. Alternatively, love is the most rational of feelings. Clarity will give us a real view of what love is and what it is not. Genius, like love, is a clear view of reality while insanity and a lack of love are anything but a clear view of reality. Illusions only exist, and indeed persist, when they are left unquestioned and viewed as anything else. Clarity and understanding reveal the truth hidden in illusion, the peace disguised as fear, and the present moment veiled in the construct of time. Clarity integrates all the diverse aspects of reality into a singular, infinite dimension. Clarity does not exclude reality. Denying that which we perceive as negative only serves to strengthen the mistaken views of the good and bad duality. The denial of the unity of reality, for whatever reason, is the very reason why these dualistic and antagonistic views exist in the first place. The intention and awareness of what truly is and what you truly are is crucial to refrain from falling into the vicious growth cycle of the conflict/separation illusion.

Make a sustained effort, if you would, to see the love and preciousness of a loved one not as its narrow form of the individual person, but as a process of absolutely everything seen and unseen blanketed over the entire spectrum of existence. This is heaven and this is the unseen dimension in everyday life. We create a heavenless vision because of our heavenless viewpoint. We create disharmony by our conflictive and individual intentions.

We extend our love of certain things only partially. We are *part*icular. Some people will do anything to acquire and keep the things they love. It is a prime motivation. People will kill, steal, contaminate the air and water, and do other damage to their environment, if that's what it takes to give the family they love a full stomach and a roof over their heads. We devise our modern society to enable us to pursue happiness, and civilization goes just about as far as it can through technological comforts and an abundance of entertainments, material things, lifestyle options, and other pursuits aimed at sustained satisfaction. But they all fall short of meaningful happiness; simply look around for proof. Are the majority of people on Earth happier now than in the past? People largely feel that our modern way of living is an improvement over the past. All things considered, I believe we have taken certain steps in our information/knowledge and technological fronts, but as a consequence of these fixations we have taken about ten times as many steps backward on the happiness/wisdom front. We live a superficial, comfortable life at the expense of what is important: a truly happy and meaningful life. What is gained doesn't compare to what is lost. We focus on the entitlements of man-made luxury and excess over the humble appreciation of the basic necessities that nature gives us, and as a result we have become ungrateful and thus fundamentally unhappy. Even as an intelligent species we generally don't really see the beauty that nature radiates. Instead we seem to want to subdue, conquer and use it because we fear its energy and its power to "take away" what we love. It's a clash between the way nature works and our attachments to what nature transforms, and the conflict that this creates in us has spilled over into the world we live in. Imagination is seeing with the mind, and we have imagined a future and a past that only serve to dim the clarity of the now. There is no good or bad until these concepts are created by the act of perceiving them, thus emerging from the illusions of divisive perceptions, motivations, and attitudes and antagonistic consequences. Our hands are tools of the mind and together they have constructed a world built on conflict through a grave misunderstanding of nature and our interconnected relationship with it.

Our individual personal identity, generally speaking, is what we call ourselves, as well as all of the preferences, appearance, views, characteristics, and so on that we attribute to ourselves. In describing yourself you will focus on the things you relate to or identify with as being part of your intellectual, physical, and even spiritual makeup. Is it possible for us to see that we are deeply interconnected and related to everything, without completely distorting reality through the myopic lenses of our personal agendas?

Humanity craves security and convenience, among the multitude of other desires. We believe that technology will sweep away our outer struggles and in effect address or solve our inner discontents in one swing. Utilizing nature for our own purposes creates technology and this allows us to create a safer, more comfortable society. However, the use and manipulation of nature, like the fight or flight response, should be, and indeed for thousands of years was, kept to a minimum. Using technology addresses only the symptoms that emerge from our psyches to the surface, which we then see in our surroundings. Technology as a tool to fix our outer problems is inadequate; it's like treating tuberculosis with cough drops and a scarf, or acne with a mask of makeup. When all's said and done, the problem of unnecessary suffering caused by humanity's mistaken perceptions of division remains, and even worsens, as is the case whenever an attempt to heal an affliction in such a way naturally only treats the symptoms. The problem is too far advanced to be prevented and apparently too difficult at its current, advanced stage of growth to be treated in any preventive or conventional way. Despite the many benefits of using knowledge to survive within the less-than-ideal circumstances of nature, technologies ultimately cost more than the benefits they bring in the short term, because we created them out of our antagonistic psyches, and thus, in any tool's form, function or purpose incorporates this conflict and separation from the way of nature. A simple stick is technology because it can be honed for a specific purpose such as raking, walking or killing. Technology isn't neutral or feasible in the long term simply because of its inherent intention to fix or improve on the perfection of nature, which can effectively makes things worse. Nature isn't broken so we shouldn't try to fix it; humanity is broken and technology is certainly not the tool to correct this damage. The solution to the consequences of our meddling with nature is not in further meddling but in understanding how to enjoy and compliment nature. Take the care to see the reality of things. Humanity's irrationality, and even insanity, may still be curable, because it is possible, however improbable, to abandon our belief in separation.

Death has touched and hurt us all. We have amplified the "profoundness" of death through the religious ideologies and theologies of generation after generation and we have sought refuge from this illusion of death by following these theologies, as well as in myriad other ways. This is essentially a collective pain or sorrow that we have created and chosen for ourselves, and then consequently spread to others and to all aspects of our world. We are all artists and many are tormented, as is quite evident in the splattered worldly canvas we have painted. We have bought into it. Death is a scar on the human psyche that is deeper than for other animals, because our conscious thought-machine keeps the negative idea of death alive longer than is necessary or prudent for our overall health. It's an illusion that is past its point of necessity. We seem to crave a structured society in an attempt to create security. We crave authority. We have so many leaders, institutions, governments, clubs, societies, schools, communities, organizations, and so on. We love to follow because it gives us a sense of power, security, and belonging, and it seems to sate our need for personal esteem and social connection. Following can be an advantage in many, mostly socially functional aspects of life, but not for the deepest and most important. This is a manifestation of the human separation mentality and has its uses, but, as with all beliefs, choices, or compromises, it has its divisions, exclusions, and problems. All clubs or organizations in all their various forms incorporate exclusions that create the us and them or we and they mentality. We are living backward from the natural way and we are closing in on a period of change that will flip nature back onto its feet. The journey will not be without transitional tribulations along the way. On the other hand, we could simply destroy the Earth in the process of destroying ourselves. There is no absolute guarantee that humanity or Earth will survive these turbulent times.

Beauty

Genuine beauty can be described as the feeling one gets when a glimpse of the pure truth of nature has taken place. Beauty is perfect just as it is. Anything and everything can be looked at as the most beautiful thing in the world; a fly, a cup, a voice, a drink of water, a leaf, a rock, a wind, a handful of sand, a mosquito, a hug, a laugh, a kiss. Reality is no more and no less than a beautiful gift to itself. It doesn't need to be changed or altered with addition or subtraction and even when it is it remains as perfect as it was. It is a timeless perception into the unification of the reflection of nature and oneself. Beauty is the captivating awe of truth which allows one to stop and be silent enough to hear nature's song. With the unimpeded inspiration of reality comes the divine perfume of all things in a single breath and the view of heaven in every blink. Beauty is the clear understanding of the perfection of *the* moment.

When we experience something utterly beautiful, the compulsion is to tap a neighbor's shoulder and point to it so they can also enjoy it. That person will probably not look at our pointing finger, but will rather intuitively understand that the finger is not of any particular importance except to be a signal to what is. However, when one has not directly observed someone else's experience of beauty and they try to explain it with the limits of communication, then people do tend to focus on the limited navigational fingers or concepts and ideas, methods, systems, symbols, customs, and descriptions which are then the only things we can use to attempt to understand, instead of seeing the meaning and full reality behind the arrows, conveyances and vehicles of truth. We focus our attention on the concepts and interpretations, thus losing the total sight of the reality being taught or revealed. The natural behavior of the mind turns the overbearing quantity and quality of beauty into limited and thus much more manageable ideas, symbols, and concepts, and so we not only miss the true beauty behind others' attempts to describe reality, but we also miss the true beauty behind what our very own minds are attempting to portray. As a result of our out-of-focus and grainy picture of reality, we create a less-than-beautiful manmade world, because of our limited and symbolic mental process. We place so much undue trust in the accuracy of our minds that we effectively misuse our minds and abuse the beauty of reality. Whenever our minds are preoccupied, all we are focused on is the pseudo-reality created by the thought process. Only a revolution of insight, however it occurs, can allow us to bring the fullness of beauty into ourselves and totally combines ourselves with that beauty or love. Beauty is its own guide, and points to you, the observer, as the crucial factor in seeing it.

Roger Penrose, Murray Gell-Mann, and countless other mathematicians and physicists believe that a fundamental unified theory will be beautiful, because all successful theories explaining the universe are. Einstein was also a believer in beauty as a pivotal criterion for a successful theory. What makes something beautiful? Beauty is more than just pleasing smells, tastes, sounds, colors, proportions, and symmetries but in a fuller sense it is simplicity, recognition, and the reflection of these things in ourselves. In terms of scientific theory, it is also effectiveness and efficiency, or what we call elegance, grace, and truth. And to think that most people still do not see or understand these poetic and artful aspects as being an integral part of physics and mathematics! Wouldn't the characteristics of beauty hold true in everything in life? Beauty is something perfect that doesn't need to be made better or more beautiful and, like symmetry, however it is changed it remains essentially unchanged. Beauty truly is everything. The departure on the road to awe will bring one right back to where one started, but will be accompanied by a new view. It is regrettable that surface awareness is all that most people tend and intend to see.

Our breath is the beauty we recognize in the cloud. We feel connected to it. We are it. We are the oceans where the clouds have fallen and we are the clouds where the oceans rise. We are the water and sunlight we bathe in, which creates rainbows and the fluid in our eyes that catches this sublime spectrum. Breath after breath and drink after drink, we are more than we think. Reflect on these things.

The Eye of the Beholder

We see the surface of things. This is why many people are so superficial. For whatever reasons, we usually only experience an individual's persona; we see only their skin, face, and clothing, and hear only our personally and socially molded meanings of the words they, and we, select We are a mainly visual species and what we "see" isn't even close, on its own merits, to the full reality. Get to know creation like a person. Engage it; talk to it. Get to know yourself. Go outside for a walk. Explore a forest. Actively observe not as a spectator but as a part of the spectacle. This is how to recognize beauty. It is connected in the same way two people that know each other suddenly see and recognize each other. This is also the way it is with nature when you experience love, truth, and beauty. It has all been connected before, and we seem to spend our lives constantly reconnecting or re-recognizing, successfully or not. This is connection or discovery of the beautiful and the true. Inspiration has always been here for us to recognize and discover. We do this in various natural ways, just as the infinite forms of beauty magnificently arrayed themselves around us. All recognition, love, insight, and epiphany are connections, whether this is sustained or as a more turbulent oscillation of touch and go. Connection is a defining characteristic of beauty.

CULMINATION OF SORTS

We are the world around us. How we view it is important. Unfortunately, we do not view it as precious and beautiful because of our own blindness, which has led to and continues to create the deteriorating conditions of our world. If we are a part of our world and the universe, then we *are* the world and the universe, and we should act as if it matters. The concepts expressed in this book might be a stretch for many, mostly pragmatically thinking people. Truth has to be simple and therefore understandable, reflecting Occam's Razor, the scientific axiom which states that a theory or explanation must not be multiplied beyond that which is necessary and essential. Ironically, simply saying that "everything is connected" is probably more acceptable and understandable to an unlearned child, but not to too many knowledgeable and categorizing adults. Nevertheless, sometimes the simple things are the hardest to understand. The idea that everything is combined may be difficult to absorb all at once. No matter how I explain it, unobstructed understanding begins with an extremely open mind that truly pays attention instead of constantly chattering on with its own thoughts and interpretations. Living requires that one filter the mind/ego and remain active in order to think, learn, remember, and predict, all of which have obvious survival purposes; however, these only go so far. Self-actualization is beyond the ego and so cannot be reached by the ego alone. Only by transcending the mind/ego/self can this crucial step be reached. The thought process, or ego, is utterly necessary and indispensable in supporting the life of an organism. We must use this survival behavior of cognitive awareness as we travel through life, but a conflict arises when we use this behavior exclusively, beyond requirement and without insight. We make a home of this behavior instead of using it as a compass, because one must remain a nomad of the mind in order to allow the ever-changing reality to be traveled accurately. In life, one must travel light, without either too many mental collectables or the dangerous attachment to forms which are ever-changing yet set in concrete by memory. Thought, ego, and fear are intrinsic aspects of a complex survival mechanism and are not destinations in themselves. Denial and indifference both numb us to the reality around us. It would be like running into ice cold water and losing the feeling in your limbs, and worse, simply not caring, because you would soon be numb and insensitive to it. Conversely, to actively accept reality and to be fully sensitive and aware of it is not numbing, but totally liberating in terms of experiencing the totality of yourself and of life. Thought, ego, and fear are not bad in and of themselves. They just have their place and balance point. They are the often misused tools that seem to have minds of their own.

In discussing the prospects for a correct and revolutionary theory that, at first glance tends toward a paradoxical view of unity while going against many common views of reality, Richard Feynman (1965) said in *The Character of Physical Law:*

> *What we need is imagination, but imagination is a terrible strait-jacket. We have to find a new view of the world that has to agree with everything that is known, but disagrees in its predictions somewhere, otherwise it is not interesting. And in that disagreement it must agree with nature. If you can find any other view of the world which agrees over the entire range where things have already been observed, but disagrees somewhere else, you have made a great discovery. It is very nearly impossible but not quite...*

Stephen Hawking (1988), in *A Brief History of Time,* writes:

> *If we do discover a complete theory, it should in time be understandable in broad principle by everyone, not just a few scientists. Then we shall all, philosophers, scientists, and just ordinary people, be able to take part in the discussion of the question of why it is that we and the universe exist.*

Einstein had an expectation, based on previous convictions concerning his much searched for Grand Unified Theory, which is a main reason why he negated the ideas put forth by quantum physics and, in large part, why he fell short of a GUT. In vain, he was looking for a theory of nature that would meet his expectation. He simply knew the unity of nature existed but, understandably enough, could not mold it into a formula. Unity is simple and covers everything. I think Einstein knew quite a lot about the unity of things because he took the time and effort to observe it.

Reflect on these things, because an unchecked habit and/or a stilted perspective will never allow us to get out of our rut; we must find an effective motivation for ourselves to think openly and freely. Our perspective needs awareness, understanding, and then sometimes a big push to get us unstuck from our tendency toward narrow-mindedness. Personal belief based on memory and experience and our collective, social "common sense" can and do reject many possibilities. We are reactive biological systems that protect ourselves in order to fulfill our basic instinct for survival. We receive stimuli and respond mostly automatically. This process needs deliberate awareness in order for us to function properly. Economic pressures, wars, and our assault on the environment are all dynamic and emergent creations of stimulus/response, cause/effect, and supply and demand. They are interactive and self-preserving. We have created a monster called the global economy and it is now spiraling out of control, as if we really had it under control in the first place. In order to be in control, we must understand ourselves and our projected manifestations totally and completely; then there will be no need to control. This is called freedom and love.

When all things are considered, people will either believe or disbelieve and will cling, rationally or irrationally, to whatever view that they wish to be true or to be false. Raising awareness does nothing if it does not spark more balanced action. In the case of humanity, awareness can be the action that spreads into everything else. If the observer sees love not "in" but "as" a part of him- or herself and all their observations, then action becomes spontaneous, intuitive, and flowers just like the natural tendency that a flower and all life exhibits. Connect with yourself and everything in the universe and you will see things as they are, not as we selectively wish to see them. Contemplate things, but don't strain your efforts toward fully understanding them. If one simply enjoys the discoveries and the beauty then this inspired joy will discover the freshness and beauty of things all on its own and for its own sake. Enlightenment, or a breakthrough of insight, is similar to the moment and the feeling that one actually experiences when they have solved a puzzle. Discovering the solution to something you have been pondering for a long while is a feeling of truth and beauty that finite language falls short of capturing, betraying its true indescribability. It may feel impossible, but as soon as you get it, it all seems so simple afterwards and you are amazed that you never got it before. Being human, we forget. We come back to the puzzle of reality after a time and we've forgotten, and it is almost as hard as it was before to reconstruct it. We forget, lose sight of the big picture, get distracted or lost or chained to the grindstone of work, pain, or the sensory pleasures of entertainment, activities, and the satisfaction of progressing toward goals. Unnecessary things frequently and incessantly crowd the way. It is the art of discovery in full bloom when one actively participates in discerning truth from illusion. Seeing this all the time can be effortless, although as humans we tend to make things more difficult for ourselves. In life people sometimes cover their eyes and ears when they know an unpleasant scene is approaching, like when they watch a horror movie. Instead of this willful ignorance, try opening your eyes and ears. Also, in times of great change people will inevitably seek comfort. People will go to the pub or to church for solace or escape. We go looking for someone to follow, someone, be it a deity or otherwise, with answers outside of or beyond us, but we need only look more deeply and more clearly inside first. I have no motive to scare or force people into believing what I believe. This forcing of beliefs is in large part why the world is in the declining state it's in today. Believe it or not, you are the key to it all, and it's turning yourself that seems to be the hard part.

I have said throughout this book that all is one and that the denial of this is what is destroying the world. This is the truth that, once found, must be shared with all who are willing to receive it. I can't help but share this awareness because of the impact it has had on my life. Nothing ever dies or is lost; everything is simply turned into something else that is just as beautiful. Whether you see it or not, the spirit or energy of the universe is still in you and everywhere else. I can keep explaining it to my heart's content, but it will never be anything more than guidance.

You have to see it for yourself to fully feel this beautiful truth. It is you who accept or deny; it is you who receive or reject.

All social revolutions start from the inside; all global revolutions start with nature. The universe is an ocean of heaven that we see as conflicting droplets creating the illusion of hell. Another way of looking at creation is that it is a beautifully woven blanket that, up close and personal, we see as ugly and tangled threads. It is in this fragmented view where all views of conflict and separation originate. When one sees this miracle for what it is—the whole, broad, infinite spectrum—hauling water and chopping wood will never be the same. Our hubris, greed, excessive expansion and growth, and our wars collapsed the Roman Empire, the Mayan civilization, and countless others. Many believe that the next society to collapse will be America, but it is the American way of life that the world follows, so it would appear that if there is a collapse, the world will fall headlong with America. It's not so much the society but the way the society thinks and lives that will crumble. The ideology and sense of value which is the foundation inside the collective is what collapses our way of living, which spreads into the things we create, whether it is buildings or social structures or governments. It won't be the American nation that falls, but the whole world. We have seen a preview of this with the global sprawl of western ways of living and the 2008 global recession that began in America and spread around the world. The movement of a cycle from any point to the same point is called a revolution, which is in essence a return to the previous cycle. It is a slate wiped clean to an earlier state and at the same instant a step forward to a new state. It depends on the nature of the cycle's behavior and what has been done to maintain its sustainability or create imbalance during the cycle. Life on Earth may go on but, in all probability, not as it has in the last few hundred years. Maybe the only survivors will be simple microbes and cockroaches, or maybe the fragile biosphere will be so damaged that it will be too inhospitable for any biological life at all to exist such as our sister planets, Mars and Venus. Given the resourcefulness of nature, that is most unlikely. What sets our Earth apart from other celestial wonders is our biosphere. So far, astronomers haven't seen anything else like it. It is fully accommodating for "complex" carbon based-life, and our Earth is a perfect hostess who gives endlessly, to her heart's content. We are depriving her of her life and ours. We are a virus that is too clever for our own good, in that we are exceeding our survival mandate with an excessive population and exhaustion of Earth's resources, and we are killing our hostess in the process of killing ourselves. What we are doing is unnecessary. It doesn't have to be this way. However, we have passed a critical phase, and without coming to understand this, because we are so far along in this process, I believe we must pass through this phase to a new stage of equilibrium. And, make no mistake, nature has no vested interest in making mankind "survivors." In a wider view of change, nature doesn't lose in this deal; we do. One can't stop the inevitable. The storm is coming, but so is the calm afterwards. Truth or purpose is a feeling of connection and openness that we have all felt at one time or another. Love is self-sustained until something breaks the awe through thought, ego, or fear, which turns us away from this revolution of life and beauty and becomes a self-fulfilling, vicious cycle with no new revolution or understanding or love. There are many deceptive things that take away from and distract us from the awareness of truth. It is this cycle of limited awareness that we are in that has separated us from God or nature. Look at the world. We are always in the cycle we see and create. The word "heal" means to "make whole." To be healthy is to be happy, because when one is healthy, one is filled with life. Many people are unhealthy and depressed because they feel disconnected and this could not be further from the truth. They are not transcending beyond their ego and into a fuller view of reality. The mind's eye stops at the ego because we are distracted by desire. This limited awareness exists for many reasons. We ignore the constant opportunity to observe the nature of our true selves and, as an immediate result, we are only aware of our partial, individual little selves. We are unnecessarily disconnected from the whole and thus continuing the multi-generational chain of mental and physical ill health and unhappiness.

Much like our Earth's weakening magnetic field, humans appear to have no overall collective will or the strength to heal our cumulative psyche. Our immune system is a wonder at healing our body, but only the self can heal the mind. With nearly seven billion people creating massive imbalances, an open and weeping internal wound, we are scattered, half caring for ourselves through piecemeal, temporary and superficial fixes instead of healing ourselves and, on a larger scale, the world, making it healed and whole. There is much healing to be done and soon. We are nearing our global flatline. This healing might not take place in the way that we want or think it will.

I see children behaving like adults when it should be the other way around also. We can learn from children, just as they can from us. Just sustaining the human life that currently exists creates a great demand that Earth cannot sustain. What will be the first domino to collapse and cascade in its effects: the demand, the supply, or both? We think an opposing force of attack or some form of protest will completely solve problems, but these only create the resistance the opposing force needs to feed and endure. We think if we battle against injustice, distress, or fear or anything else we dislike this struggle will solve the problem and lead to that which we feel is just and peaceful. This aggressive method only aids in survival; however, it has not, does not, and will not bring peace and understanding; it only makes things more conflictive and unstable. See the truth of this. Conflict begets conflict, aggression begets aggression. A war against war is still war, which will not bring peace to conflict. This is why all wars, psychological and physical, are the continuum of a single war with apparent lulls in between; however, these gaps of respite are only transformations of aggression from the outer world into the psyche. Acceptance of our common needs and our common bonds on Earth dissolves factional and artificial affiliations, and shows us that there is a middle ground which brings the real peace of the "what is" or the "now." We are looking to connect the micro and macrocosms, to find our place and meaning between these scales of reality, searching for a theory of everything or complete description of our universe with ourselves included. We are all innocent, whether we walk in our own light, being that of the whole, or obstruct it and live in our own shadow. There is more beauty to see in the light. We are selective, and because of this we are conflictive. However obvious it is, humanity still suffers a collective ingrained obstructionism that hinders our awareness; if we were to understand reality clearly we would act in alignment with nature. This simple truth eludes us. We can't confine our feelings of love to the memories and situations that evoked them in the past. These instances are left dormant and are only tapped in times of need, such as when we want to find comfort in an escape from reality. Spread this love throughout every moment and situation instead of keeping this feeling, which we all feel, contained and separate from everything and creating a misplaced and passive perspective, which we then see as the face of an ugly, conflicted world instead of a vibrant and beautiful reality. Spread this love, and then you will haul water and chop wood as if you were the wood and water. This is the real world we have forsaken…until now. What is gained in our modern world doesn't begin to compare to what is lost. This revolution we are in is the end of distortion and the beginning of clarity. This is an everyday thing that is self-sustaining. Think of something you really enjoy. If you are inspired or "in spirit," meaning to inhale or breathe, you are then passionate about something. Think of how easy it feels, think of the seemingly endless energy and motivation you have when you are immersed in the flow of your inspiration and passion. People have a hard time getting inspired. Can an insight be sustained in one's daily life, not lost or exclusive to the past or projected into the future, but actually lived and felt in the here and now? An extension of that flash of awareness into the undivided, singular, and eternal moment, encompassing past, present, and future is life—it is life itself. Not something left in the mind as an ideal or spiritual abstraction to play with, or to throw around in books or conversations at our leisure, or whose goal is to achieve separation from the reality of which it is the very essence. Life has its flow. That flow is you, in and beyond the horizon of all events.

We require liberation from ourselves. We are a central ingredient in reuniting, perceiving, and restoring the harmony and proportion of nature and ourselves within it. Reality filtered by the mind is a pseudo-reality, and this leads to misperceptions of what reality is. Are we too ill-equipped to deeply, adequately understand the beauty of this reality? Is the unavoidable byproduct of a sense of self and healthy fear always egotism and unhealthy fear? We, along with all of creation, are an energetic spiritual fire. Some may say these facets of unity, of the many in one, are all well and good in theory but have no place in reality. To this I say, it doesn't get any more real. There is no need to count our blessings because they are infinite. In fact, we don't even have the time to count them! Just be aware of the singular and infinite blessing of all that is life and you can't help but feel love, gratitude, appreciation, and awe. Enjoy the wonder of creation as yourself because we are a single organism on Earth and of all that exists. The world is our mirror and the focus is becoming clear. This book has no conclusion; that is why this final section is called a culmination "of sorts." People are always looking for a conclusion to things, and there isn't one…

REFERENCES

Blake, W. (1801-1803/1988). Auguries of Innocence. In D.V. Erdman (Ed.), *The Complete Poetry & Prose of William Blake* (p. 490). New York: Anchor Books.

Blake, W. (1793/1988). The Marriage of Heaven and Hell. In D.V. Erdman (Ed.), *The Complete Poetry & Prose of William Blake* (p. 39). New York: Anchor Books.

Blake, W. (1792/1988). Several Questions Answerd. In D.V. Erdman (Ed.), *The Complete Poetry and Prose of William Blake* (p.474). New York: Anchor Books.

Clugston, M.J. (2004). *Dictionary of Science-Penguin Reference*. London: Penguin.

Cole, K.C. (2001). *The Hole in the Universe: How Scientists Peered over the Edge of Emptiness and Found Everything* (pp. 35, 65, 73, 163). Orlando, FL: Harcourt.

Darwin, C. (1859/1951). 6th edition reprint of *On The Origin Of Species-by means of natural selection or the preservation of favoured races in the struggle for life* (p. 4). London: Oxford University Press.

Donne, J. (1624). Meditation XVII. In *Devotions upon Emergent Occasions*.

Ehrlich, P.R & A.H. (2008). *The Dominant Animal: Human Evolution and the Environment* (p. 207). Washington, DC: Island Press.

Emerson, R.W. (1841/1993). Self Reliance. In S. Appelbaum (Ed.), *Self Reliance and Other Essays* (p. 36). Mineola, NY: Dover Publications.

Ereira, A. (1992). *The Elder Brothers: A Lost South American People and Their Wisdom* (p. 10). New York: Knopf.

Feynman, R.P. (1965). *The Character of Physical Law* (p. 171). Cambridge, MA: MIT Press.

Feynman, R. P. (1972). *Take the World from a Different Point of View* Part 2 of 4
Editor: John Watts. Produced and Directed: Duncan Dallas. A Yorkshire Television Color Production. Retrieved Aug 15, 2010 from: http://www.youtube.com/watch?v=Ee3QLbmXJzw

Gell-Mann, M. (1994). *The Quark and the Jaguar: Adventures in the Simple and Complex* (p. 27). New York: W.H. Freeman.

Gibbon, J. (1984). *In Search of Schrodinger's Cat: Quantum Physics and Reality* (pp. 5, 164, 159, 231). New York: Bantam.

Gleick, J. (1993). *Genius: The Life and Science of Richard Feynman* (p.13). New York: Vintage Books.

Hawking, S. (1988). *A Brief History of Time: From the Big Bang to Black Holes* (pp. 11, 175). New York: Bantam.

Lama, D. (2005). *The Universe in a Single Atom: the convergence of science and spirituality* (p. 208) New York: Morgan Road Books.

Lauterwasser, A. (2006). *Water Sound Images: The Creative Music of the Universe* (pp. 67-68, 72). Newmarket, NH: Macromedia.

Mails, T.E. (1997). *The Hopi Survival Kit* (pp. 148, 153). New York: Welcome Rain.

Moring, G. F. (2004). *The complete idiot's guide to understanding Einstein-* Second Edition. Chris Eliopoulos (Illus.), (p.132). Indianapolis, IN: Alpha Books.

Mowat, F. (1972). *A Whale for the Killing* (p. 81). Toronto: McClelland and Stewart.

National Center for Atmospheric Research (NCAR). National Science Foundation (2006, March 6). *Scientists Issue Unprecedented Forecast Of Next Sunspot Cycle.* Retrieved Oct 17, 2010 from: http://www.nsf.gov/news/news_summ.jsp?cntn_id=105844

Ovid. (8AD). *Metamorphoses.*

Pascal, B. (1670/1980). Pensees. In M. Collison & R. Collison (Eds.), *Dictionary of Foreign Quotations* (pp. 218, 240). New York: Everest House.

St. Augustine of Hippo. (398/1953).*Confessions.* In *The Fathers of the Vol. 5.* Washington, DC: The Catholic University of America Press.

Seneca. (1st Century B.C./1980). De Beneficiis. In M. Collison & R. Collison (Eds.), *Dictionary of Foreign Quotations* (p. 242). New York: Everest House.

Shakespeare, W. (1599). *King Henry IV* (Part 2).

Shakespeare, W. (1601). *Hamlet.*

Tzu, S. (6th Century BC/2009). *The Art of War.* Classic edition (p. 5). English translation and commentary by L. Giles. El Paso, TX: El Paso Norte Press.

U.S. Department of the Interior/U.S. Geological Survey (page last modified: May 06, 2010) Retrieved Oct 14, 2010 from: http://geomag.usgs.gov/faqs.php

Wells, H.G. (1936). *Things to Come*. Directed by William Cameron Menzies. Produced by Alexander Korda. A London Film Production.

Whitman, W. (1855/2007). *Leaves of Grass* (pp. 21, 22, 25, 34). Mineola, NY: Dover.

INDEX

democracy, 9, 101

denial, 79-80, 126, 145, 252-53

Descartes, Rene, 42, 76

desire, 92

DiCaprio, Leonardo, 125

dimension, 203-4, 212, 230, 249, 254, 258. *See also* spacetime

dinosaurs, 20, 122, 143, 183

Dirac, Paul, 206-7

discovery, 24-26, 41

disease, 91-92, 98, 100, 106, 110, 116

disorder, 164, 211, 213, 225-26. *See also* chaos

diversity. *See* variety

division (*see also* separation), 23, 33, 61, 66, 221-22, 275, 283, 316, 318

DNA, 34, 38, 185, 187, 191, 194-95, 287, 289, 293

dogma, 12, 91, 223, 311

domestication, 23

Donne, John, 7, 329

double slit experiment, 260

doubt, 24, 27-28. *See also* skepticism

Drake equation, 29

dream, 41-44

drought, 66

dualism, 273, 292, 300, 312. *See also* separation

duality, 84, 90-91, 166, 260-61, 289, 291-92. *See also* separation

E

earth, 9-10, 12, 16, 116-18, 120, 122-25, 127-43, 145-53, 155-57, 159, 162

earthquake, 131, 147, 157

Easter Island, 91, 135

economy, 9, 94-95, 100-105, 107, 109, 116, 119, 121

Edison, Thomas, 93

ego, 51-52, 55-60, 62, 64-65, 68, 75-76, 78-79, 81. *See also* thought; observer; observation

egocentrism, 53, 76

Egypt, 135

Einstein, Albert, 8, 244, 249, 253, 258-60, 264, 273, 275, 288, 297, 308, 319, 323, 331

electricity, 16, 137, 140-41, 208-9, 234-36. *See also* light; magnetism

electromagnetism, 45-46, 233-41, 243, 247-48, 256-61, 263-64. *See also* light; photon; rainbow

electron, 189, 206-8, 236, 258, 260, 263, 265, 270

electroweak force, 273-74

Eliot, T. S., 125

emergence (*see also* evolution; feedback), 192-93, 196, 202, 207, 245, 248, 257, 262, 270, 273

emergency, 126, 145

[Created with **TExtract** / www. Texyz.com]